A HISTORICAL GUIDE TO
FLORENCE

Frontispiece: The heart of old Florence, including the Palazzo Vecchio, Giotto's tower, and the cupola of the Duomo.

A HISTORICAL
GUIDE TO
FLORENCE

JOHN W. HIGSON, JR.

UNIVERSE BOOKS · NEW YORK

Published in the United States of America in 1973
by Universe Books
381 Park Avenue South, New York, N.Y. 10016
Copyright in 1973 in all countries
of the International Copyright Union
by Universe Books

Library of Congress Catalog Card Number: 72-91632
ISBN 0-87663-180-4

Printed in Great Britain

For Eleanor

CONTENTS

The city's unchanged aspect one hundred years ago . . . its appearance today after the consequences of the unification of Italy, an increasing population, industrialization, the automobile, and other manifestations of progress . . . World War II and the flood of 1966 . . . the things preserved unchanged, including the surrounding countryside.

The traditional character of the Florentines, their commercial success and its effects on thinking, art and literature . . . current conditions of life and society and their historical background . . . a visitor's impressions and reactions, positive and negative . . . the problems of tourism, crowding, and modernization . . . the influence of the church, the state, and the foreign colony.

The art collections . . . the daily cycle of life . . . the city's topography.

The beginnings as an Etruscan settlement . . . the Roman rebuilding . . . the Teutonic invasions and the Dark Ages . . . the revival of the Empire, of trade and of town life.

The religious reform movements and the reconstruction of the Florentine Baptistery . . . other 11th-century churches . . . the Society of the Towers . . . the struggle between pope and emperor aids the towns . . . Florence's population, wealth and jurisdiction expand . . . the few surviving art forms of the time.

The Guelph and Ghibelline parties create widespread civil turmoil . . . the influence of the mendicant orders and of

ILLUSTRATIONS

8 ILLUSTRATIONS

PREFACE

In today's world of jet planes and pay-later plans, more people than ever before are able to visit the great cities of Europe. Many, who twenty years ago would never have considered such a trip, find themselves walking the streets of Paris or wandering in the Roman Forum. Yet, while the physical and economic obstacles that once limited world travel have been largely removed, less progress has been made in providing adequate interpretation of the European heritage we all enjoy and want to comprehend.

That is particularly true of the contributions made by Florence, which, with the possible exception of Athens and Rome, is more universally and singularly identified with the culture of Western civilization than any other European city. Americans and Britons, especially, cherish Florence with a fondness and attachment they reserve for few other places; and of the more than a million Americans, and almost as many persons from the British Isles, who visit Italy each year, most spend some time in Florence. Yet the history of this birthplace of new styles and ideas in Western architecture, sculpture, and painting, as well as in literature and music—a history that can be especially meaningful to the modern traveler who is neither art specialist nor professional historian—is little known to these multitudes of visitors.

Many earlier books on this subject—long, rambling commentaries or impressions, ponderous histories, labored and pedantic art critiques—are hopelessly dated in content and approach, or out of touch with reality, or have been written by specialists, antiquarians, and long-time residents of Florence for the leisurely, sophisticated few. Many of these works, reflecting the scholarship and values of a different era, are often concerned with only segments or phases of the total story. Their authors could hardly have contemplated the changes wrought by World War II and its aftermath, the revolution in travel, or the requirements of the modern reader.

At the same time, reinforced by some romantic literature, the popular, traditional image of the city—the picture postcard or travel poster view of Florence—deceptively suggests a peaceful scene of static artistic glories and of happy craftsmen at work under a benevolent southern sun. But this, of course, does not encompass the full reality. Today, as in the past, the essence of Florence can be found in its need to create and at the same time preserve, in its unending struggle between the demands of the present, the expectations of the future, and the conditions and restraints imposed by history. Just as Old Florence was a product of the tension between solid traditional and dynamic new attitudes of mind and behaviour, artistic styles, and sociopolitical systems, so the Florence of today is still a city of conflicting points of view, of vivid contrasts and a varied character.

One customarily thinks of Florence as the embodiment of the 15th-century Renaissance, but it is really a mixture of many eras and styles. A number of its religious foundations date back to the first millennium of the Christian era, while the recent design of a new church near the Autostrada would be "modern" in the 21st century. In contrast to the early Renaissance basilica of San Lorenzo with one of the most elegant, well proportioned interiors in the history of architecture, the inside of the nearby Gothic Cathedral is gaunt, bare, and cavernous, while the most popular church in the city—the Baroque Annunziata—is overloaded with lavish, exotic decoration. Some of the city's buildings have a harsh, forbidding appearance—the Palazzo Vecchio and the Bargello were really fortresses—but others, like the Ospedale degli Innocenti (Foundling Hospital), with its open portico and coloured terracotta medallions of babies in swaddling clothes, are gentle and inviting. There is an inevitable hardness in the presence of so much stone, but, in contrast to some other medieval towns, the effect is softened by the warm colors of stucco walls and tile roofs and by the green of the surrounding hills.

But diversity is not confined to the city's architecture. The Florentines themselves, at one moment maddening, are, at the next, disarmingly pleasant. So is their climate. There are periods of the year when torrential rains, coming down as in the tropics, continue for days and swell the Arno and its tributaries to their flooding, destructive potential; other periods of protracted drought when there is not enough water for domestic use and Florence's river is no more than a sluggish series of stagnant, shallow pools. Some winter days are so cold that fountain jets freeze in midair; on some summer days, the sun beats down unmercifully on the jostling hordes of people and vehicles amid the humidity, fumes, and dust. Still, other, more temperate days —away from the congestion and noise, when the air is clear and sharp and the earth colors of the town and the surrounding hills are outlined against the bluest of skies—make an impression on the eye and on the soul that will never be surpassed or forgotten.

Whatever else it is, however, Florence today—a busy, crowded city of over half a million inhabitants—is suffering from the problems of congestion, smog, and the breakdown of services that plague other cities. Class antagonisms, student riots, strikes are endemic; daily life is hectic, competitive, noisy, and at times contentious. Not that urban strife and friction are new to the Florentine scene. The city of the late Middle Ages and the Renaissance was also a vital, humming, discordant commercial center. Feuding, factionalism, and bloody uprisings were commonplace, and life for the citizens was often one long series of crises. Nevertheless, those were the city's most productive years—so productive that it became one of the wellsprings of Western culture, until, exhausted by its own pride and divisiveness, it fell victim to external forces beyond its control and ceased to be a dominant factor in the life of Europe.

It was the 19th century that first saw a renewed consciousness of the city's importance and great historic value and that prompted the well-circulated literacy appreciations from which our traditional view derives. Since then, the list of Florence's remarkable contributions to Western civilization has been ever more thoroughly documented. It is impossible in a book of this size to do more than touch on any but the most significant; and, accordingly, a degree of selectivity has been essential in order to present a clear overall grasp rather than a crowded tabulation of specifics. At the same time, an effort has been made to relate in an instructive way the intangibles—the cultural achievements, the personalities, the customs and institutions that grew up, the chronological record and events of history, the organic growth and flowering of the city—to those tangible remains that have survived and that we can see and touch. For only by placing these material things—the paintings and statues and monuments—in their historical context, in their own era and environment, can the salient features of each be fully appreciated.

Inevitably, the ever-swelling complexity of our contemporary life tends to obscure its origins. It is therefore worthwhile to turn back occasionally to examine an antecedent society—especially one of such an extraordinary combination of energies, brains, and talent as that of Florence—to trace the achievements that not only shaped men's minds, but also so stirred their esthetic and pleasure senses for the enjoyment of life.

Of course, the story of a city is many things—its people and social patterns, business life, political institutions, military record, external relationships, literary and artistic production, and so on. But perhaps more clearly definitive than any other is its architecture. Architecture has been called the mother of the fine arts, and certainly in Florence its practitioners not only determined the future direction of their own speciality but influenced the parallel development of their fellow painters, sculptors, and other craftsmen. Over the centuries, almost all phases of the city's life have been reflected in its churches, monastic establishments, civic buildings, guild halls, workshops, houses, palaces and gardens, walls, fortresses, and bridges, many of which still survive. These building blocks of history are often the most revealing remains of a society or culture. They may also appear to be the most substantial and permanent works of mankind, but exposed to the elements and man's caprice, they are increasingly vulnerable. It was in the hope that they will continue to be properly maintained and protected that this book was written.

PART ONE

The City of Florence Today

Little more than a century ago, the weary traveler making his slow approach to Florence by carriage or horseback over dusty and difficult roads, and at last catching sight ahead of that legendary city nestled in its green valley, must surely have experienced a deep, soul-tingling thrill. There in the distance loomed the familiar shape of the Cathedral's great dome, while around it crowded the jumbled, irregular rooflines of the city, still confined within the orderly limits of its ancient wall. From every direction, a countryside of spectacular beauty, unmarred by industrial suburbs, extended to the great stone gates themselves.

Here on the banks of the river Arno lay a city with a unique character, its general appearance almost unchanged since the 16th century. Bell towers, cupolas, and the rugged battlements crowning its more imposing structures still dominated the surrounding mass of the town. Dun-colored stones and terracotta tiles blended serenely with the encircling hills. No jarring contrasts unsettled the eye. A hazy atmosphere, diffused with the golden light peculiar to Tuscany, enveloped the scene—a happy collaboration of man and nature.

Florence attained this essential form during the twilight of the Middle Ages and in the glorious period of the Renaissance that followed. In those years it played a prominent part in the European drama, profoundly influencing the course of events in Italy and across the continent. But in the 16th century, the conquest of the peninsula by foreign powers extinguished the city's independence and creativity, and Florence gradually slipped from the mainstream of history, no longer to shape or be affected by the great movements of the times. The extravagances of the Baroque era, which so altered Rome, left scant trace in Florence. The age of exploration and discovery provided no new opportunities for the city but in fact accelerated its decline. Even during the turbulent period of the industrial revolution, Florence remained

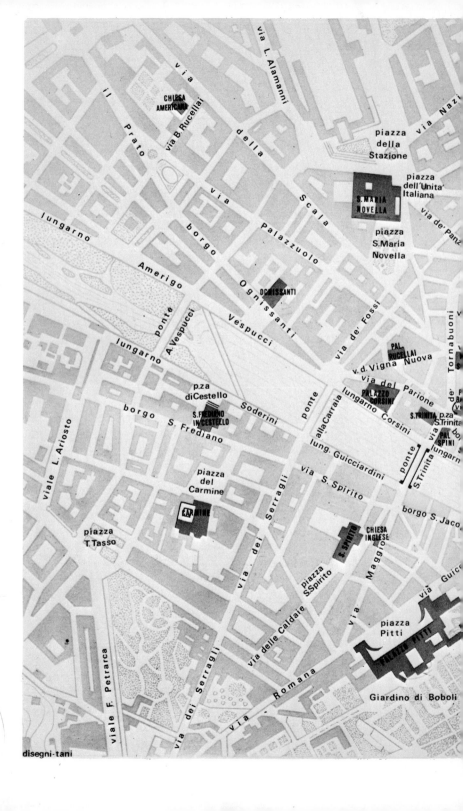

View from the north of Florence within its old walls, as depicted by the 18th-century Florentine artist Giuseppe Zocchi.

quiescent. The population continued relatively static* and little new building took place. Maps dated around 1850 show a city scarcely altered from the time of Michelangelo. Considerable areas still devoted to agriculture remained within the walls. The medieval heart of the city survived intact, and the beautiful Tuscan country side reached out on all sides, undisturbed. To have rounded a bend in the road and beheld ahead that famous city, towered and domed, girded by its wall and set like a jewel amid the green of field and vineyard, must have etched on the mind of many a traveler a vivid and unforgettable picture.

But in many respects this peaceful scene was not to last, and today the traveler to the valley of the Arno experiences a less romantic introduction. The approaches to Florence itself have been drastically changed by the inevitability of progress. The old Via Bolognese from the north and the Via Senese from the south happily still retain something of their ancient appearance, but there is little to admire along the other principal roads, including

* Around 100,000. Today it is more than 500,000.

the connections to that main artery of travel in Italy, the Auto-strada del Sole. These follow the plain of the Arno on almost flat land and pass through acres of commonplace suburban development, the hallmark of our 20th-century civilization. Here, where a rich soil once supported an abundant agriculture, factories, apartment blocks, gasoline stations, and all their attendant phenomena have steadily encroached, and the sprawling suburbs have progressively insulated the city from the surrounding countryside, which no longer provides a complimentary and nourishing influence to Florentine life.

One's first impressions, therefore, on entering the city are somewhat disappointing, but past the suburbs, the relatively unspoiled character of old Florence becomes increasingly apparent, until reaching the core area we discover that, in spite of much rebuilding, there still remains a significant part of the ancient city yet undisturbed. In fact, it is an interesting paradox and a measure of the inherent quality of the city that, even after the unfortunate changes that have taken place, Florence still somehow remains more closely linked to its past—less violently wrenched into the 20th century, and hence more truly its historical self—than most other important European cities. That being said, it is nevertheless worthwhile, for a better appreciation of the things that make Florence famous, to identify and distinguish those alterations to the city for which our modern age must be held accountable.

The beginning of major change in Florence may be traced to the middle of the 19th-century, at a time when profound new forces disrupted the stability of Europe. The consequences of the industrial revolution had altered social and economic relationships of long standing, creating problems that taxed the resourcefulness of every government and threatened the very existence of many. Radical new doctrines challenged the existing political order and demands for reform echoed across the continent.

Italy, on the fringe of these developments and long split into a number of separate kingdoms and principalities, responded in its own unique way. An impetus was given to the old but languishing idea of national union—the welding together of the diverse states of the peninsula, the overthrow of the various regimes and tyrannies, including the temporal rule of the Catholic

Church, and the achievement of a national purpose and a national government. At last this became not only a dream but a possibility. Known as the Risorgimento (literally, Resurrection), this dramatic and turbulent phase of Italian history culminated in 1861 with the effective unification of most of the peninsula under the benevolent rule of the House of Savoy.

Florence, selected as the provisional capital of the new Italy, partly for its central position and partly for its favourable political climate, experienced an influx of court and government officials, soldiers, and businessmen, all impatient to refashion the life of the nation. Thus began the process of destruction and rebuilding which, uninterrupted by the removal of the central government to Rome (when the Papal State was incorporated into the new kingdom in 1870), and continuing down to our own day, has in some respects forever altered the city's traditional character.

Looking back to the years immediately following the unification, it is not difficult to understand why so little concern was given to the preservation of the old appearance of the city. Strong feelings, long pent up, had been released by the Risorgimento, sweeping aside the forces of conservatism. With the pope in retreat and the Tuscan grand duke deposed, the new politics required a break with the past and the removal of the apparatus of tyranny and the symbols of the old order. Villas and *palazzi* were taken over by the royal court and by the various ministries to serve the needs of the new regime. In the space of a few years, scores of beautiful buildings were cut up and disfigured. Monasteries and convents, seized from the church, were hurriedly converted to offices, barracks, schools, or hospitals—more often than not failing to serve adequately their new purposes.

In like spirit, to permit the anticipated expansion of the city and indeed to encourage it, the encircling historic walls north of the river were pulled down in the 1860s and a broad boulevard was laid out on their perimeter. Housing developments and an increasing population continued the transformation, and the suburbs spread out in every direction. At first, these extensions were not unattractive, but subsequent additions have been progressively more commonplace, until todays huge cubical apartment blocks, repetitive imitations of each other, appear devoid of any architectural merit.

Equally irreparable and less justified, a misconceived project, rigorously carried out in the 1880s, sought to modernize a large section of the heart of the city centering on what had been for centuries the Mercato Vecchio (Old Market). Around this piazza since medieval times had grown up a jumble of ancient towers, churches, *loggie*, tabernacles, and other historic structures amid a tangled maze of narrow streets. All this was indiscriminately swept away to make room for construction of the present prosaic Piazza della Repubblica and its adjoining blocks of uninteresting buildings.

The motive for this is clearly set forth in an inscription on an archway over one of the streets leading into the piazza: *L'antico centro della citta da secolare squallore a vita nuova restituita* (The ancient center of the city from centuries of squalor restored to a new life). Although the area doubtless needed cleaning up, it was not necessary to level it. The very buildings that seemed to be such obstacles to progress in the 19th century comprised much of the essential heart and soul of the old center. Those on the perimeter of the project that were allowed to remain are proof of that. Unfortunately, the possibilities of judicious restoration succumbed to a stronger desire to wipe away reminders of the past and to rebuild in accordance with the mood and tastes of that day.

Each century had witnessed a few changes in Florence's general appearance, but not until after the Risorgimento were alterations on such a large scale attempted. Many of these were inspired by the intellectuals and romanticists of the Victorian period, who had recently "rediscovered" the Italian Gothic style and the artists of the duecento and trecento (particularly Giotto and his followers).* Not the least influential of these arbiters of public taste were the members of the foreign colony in and around Florence, mostly British and American. To them and to local opinion in general, which they greatly influenced, it was inconceivable that churches and public buildings should be left in an unfinished state. The fact that the greatest artists of the

---

* The Italians more conveniently refer to the 1200s as the duecento, the 1300s as the trecento, the 1400s as the quattrocento, the 1500s as the cinquecento, the 1600s as the seicento, and so on, while we commonly use the somewhat misleading terms 13th century, when we refer to the 1200s, the 14th century for the 1300s, and so on.

The Mercato Vecchio before it was rebuilt in the 1880s. The column and its statue, long marking the center of the ancient city, are still in place.

The Piazza Vittorio Emanuele (now Piazza della Repubblica)
as it looked shortly after the reconstruction of the old center.
Today the statue of the king is in the Cascine.

Renaissance had apparently felt unequal to the tasks of final
completion (the most difficult part was often put off indefinitely)
did not give them pause. And so, to the many changes made in
the name of hygiene or progress, others were made in the name
of art. The great rough stone frontal walls of the Duomo and the
church of Santa Croce, for example, were "improved" at tremendous cost by the addition of elaborate façades. Castles and
other buildings, including the so-called Casa di Dante, were
"restored" in an exaggerated and artificial way, according to the
then imperfect understanding of medieval architecture.* Landmarks were removed and statues in the eclectic style of the times
placed about the city. Frescoes, which had long been left to
molder and decay, were inexpertly patched up and repainted, with
unfortunate results. Looking back today, we see more of the
attitudes of the 19th century in these works than was perhaps
intended.

* It has been recently determined that the great poet Dante Alighieri did
not live in this building but in another nearby.

But on an even larger and less restricted scale, and at a progressively faster tempo, the compelling realities of our own era have everywhere left their mark. These are especially apparent if we enter the city through the ever-widening sprawl of the eastern and western suburbs which have grown so rapidly since World War II. Zoning here, according to occupancy and use, is unheard of, and few districts are set aside exclusively for residential purposes. Instead, Italians customarily live in congested and diverse surroundings so as to maximize social contacts at all times. The newer sections therefore include shops, offices, factories, apartments, markets, bars, and restaurants all mixed up together. Here all of the paraphernalia of postwar prosperity seem to have mushroomed in super-abundance. New buildings rise up everywhere. New businesses manufacture and display their products. Neons and advertisements crowd upon one another. Traffic becomes increasingly congested despite the devices employed to control it—signals, painted lines, signs of all kinds.

The consequences of progress, however, are even less acceptable in the older parts of Florence, but the urgent quest for modern conveniences and for a higher standard of living have dictated the course of civic development. An attractive inner courtyard of an old Renaissance palazzo, once filled with the sight and sound of a splashing fountain, is now marred by the creaking mechanism of an elevator. A noble façade or roofline is disfigured by the electric wires and television antennas that grow thicker daily. A little vegetable stand, which has displayed its profusion of color in front of an old, stone building since beyond memory, must surrender its place so that a few more automobiles may park; a weathered shrine to the Madonna, with its devotional image set up centuries ago, must accommodate itself to a "no left turn" sign; ancient piazzas, formerly reserved for human activity, now are packed tight with motor vehicles of all kinds, their pavements marred by oil and grease.

But all change has not been gradual or within the practical control of Florence's citizens, for in recent years two unavoidable and catastrophic events—the German demolitions of 1944 and the flood of 1966—have underlined for the world the vulnerability of the city and its treasures.

The former disaster, growing out of the Nazi occupation of Italy during World War II, was to leave the more lasting scars. Throughout the course of the war, Florence had suffered practically no damage—the Allies had specified it a national monument and the Axis powers had declared it an open city—and all expected that it would escape unharmed. However, as the British advance approached the city near the end of July 1944, the occupying Germans abruptly ordered the inhabitants to evacuate the buildings on both sides of the river, at the same time requesting detailed maps of the area. Alarmed by the apparent intentions of the Germans, a delegation of high-ranking Italians immediately put before the commandant a memorandum citing a number of positive assurances, including those of the German Ambassador, Field Marshal Kesselring, and even the Führer himself, that nothing would be done to damage the city or to furnish the Allies with any military motive to attack it. In reply, the delegation was assured that the measures being taken were only precautionary.

However, on July 31 the bridges and the adjacent areas were declared out of bounds and no one was permitted to cross the river. The city in effect was cut in two. For the next several days, the Florentine populace waited. Then, after dark on August 3, a fearful explosion shook the city, and others followed throughout the night. Dawn revealed the devastation. All the bridges had been totally demolished except for the Ponte Vecchio. The approaches to it, however, were more than effectively blocked by the indiscriminate destruction of all the ancient buildings in the vicinity on either side for 200 yards. They had been mined in the basements and blown up vertically, so that nothing remained but a vast mountain of debris, thus resulting in as great a loss as the bridge itself. Some of Florence's oldest and most characteristic streets—Por Santa Maria, Via Guicciardini, Via de' Bardi, and part of the wonderful Borgo San Jacopo, with its houses over hanging the river—disappeared forever in the rubble. Why this act was considered necessary has never been explained. The Germans, with only a handful of soldiers in Florence, had no intention of holding the city. The Allies, proceeding slowly and steadily north, had a choice of several places to ford the Arno to the east and west. As it was, Allied engineers had steel bridges thrown

The shoplined Ponte Vecchio (*right*) and medieval houses along the Via de' Bardi as they appeared before their destruction during World War II.

across the river in a few days and the advance continued without interruption.

According to one account, Hitler himself, at a meeting with Goering and Kesselring, gave the order to blow up the bridges, saving "only the most artistic one," by which he meant the Ponte Vecchio, with its famous shops. The preservation of the Ponte Santa Trinita, regarded by some as the most beautiful bridge in Italy, with its subtle curves and tense, springing arches, was apparently not even considered.

After the war, these areas, with the exception of the Borgo San Jacopo, were quickly rebuilt with varying results. Agreement could not be reached on whether to try to reconstruct the buildings as they had been or to break with tradition and erect structures representative of the 20th century. As a consequence, an unsatisfactory compromise prevailed, and the new buildings were designed on both theories. Stone was to be used only as a facing and only in parts. The old irregularity of mass and form was to be retained, with certain improvisations, but windows and store fronts would be contemporary. The streets themselves would follow the old plan but would be doubled in width. It is only necessary to compare the present Por Santa Maria or the Via de' Bardi to old photographs to understand what has been lost. In fact, the torrent of criticism engendered by these hybrid buildings held up all work on the Borgo San Jacopo until 1962, when the interminable arguments finally led to another compromise. This time it was agreed to retain more of the character of the old quarter with fewer concessions to 'progress,' but even these new structures were built too high and their window patterns were altered to allow the owners to squeeze in several more floor levels. Though the river bank at last resembles its prewar appearance, no one will mistake these buildings for their ancient neighbors that survived downstream.*

The other major catastrophe suffered by Florence was the dramatic flood in the autumn of 1966, which focused on it the shocked attention of the world. For three days and nights a heavy rain had fallen continuously along the Apennine chain and the River Arno had risen steadily, until by the evening of November 3 it had reached the curved arches of the city's bridges. This in itself was not unprecedented and did not cause any general alarm. People went to bed as usual. During the night, however, the river continued to rise, and a few of the shopkeepers on the Ponte Vecchio were at last advised to remove some of their stock. By early morning, it was still raining and a flood seemed inevitable, but, as the 4th was a holiday, most Florentines remained asleep in their beds, unaware of the impending tragedy. By about 7.00 a.m., the Arno had begun to lap over the top of the parapets along its banks and into the streets alongside. At the same time, a tremendous wall of water rapidly built up against the Ponte Vecchio, whose broad piers, acting as a dam, forced the water to either side. In the gray light of dawn, the few witnesses felt sure that the ancient foundations of the bridge would soon give way to the pounding weight of rushing water

* It has been argued that exact reconstruction would have been quite feasible. Many detailed photographs exist of most of the buildings, especially those along the Arno; ground plans are known; fragments could have served as models of various parts; plaster color could have been closely duplicated. For economic and other reasons, this course was not followed.

(*above*) Pulverized remains, after they were mined and blown up, of the old houses adjacent to the Ponte Vecchio on the Borgo San Jacopo and those that survived downstream. (*bottom left*) Via Por Santa Maria and the Amidei tower as they appeared before World War II, and . . . (*bottom right*) what was left after they were blown up.

Via Por Santa Maria today, wider but still inadequate, with its controversial postwar buildings. The restored Amidei tower may be identified by the lion's head.

Early morning—November 4, 1966—at the south end of the Ponte Vecchio as the Arno began to overflow its banks.

and the massive tangle of tree trunks and other rubbish that had accumulated against it.

From then on, the pace of events accelerated rapidly until, within half an hour, the river suddenly burst over the parapets in full flood and rushed into the city. People living in ground-floor or basement apartments were literally awakened by an onrush of muddy water. A few were drowned, but most escaped upstairs, leaving their possessions behind.

By mid-morning, half the city—some 3,000 acres—was inundated to a depth of up to 14 feet. The Santa Croce area was especially hard hit, but even the streets around the famous Baptistery, half a mile from the river, stood in several feet of fast-flowing water, now laced with large quantities of heavy fuel oil that had been forced out of underground storage tanks.

Throughout the day, the rain continued. Finally, by nightfall, it stopped and the river crested. The next morning, the receding waters disclosed a ghastly mess. Street pavements had been torn up and swept away. Underground pipes were dislodged or broken, and the city was without fresh water or electricity. Thousands of cars had been hurtled through the streets and piled into twisted mounds of wreckage. Vast stocks of merchandise waiting the Christmas season were destroyed. And over all lay a thick layer of foul, stinking mud and oil.

Amazingly, the Ponte Vecchio had held, though the river had broken through the walls of its shops and flowed over it. At times almost submerged, the other bridges—all postwar reconstructions—also survived. Large sections of the embankments, however, were torn away, leaving gaping holes in the streets along the river.

But great as was the world's sympathy for the Florentine people and for the city itself, an equal concern focused on the damage to the city's art treasures, which, though considerable, has fortunately proved less than feared in extent and much of it repairable. The most important single work almost completely ruined was Cimabue's famous life-size crucifix, which had been in the Santa Croce museum. Other paintings temporarily in the basement restoration rooms of the Uffizi were badly damaged, as were thousands of books and periodicals in the lower floors of the National Library, which is vulnerably located at a point on the

When the flood receded, much of the city was left coated with mud and oil.

river bank where the greatest volume of water was unleashed. But the great bulk of the city's treasures were either beyond the reach of the flood waters or have been completely restored.

This was not the first time that the rampaging Arno had swept over the city. It had done so before many times, though only once or twice were those inundations comparable to that of 1966. One of similar scale and intensity occurred on the same day— November 4—in the year 1333, of which we are given a detailed description by the early chronicler Giovanni Villani. After describing the torrential rains (which also began on November 1) and the fear that filled the hearts of the people, he goes on:

By Thursday morning, November 4, the Arno, swollen by the Sieve and other tributaries upstream, overflowed the fields east of the city and backed up against the city walls to a depth of some 12 feet, until the gates and wall itself were broken down, and the water flooded into the streets filling the entire city north of the river. In the baptistery of San Giovanni, the water rose over the altar. South of the river, the water extended almost to San Felice and ruined many houses of the poor.

Villani then records that the bridges at that time were not so fortunate:

> First, the Ponte Carraia was carried away, except for two arches on the north side. Next fell the Ponte Santa Trinita, except for one pier near the church. Then it was the Ponte Vecchio, its arches blocked up by logs and debris, that was overwhelmed and with all its houses and shops collapsed and swept away. . . . At the same time, the water destroyed many of the buildings standing along the river bank on both sides between the Ponte Vecchio and the Ponte Carraia, where all was destruction and chaos. . . . When at last the water returned to the Arno, it left the streets, houses, and cellars loaded with foul smelling mud, which took more than six months to be finally cleared away.

Can a recurrence of such catastrophes be prevented? Those in a position to judge point out that, short of a vast increase in the reforestation of the Apennines and the construction of many large reservoirs upstream, only a deepening of the Arno's channel and the construction of a huge underground overflow tunnel can avert another such flood. But the money seems not to be available. In the meantime, however, steps can certainly be taken to protect the city's art treasures and libraries and to set up a warning system so that at least some property can be removed in time to higher ground.

Such, then, are the adversities to which Florence has been subjected. Some could not have been avoided, but others were within the purview of public opinion and government action. Since the war, several proposals have been made to restrain the wholesale modernization and rapid, poorly planned expansion of the city, though with little effect to date. Once there was a scheme to build a satellite city in the nearby plain to accommodate new industries and the excess population, as there is now a project to prohibit autos in some sections. But these ideas are yet ideals. Nevertheless, there is a growing awareness that the city's unique, historic character should not now be sacrificed piecemeal to poor planning or the lack of it, or to the questionable "necessities" of the times.

Occasionally, progress has been interrupted, not merely adjusted, to preserve something of the old, as when vehicular traffic was prohibited on the Ponte Vecchio, for fear it would collapse. Perhaps the most heartening achievement in recent years has been the rebuilding of the Ponte Santa Trinita, exactly as it was before the Nazis destroyed it. In this instance, the advocates for a more modern and efficient bridge were forced to give way to those who insisted on an exact reproduction. Many of the original parts and fragments had been found and collected after the liberation of Florence and carried by hand to the Uffizi and Pitti, where they were one by one identified, numbered, and stored. To replace those sections that were missing, even the old quarries in the Boboli Gardens were reopened to obtain stone of the type originally used. Finally, after years of discussion and laborious study, they were faithfully reincorporated in a new structure, which was completed in 1957. Today, the bridge arches the river, exactly as it was before—a tribute not only to its original creators but also to those who called it back to life. The rebuilding of the Santa Trinita may signify a reversal of trend. Perhaps solutions may yet be found to preserve and revitalize the old character of Florence while accommodating the demands of modern life.

Fortunately, it is not too late, for although the extent and magnitude of change cannot be minimized, the city's essential charm and character—its unique ambiance—have not been lost. Remarkably, in spite of all that modern man has done and of the unending assault by the elements, for many, Florence still holds a fascination unequaled by any other city in Europe. Perhaps the best way for today's traveler to understand something of the magnetic force that has gripped so many admirers in the past is to climb the hills overlooking the city, where some of the most charming residential districts in the world and much of the beauty of old Florence are yet to be found. Here, narrow, wall-lined roads still wind among the olive trees and vineyards, past graceful and distinctive villas unspoiled by change. The mellow age of these dignified homes, the golden color of their stucco walls, the weathered terracotta tiles of their roofs, and the dramatic Old World formality of their terraced gardens, all contrasting with and yet complementing the humble farm buildings and surrounding fields, make these hills one of those vanishing

Old photo of life along the Arno and the Santa Trinita bridge.

regions where a restful and more elegant age has managed to survive.

It is from vantage points along these slopes above the river, removed from the distractions and annoyances of the modern city, that we can still enjoy the famous views of Florence, well known from so many pictures. From a convenient place like Bellosguardo, the Piazzale Michelangelo, or Fiesole, the city, with its towers and cupolas rising majestically above the massed, red-tile roofs, perhaps still deserves some of the more romantic descriptions that have so often been lavished upon it.

A large part of the history of Florence has been bound up with its *contado*, or surrounding farmland, ever since the Middle Ages, when the control of this area was wrested by the city from the power of the landed nobles. The distinctive beauty of the country-side, with its rolling hills of olives and vines, artistically laid out and painstakingly tended, visibly expresses the rational order, harmony, and balance for which Tuscany is famous. It is as though the land had been arranged with the care and foresight of a giant garden—which, in fact, it is—where nature is strictly controlled and where the appeal is primarily to the mind, not the emotions.

The simple aspects of the *contado*—the humble farm houses, the conical haystacks, the hilltop villages—as well as the sublime —the stately villas, the tall cypresses, the ancient monasteries— have all had their effect on the eye and mind of the Florentine artist and, hence, on European culture. However, with the growth and insulating effect of the suburbs, with the migration from the land to the city, and the gradual breaking up of the old patterns of life, such influence is now, unfortunately, more remote and diminishing. This is a distinct loss, as one of the most attractive aspects of life in old Florence, and one mentioned so often by the 18th and 19th century writers, was the intimate contact between the townspeople and their rural neighbors. Today, in order to enjoy something of this disappearing flavor, it is necessary to penetrate well beyond the suburbs on one of the less traveled roads, stopping in a village or in the surrounding countryside, where life still remains comparatively unsophisticated. In these more remote areas, the farms, generally small and almost self-sufficient, produce modest quantities of many crops, the most important of which are olives and grapes, the latter yielding the famous red Chianti wine. In the past, the income from these crops was customarily apportioned on the *mezzadria* system— half to the tenant and half to the landlord who supplied the land, the buildings, the equipment, and the beautiful white oxen, which may still be seen in pairs, red braids twined in their horns, pulling the primitive plow and maneuvering among the olive trees and vines. (The *mezzadria* system, which probably originated during the Middle Ages on church lands administered by abbots and bishops, was initially a more liberal scheme than the prevailing feudal system, since it implied that the peasant was not a serf but a partner in the enterprise.) However, this 50-50 split arrangement has been altered since World War II in favor of the farmer, who now receives 60 per cent or more, or has been completely eliminated, and operations are conducted by salaried employees.

Until recently, farming methods, too, had changed but little. Grass from fallow land was tediously cut by sickle and fed to the domestic animals. Nothing was wasted. Limbs and twigs from pruning were tied in bundles with strips of bark and stacked for future use. No square foot of arable soil was overlooked. In the past few years, however, there has been a distressing exodus of young people from the less productive farms to the cities, and many areas have been left untended. There is also evidence that the modern world is beginning to catch up with Tuscany— tractors replacing oxen, cement posts replacing trees and stakes on which the vines have always been trained, diversification giving way to a single crop, and here and there the jarring sight of a factory in the midst of a rural landscape. If the present trend continues, the unique appearance of this beautiful land will probably be drastically altered in a decade or so.

Prior to these recent developments, rural change was almost nonexistent and the mental attitude of the *contadino* remained as in ages past. Generally this meant that he was concerned not so much with modernizing his techniques or in the monetary success of his individual enterprise, but rather in the unending contest with the landlord, the tax collector, and the soil itself. Genuine satisfaction was therefore achieved not by greater production or by a reduction in costs, but by the gradual, though often delusive, resolution of these traditional struggles in his favor.

But whereas the *contadino* has always looked upon farming not as a business involving profit and loss, but rather as the traditional basis of social relationships and the source of his inherent right to a livelihood, the Florentine city dweller has, on the contrary, been ardently concerned with the monetary success of business enterprise and the accumulation of capital. The application of new ideas to the processes of production and distribution, and the daring to take great risks, made the Florentine entrepreneurs a factor in the commercial world at a rather early date. Never content with the traditional way of doing things, they were among the first to break away from the inhibitions and restraints of the Middle Ages and to seek a richer material life through inventiveness and self-reliance.

It was, in fact, their early recognition of the inevitable triumph of the mercantile capitalism of the towns and the demise of feudalism, their awareness of the actualities of a changing situation, that prompted them to take advantage of it. Their overriding characteristic seems to have been a strong sense of the practical, of the tangible realities around them, not only in business and politics but also in their approach to life generally. To probe beyond the limits of the visible world into metaphysical subtleties held no appeal for them. They produced few, if any, religious leaders, theologians, heretics, or original philosophers. Instead, the more earthy subjects involving man and his environment—history, physical science, practical politics, architecture and figurative art, and above all commerce—absorbed their minds and energies. Money changers and cloth merchants, they excelled at book-keeping and weaving. For several centuries (the 13th to the 15th) the output of their woolen mills, and later their silk industry, two of the principal sources of new wealth at the time, was of the highest quality, while the scope of their marketing opera-tions throughout Europe surpassed all others. To overcome the competition of traders from neighbouring towns, the Florentines employed every ingenuity and device. They became the foremost bankers of Europe and financed not only a large part of inter-national trade, but even the governments of the greatest states of the day, including France and England. Their coinage became the standard of value and principal medium of exchange for long periods, and their leading businessmen were sought by numerous foreign powers for their services in industry, government, and finance.

Why, we ask, was Florence able to compete so successfully? All the cities of northern and central Italy straddled the ancient trade routes and benefited from the increased activity following the Crusades, but whereas Venice, Pisa, and Genoa were seaports and maintained large fleets, Florence had no such advantages. Neither was the city endowed with any great natural wealth from agri-culture, mining, or grazing. Its geographical position alone gave it an advantage as a crossing point of trade routes, and the citizens capitalized on this at an early date. At first, they did so by acting as the middlemen for the exchange of goods between more wealthy regions. Later, they ingeniously devised methods for taking over this trade, especially wool, through loans or outright purchases of cargoes. In time, a new class of capitalists was formed whose continued existence was dependent not on nature's bounty, but on their own ingenuity, and whose minds were engrossed in the present and future possibilities for shaping their own destinies and fortunes.

The Florentines early realized that they could not depend solely on the carrying trade, could not be merely a conduit for goods, but would also have to enhance the value of those products passing through their hands. For this reason, Florence, near the end of the Middle Ages, gradually turned itself into a giant processing center, a beehive of craftsmen, reworking and finishing silver and other precious metals, gems, stone, marble, leather, furs, wool, silk, and other raw materials that filtered through its gates on their way to the world's markets.

As the population grew and the workshops flourished, the city's prosperity more and more depended on the ability and creativeness of its artisans no less than on the wits of its entrepreneurs. This need to improve a thing, to impart an increased value to it by making it a little better, more durable or more beautiful, to treat and tool leather in a unique way, to dye silks and woolens with more vivid and unusual colors, to design and shape and embellish the precious metals in a superior fashion, became the primary concern of almost the entire citizenry. Out of all this evolved not only the material wealth that was to sustain the flowering of the Florentine civilization, but also a tradition of excellence, of superior workmanship. Here were established by the gold- and silversmiths, the dyers and designers, the stone masons and others, the standards, the techniques, and the apprenticeship requirements that were later to guide the men who undertook to master the higher arts of sculpture, painting, and architecture.

Largely responsible for this development, the Florentine merchants and bankers, through their guild organizations, gradually formed a kind of plutocracy or oligarchy that subsidized and encouraged artistic endeavor. Attempting always to produce and offer the best of the commodities and services in which they dealt, they demanded the highest excellence from the artisans who did their bidding. The standards by which this work was judged were imposed by the same men who supplied the funds. Unaccustomed to abstract ideas or symbolism, these men dealt in material goods and hard cash values. In art, as in business, they required a straightforward delineation of the subject matter.

In painting, a man should look like a flesh and blood human being, not a two-dimensional abstraction, as had been the case during the Middle Ages, when art had been under the sway of the church. Instead of priests, men of affairs now provided the inspiration and influence.

By good fortune and the facts of geography, the city during its heyday never fell under the direct rule of either the pope in Rome or the emperor across the Alps. Both were too far away and were preoccupied with their more immediate neighbors—the emperor with the cities in the Po Valley and the pope with the territories of Umbria and Romagna. Nor did Florence succumb to a family of hereditary despots. The nobles were expelled at an early date or otherwise excluded from power, which was consolidated in the hands of the merchants and bankers and their guild organizations. Though most Italian cities harbored such guilds, which to varying degrees exerted political influence, only in Florence were the guild officers also the city government leaders continuously for several centuries. These men revealed a decidedly cosmopolitan turn of mind, stimulated by the extraordinary range and multiplicity of their foreign commercial arrangements and their consequent involvement in the politics of Italy and Europe on a scale out of all proportion to the size and military power of Florence. In turn, these commitments encouraged the adoption of an aggressive policy of conquest that sought to widen the population base of the city, increase its territorial resources, and obtain direct access to the sea.

Such far-reaching contacts had another important result. They led to a reappraisal of traditional opinions and dogma and incited a condition of intellectual inquiry among those who were in touch with alien customs and ways of life. No longer could the probing curiosity of these men be confined within the limits of medieval philosophy and practice, so laboriously built up by the western clergy and the *doctores scholastici* (schoolmen) throughout the Middle Ages. Instead, a new secular attitude of mind was born, which became known as humanism. Generally, this has been defined as the shifting of emphasis in man's principal intellectual preoccupation away from matters of faith and the hereafter, the primary concerns of the medieval era, toward the living human being and his immediate environment. Henceforth, priority of thought was centered on earthly business—on the profits from buying, shipping, and selling valuable cargoes over vast distances, on loans and interest return, on the possibilities of converting handicrafts into large-scale industrial production— and, concomitantly, on earthly pleasure—on the revival of those seductive aspects of classical culture of which there were remnants, legends, or memories. Pagan myths and rites lingered on among the people, sometimes in Christian guise. The languages spoken on the peninsula were the direct descendants of classical Latin. Roman ruins survived throughout Italy. Classical manuscripts and Roman law had been preserved in many of the monasteries. These were the elements for the making of the Renaissance.*

No city was more responsible for cultivating this new mental reorientation or for undertaking the investigation of the pre-Christian world than Florence. As was long their custom, the citizens looked back to ancient Rome for precedents and inspiration, so that it was natural for Florentine humanism to give birth to a fresh search for and reappraisal of classical literature, which had for centuries lain dormant or obscured by medieval interpretation, in an attempt to find justification and meaning for the things of this world in which they took increasing pleasure. Moreover, these endeavors did not remain the preserve of a small elite but were widely diffused among a stratum of prosperous and educated laymen and the scholars they supported and encouraged. In the process, the first libraries outside the church took form, and critical studies probing the grammatical, rhetorical, and literary aspects of the ancient texts were systematically carried out.

Even more important, the Florentines found in these manuscripts principles of political philosophy analogous to their own institutions of a republican nature and their ideals of political liberty, which served to justify and strengthen them. These discoveries also provided the city's spokesmen and writers the means and incentive to articulate these principles to others and to thereby hand them on to posterity.

* It was the Florentine historian Giorgio Vasari, writing in 1550, who coined the term *la rinascita* (the rebirth) to describe the period from 1350 to 1550 of revived interest in classical civilization, later called the *Renaissance* by the French.

At the same time, the renewed emphasis on classical literature encouraged a new interest in Greek and Roman architecture and art. Men turned to study the ancient ruins that surrounded them. Buildings, statues, and mosaics were literally unearthed, pieced together, and measured, and their beauty was assessed. The simplicity and purity of classical architectural forms—the rounded arch, the pillar, the three capital orders, the pediment, the frieze, the cornice, all abandoned during the Gothic period—were tastefully reintroduced. At the same time, credit and acknowledgment were extended to the individual architect or artist who assumed personal responsibility for his work, unlike the older practice of submerging it in a collective effort of many people. In Florence, the fact that the guilds were largely responsible for the improvement and decoration of many of the churches and other buildings placed the guild members in direct contact with the artists and architects who were engaged in these studies, so that the revived interest in classical art did not remain the private preserve of specialists but became of general public concern. It was this interplay between the professional and amateur, between the worlds of the scholar, the artist, and the merchant, between academic ideals and practical application, that contributed to the unique character of the Florentine Renaissance.

Before the 14th century, Florence had no native schools of sculpture, mosaic, or painting, but had had to import foreign craftsmen—Byzantine, Venetian, Pisan, Sienese. Pisa and Siena had already commenced their special contributions in sculpture and painting and had completed their cathedrals before Florence, a late starter, had entered the field. Yet, though the city was without any continuing artistic tradition, except to a limited extent in architecture, there occurred in the trecento and quattrocento a stupendous outpouring of native genius and innovation in the arts, which eventually spread outward, touching every corner of Europe and forever altering the course of Western culture.

Though this process of artistic development went on almost continuously for several centuries, three well-defined periods of exceptional importance stand out, each punctuated with the names of men familiar to us all. The earliest phase, during the last part of the duecento and the first half of the trecento—before the Renaissance proper—was dominated by the great Giotto in painting, Andrea Pisano and Orcagna in sculpture, and Arnolfo di Cambio in architecture. Then, after a lull, the first part of the next century—the quattrocento—saw the appearance of four outstanding artists who carried forward the earlier achievements onto a new level of creativeness: Ghiberti and Donatello in sculpture, Masaccio in painting, and Brunelleschi in architecture. Finally, toward the end of the 1400s and into the next century, a last momentous phase culminated with the incomparable achievements of Botticelli, Leonardo, and Michelangelo, the last two of whom combined within their persons the ultimate artistic expression of the Florentine Renaissance in all three branches of the fine arts.

Though it was in painting that the Florentines may be said to have made their most original contributions, architecture and sculpture, often practised by the same artists, were especially favored.* Stone and marble, the principal mediums in both these arts and readily available in a variety of types, possessed the earthiness and strength they so admired. But to the natural and appealing qualities, the color and texture of these materials, and to the basic techniques of the stonemason's craft, they added an exceptional genius for carving statues and designing buildings full of power and character on the one hand and grace and proportion on the other.

These qualities are especially apparent in the great city palaces built during the Renaissance with their massive bulk and rugged, though balanced exterior façades, combined with their graceful and airy *loggie* and courtyards. Here, as in painting, the rudiments, the essentials had to be clearly and honestly set forth—the columns, windows, pediments in a building must be intelligently assembled, each part beautiful in itself and in proportion to the whole. Each had also to be directly related to man. Just as the study of the human figure and anatomy led to a more accurate representation on canvas, so it set the scale for Florentine buildings, the parts of

* Few of the artists of the trecento and quattrocento confined themselves to one medium of expression. Many were first trained as goldsmiths or wood workers in *botteghe* (workshops) or as stone carvers in the quarries. Giotto started out as a mosaicist before he went on to sculpture, architecture, and painting. Orcagna, Brunelleschi, Alberti, Verrocchio, Leonardo, and Michelangelo all excelled in various branches of the arts.

which made sense only to the extent they satisfied man's physical and esthetic needs. In return, the new studies of rational and planned construction produced for the painters the new science of perspective.

The Florentines were never greatly influenced in either architecture or painting by the excessive decoration of the Late Gothic style, nor by the Venetian infatuation with color, nor by the drama of the Baroque. Rather, they strove for a realistic statement, for a just synthesis of strength and grace. This masterful union, symbolized in a sense by the city's principal emblems—the lion and the lily—became the touchstone of the Florentine achievement.

In painting particularly, the ability to depict the essential features, the substance of a thing, and to do so without distortion —to do so realistically—became the test of worth. Accurate perspective, correct anatomy, the true play of light, and balanced compositions were for the first time carefully worked out. But the great emphasis laid by the Florentines on artistic achievement and the search for perfection had a negative side, for by setting their standards so high, few artists could measure up to them. As a result, projects were seldom undertaken or work finally accepted without prolonged and bitter debate. Derisive criticism and ceaseless fault-finding became epidemic, sometimes degenerating into mockery, persecution, and violence.

Along with the Renaissance study of Roman literature came the discovery of the satire, that form of written criticism intended to ridicule, which the Florentines, especially after the invention of printing, used unmercifully on one another. The painter Vasari says, for example, that though the greatest artists were to be found in Florence, the great rivalry between them and the intense criticism and "evil-mindedness" of the citizens, though sharpening their wits and their talents, often made life in Florence unbearable. In addition, he suggests that though the painter or sculptor might perfect his art in Florence he should "market his works and his reputation elsewhere" for the city "treats its artists like time treats their works—having perfected them, it little by little destroys and consumes them."

Elsewhere, Vasari says that Brunelleschi was in a state of terrible bitterness and despair caused by the "impious spite of his fellow citizens, who are so blinded by envy that they let their jealousy and ambition threaten the honor and fine works of others."

The Umbrian painter Perugino was advised by his teacher to remove himself to Florence to improve his art. He did so, but finally left the city, unable to accept the insults and slanders aimed at him. In a different vein, after a long residence in Padua, Donatello said that he would soon be worthless as an artist if he continued amid the flattery of the Paduans, and he longed to return to Florence, where he would be constantly criticized.

Another cause for this atmosphere of discord may have been a peculiar feature of the city's constitution which, for several hundred years, required that the terms of office of the Signoria— the governing body—be limited to two months, and that during this time they be confined to the inside of the Palazzo Vecchio, out of touch with the citizens. The purpose of these restrictions was, of course, to prevent bribery and to inhibit any one man or group from acquiring permanent control. But the very distrust and suspicions that prescribed these limitations also prevented the formulation and execution of such consistant, long-range plans as made for the stability and unity of Venice. Instead, the frequent changes in leadership often caused a continual alteration of purpose and tactics, producing a zig-zag course. Inevitably, there followed confusion and failure, especially of military and financial undertakings, leading to blame, slander, and conflict.

Certainly the Florentines were not alone guilty of these sins, but they seemed to erupt more violently and become magnified in the Florentine temperament. A colorful illustration of this may be seen in Botticelli's small painting, *Calumny*, now in the Uffizi, wherein the artist condemns his countrymen's morals and attitudes by depicting their vices. Here, amid a scene of Renaissance splendor, Truth, personified by an imploring nude figure, stands alone and ignored to one side, while Calumny, in the center, clothed in pleasing attire, together with other evil companions— 'Suspicion', 'Envy', 'Treachery', etc.—drags an innocent victim before a judge with donkey's ears, who is condemning the helpless prisoner to an unjust punishment. Though the artist took the subject matter from an ancient allegory, the picture serves as one of the more graphic of the many commentaries that record the negative side of the traditional Florentine character.

It may be that the facts of modern life are mitigating these special qualities—good and bad—but, to a degree, they remain. The Florentines still seem to combine a love of proportion and style with a sense of reality and earthiness. For many of them, perfection in their daily tasks remains a goal, and whatever the medium—rare metals, ceramics, leather, silk, or woolen fabrics— they certainly possess a sure artistic sense, as demonstrated by their patient craftsmanship in a thousand workshops and by their repeated successes in the field of fashion design. The weaknesses, too, apparently persist, for the native tendency toward intolerance and vindictiveness manifested itself in the treachery and fanaticism of some of Mussolini's Florentine followers during the Fascist period. It should be added, however, that then, as in the past, opposition to those guilty of such excesses was quick to form, and within the city, divided as usual between conflicting points of view, a continual struggle was carried on.

In fact, there are many who feel that the propensity to division and conflict, which is so marked a feature of the history of Florence, is an important element in the long list of Florentine

An ironworker in his shop—one of the many craftsmen upholding the Florentine tradition.

achievements. The Italian language itself, in the creation of which they played a predominant part, may have been shaped and molded through their incessant bent for controversy and argument combined with their equally tenacious pursuit of excellence. This euphonious and civilized tongue is actually the Tuscan vernacular, one among many throughout the peninsula that resulted from the breakup of the Roman Empire. The language of Dante, Petrarch, and Boccaccio, natives of Tuscany, it was gradually refined and perfected over the centuries until finally it was accepted throughout Italy as the official, literate form.

Pre-eminence in this matter was no small accomplishment in a country where words, written or spoken, assume an unequaled importance. A veritable torrent of language flows endlessly, as much for its own sake as for the business at hand, and the printed word is exploited without restraint. Newspapers and handbills cry out their messages in large black headlines. Announcements and posters appear everywhere, especially during elections, and few walls are immune from the propagandist's paint brush. Bureaucracy, which flourishes in Italy, continues to increase without letup the already mountainous piles of printed records. Laws and regulations issue forth unendingly, registers compile masses of useless data, and complicated printed forms are supplied for every conceivable circumstance, their original purpose often being lost once the formalities of filling them out and affixing the ubiquitous revenue stamp have been complied with.

The spoken or shouted word is also employed unsparingly. The simplest situation or question can set in motion the most elaborate linguistic gymnastics, accompanied always by the appropriate gestures and facial contortions. Verbal expression is a highly refined art, particularly on those many occasions when a difference of opinion exists. As the conversation becomes more animated, complete strangers stop to listen and judge the performances of the participants. Often, these exchanges assume theatrical overtones, which, absolutely fascinating for visitors, are only momentary and commonplace diversions for Italians.

Italian city life, in particular, has always been surrounded by a great deal of clamor and noise, a peculiarity often remarked on by foreigners. It is almost as if the enjoyment of life is in direct proportion to the magnitude of the uproar. Radios and phonographs are tuned at maximum volume. Autos and motor scooters are owned and driven as much for the engine's roar or the sound of the horn as for their convenience

The national craze for driving has, like noise, become a symptom by which to diagnose the character of the people. As the Italian's conversation is animated, loud, and gesticulatory, so his driving is fast, erratic, and egotistical. It is a direct expression of his personality, which, perhaps frustrated in so many other respects, fulfills itself behind the steering wheel. Suppressed characteristics rise to the surface—impatience, aggressiveness, resentment —which are translated into maximum use of gas pedal, brake, and horn. A car is heard roaring ahead at utmost acceleration, and moments later, the same car is skidding to a halt. Driving is thus transformed into an expression of individual self-assertion against society, each driver endeavoring to out perform his competitors. Mutual cooperation for the sake of the smoother circulation of traffic is not of primary concern.

In fact, traffic conditions have reached a state of near-chaos within the cities, where a combination of inadequate streets, too many vehicles, and the Italian temperament have produced a situation guaranteed to bring out the worst in everyone. Rome is perhaps the most congested, but Florence is not far behind. The police struggle to cope with the situation, but it is not uncommon to see them give up with a gesture of despair and stalk away from a particularly bad snarl that defies untangling.

Of a different nature are the hazards found on the wider boulevards which accommodate massive flows of traffic between major intersections, as, for example, Florence's wide Viali di Circonvallazione, where each driver has a chance to make a run for it. Here, it is well to remember that driving in a lane is unheard of and that the real object of the game is to dash ahead rapidly, weaving in and out, without actually hitting anything. A car pulling alongside may, with no warning whatsoever, suddenly cut in front at breakneck speed. The agility and skill thus demonstrated might under other circumstances be admired, but the complete lack of concern and the rude insults and fist-shaking that accompany all this leave the visitor, whose foreign license plate makes him no more immune than the native, less than enthusiastic for this phase of Italian behavior.

This attitude of aggressive self-assertion expresses itself in other ways. For example, there is no orderly queueing at the bus stop, as in England, each awaiting his turn. Rather, in Italy, as the bus draws up and the doors open, everyone pushes as hard as possible, elbowing his way to the entrance. In general, restraint and consideration for others do not animate Italians in public.

It has often been pointed out that Italians have little social conscience and little sense of responsibility to their fellow citizens. Explanations lie deep in the roots of Italian history. A great part of the peninsula, including Tuscany, was subjected in the 16th century to what became several hundred years of foreign domination, direct or indirect. This situation was especially humiliating for a people, particularly the Florentines, who had known independence and had been among the unrivaled leaders of Europe. All through the Middle Ages and during the Renaissance, their history had been one of increasing communal freedom, greater power and material well-being, and an ever-larger role in the affairs of the continent. Their contributions in literature, art, science, government, commerce, and banking were universally recognized. Yet in the space of a few decades, all this was ended, when in the 16th century, Spain and later other powers were able to impose their dominion over Tuscany and the other Italian states. As the years passed and the yoke settled into permanence, oppression and exploitation inevitably grew. High taxes and burdensome prohibitions stifled ambition and incentive. Poverty increased; life became progressively harder and survival itself a struggle. As government tyranny grew less flexible and further out of touch with the people, as was the situation in the Tuscan Grand Duchy during the 17th and 18th centuries, disrespect for the law and a spirit of contempt for authority developed. Inefficient, corrupt government and lack of justice in the courts led to the vendetta and other extralegal forms of retribution and compensation. At the same time, the individual developed a cynical, selfish attitude toward life and replaced a love for country with an attachment to the more tangible loyalties around him. These habits of mind were not magically erased by the Risorgimento or by the efforts of Mussolini. Thus life today, which still remains fiercely competitive, is carried on according to the old rules of family influence and group loyalties. With such an attitude, the transition to an affluent, modern society is more difficult, and the wonder is that so much progress has been made.

Under the circumstances, the Florentine, like other Italians, has not been able to rely on the regular rules of society to see him through, nor can he hope to achieve either security or success merely by working hard and adhering to formal standards of conduct. Instead, the business of life is carried on according to a hidden system. That is, beneath the surface of the written law and the customary social forms, the actual business of the nation is conducted by an unwritten, but more binding, set of traditional practices.

The collection of taxes, for example, is often cited as illustrative of the general attitude toward the law. A businessman keeps one set of books for himself and another for the government. Both taxpayer and tax collector know the income estimate is not accurate, and each knows that the other knows. It is, however, a starting point upon which to begin negotiations.

Generally speaking, the state is not always very highly regarded. The basic trouble is that many national laws are not considered as protections designed by and for the citizens, but as unreasonable restraints imposed from above. To a degree, this is true—in the past by totalitarian regimes insensitive to the needs of justice and today by Rome, where the central government, employing the instruments of a constitution designed to coerce unity in a diverse country and a codified legal system inflexible and difficult to change, attempts to control almost all the activities of the national life. But split as the electorate is among many splinter parties and points of view, no general consensus forms to support those programs that finally emerge as the law of the land. Thus, having surrendered most powers to Rome, the governments of the regions and municipalities find themselves helpless to do much by themselves and can only try to enforce national laws, while the people resist attempts at conformity.

The dead weight and inefficiency of the central bureaucracy are said to be staggering. To a degree, this is intentional, since many departments serve as the means of employing people who would otherwise have no jobs and who spend their time filling out and cutting complicated forms, reading, talking, making unnecessary appointments, gluing labels, and so on. Perhaps the rubber stamping of everything over and over again is the most annoying and obvious bureaucratic pastime. One looks for a glint of humor or slight self-consciousness as the pounding hand clenching the stamp flies back and forth between inkpad and paper, but instead one finds only a determination to get on with what is taken for an important function. The whole thing would be comical if it were not so absurd.

In a country where every transaction, no matter how simple, is drawn out and made much of, those involving government or public services are even more protracted. Most of officialdom is open only in the morning, refuses to accept checks, and requires antiquated forms and procedures for the most routine affairs. Infinite patience is therefore required, and waiting for services of one kind or another becomes almost a way of life.

Like other Italians, the Florentines are equally helpless to effect major changes in the attitudes of the bureaucracy or the machinery of the state. They accept the rule from Rome much as their ancestors accepted the grand ducal administration. However, patiently adapting themselves to the existing conditions, they usually find ways to get around annoying restrictions.

Excessive individualism and refusal to conform to constituted authority are notorious Italian characteristics, and Florentines especially are known for their independence of mind and determination to go their own way. To a degree, this is healthy, but it often leads to a general lack of cooperation.

That everyone should concentrate on his private interests at the expense of the public welfare was not always the case, especially in Florence during the Renaissance, when patriotism and civic concern reached a level that has been compared to that once enjoyed by the Greek city-states. But this attitude of mind withered away near the end of the quattrocento under a combination of divisive forces, foreign and domestic.

The relative lack of natural resources has also influenced the Tuscan character. Although none of Italy enjoys an abundance of essential raw materials, such as iron, coal, or oil found in neighboring countries, some parts of the nation have been able to exploit other minerals, water power, or agriculture on a much larger scale than is possible in Tuscany. Around Florence, there are few vast stretches to raise large herds of sheep or cattle, no fertile plains for mechanized farming methods, and the forests that once covered the hills have long since gone. The traditional crops, the olive and the grape, are of high quality but are not grown in quantities sufficient to form the backbone of the economy. Nevertheless, a large percentage of the rural population is engaged in the tedious and painstaking effort of nursing along each annual harvest.

Nor has there been much industry, other than on a small scale, here since the days of the wool processing in the 1300s and 1400s. Even that was wholly dependent on foreign supplies of raw material and on foreign markets, just as today the Florentines are dependent on foreign tourists. This precarious situation has therefore always existed.

Wealth there is, however, but it has not been generated out of natural resources so much as patiently accumulated through ingenuity—by the artisan's handiwork, by the creation and collection of antiquities, and by the provision of services to tourists and others. As wealth is not easy to come by, it is tenaciously held. Accordingly, Florentines always say they are poor, for to do otherwise would be to risk having to pay higher salaries and higher taxes. For the same reason, they often live frugally and are not especially fond of opening their houses to any but very close friends. Even long-time residents of the foreign community seldom are invited to Florentine homes. Hence, the Florentine reputation for stinginess and exclusiveness.

The people of Florence have also been accused of being arrogant and sharp-tongued, and in daily social intercourse one encounters a certain lack of restraint, symbolized by loud, argumentative voices. Negative impressions of the Florentines, however, generally are offset by their intensely human qualities, warm friendship, and sympathy in personal relationships. These contacts, as mentioned, are not always easy to achieve. Perhaps the unending stream of foreigners that have descended on their city over the centuries has helped to cause this attitude of exclusiveness. What other defense have they against the loss of their privacy and their own special character? Nonetheless, every visitor sooner or later experiences kindness in many forms from various quarters not remotely connected with the tourist trade.

On such occasions, one's underlying love for the country is periodically replenished.

Sometimes a short drive into the suburbs or surrounding countryside permits a glimpse into the everyday life of the people. Here, away from the hectic tempo of the congested center, one can pause and contemplate the simple aspects of daily routine that make up the Florentine scene. Even the most commonplace of these—an artisan at work at his bench, a waiter taking an order, a garbageman emptying the cans, a boy singing as he goes by on his bicycle—are worth noticing as each seems to embrace a certain unique distinction. Somehow, it is true that the Florentine and his Tuscan neighbors lend a discernible dignity and graceful individuality to everything they do.

On Sunday, everyone will be dressed in his best clothes: even the poorest laborer or peasant in his suit of coarse material is neat and well turned out, and in the evenings the younger men and women, often wearing the latest Italian styles, are particularly interesting to watch when they stroll the streets of small country towns, arm in arm, making the *passeggiata*.

Nor are the children casually or poorly dressed, for the Tuscans take great pride in their appearance. In fact, nowhere do children receive more attention. This is sometimes carried to a fault, particularly among the middle and upper classes in the cities, where a child's every waking moment is under the constant supervision of his mother or nursemaid, and he is pampered and coaxed unendingly. Often the natural love and attention that are so heart-warming to see between an Italian mother and her baby are prolonged into the child's adolescence, accompanied by a noticeable tendency to overindulge, overprotect, overfeed, and overdress. The amount of clothing piled onto small children in the wintertime is truly amazing. One sometimes wonders how they can move about under so many sweaters, overcoats, hats, and scarves.

Especially noticeable is the easy and intimate relationship that exists among all members of Italian families, regardless of age, and that excludes none of them from all aspects of daily activity. The children seem to be always around, even late into the night, as do most decrepit old people, all happily tolerated under what, at times, in many small, crowded living quarters, must be trying circumstances.

In addition, children often accompany their elders in public, and it is natural for them to be accepted anywhere at any time. Cocktail lounges of the American type hardly exist in Florence (with the exception of a few primarily for foreigners), and those places where alcoholic beverages are served are open equally to those of 8 or 80. This is probably because little emphasis is placed on drinking as such. There are no dark rooms where people sit silently at bars, glumly swallowing highballs and martinis. Rather, drinking accompanies some other pastime, such as talking, eating, or playing cards. Little hard liquor is consumed, and most Florentines drink a mild *aperitivo* of one kind or another before dinner, usually some form of vermouth.

Restaurants and *trattorie* provide an excellent opportunity to study the Florentine family in public. The noon meal on Sunday is especially important, and the happy spirit of the occasion, assisted by copious amounts of red wine, leaves an indelible impression. For the Anglo-Saxon unfamiliar with this ritual, the enthusiasm, the warmth and commotion, are fascinating to behold. So also is the manner in which the meal is consumed. Since most Florentines love to talk as much as to eat, neither activity can be sacrificed for the other. It is, therefore, with great ingenuity that a continuous stream of conversation is combined with a practically uninterrupted ingestion of the meal. Each mouthful of *pasta* or other food is accompanied by a reverse flow of words, while, at the same time, bread is torn off piece by piece with the fingers, thrown into the mouth rapidly, and sluiced down with the local wine.

Some rudimentary knowledge of Florentine dishes and specialties should be acquired beforehand to enjoy fully this phase of a visit to Italy. One customarily orders a la carte; and each item is sensibly served separately, one at a time, and of manageable proportions, in contrast to the onslaught of heaping, oversized plates that often descend all at once in American restaurants, taking the edge off the best of appetites. Dishes do not return to the kitchen in Italy with wasted food, all of which is precious, and everything is consumed with gusto.

The noon or evening meal may start off with *antipasti* (hors-d'oeuvres of fish, shellfish, fowl, meat, or vegetables prepared in numerous ways*), but more likely the Florentine will begin with a *minestra*, a term that includes soup (*zuppa* or *brodo*) as well as dry paste (*pastasciutta*) served with a sauce. Many forms of the latter are cut in familiar shapes and stuffed with meat or vegetables —*ravioli*, *tortellini*, *cannelloni*—while others take the form of long strips of varying width—*spaghetti*, *tagliatelle*, *vermicelli*—often difficult for the foreigner to eat gracefully. This is no problem for the Italian, however, whose ability to control those elusive strings was perfected in childhood. The napkin is tied under the chin and the steaming plate of *pasta* and its sauce are thoroughly mixed with spoon and fork. The spoon is then put aside—never used as a crutch—while the fork spears a generous portion which is then expertly twisted and twined up into the air and thence skillfully conveyed into the mouth with a minimum of loose dangling ends.

Florentine cooking is generally simple and uncomplicated, and, in fact, Tuscany has not made large contributions to the science of gastronomy. A steak is prepared with a bit of oil by merely grilling over a wood fire and served rare with a slice of lemon. Nothing is ever added—no sauce or trimmings to camouflage its essence. But for the average Florentine, beef is expensive so that he will probably order the less dear *vitello* (veal), since Italy does not have the ranges or the forage to fatten many cattle, and most are slaughtered very young.† Or he may settle simply for *pollo* (chicken) or *animelle* (sweetbreads) or *trippa* (tripe) or *cervello* (brains), making up for the economy of even these servings with bread and pasta.‡ Particularly enjoyable are various local vegetables, usually sautéed lightly in olive oil and served

---

* Local Florentine specialities include *carciofini fiorentina* (artichoke hearts in cheese sauce, mushrooms, and cauliflower), *crostini* (small pieces of toast with minced chicken livers), *zucchine alla toscana* (baby zucchini cooked with minced pork, tomato, and onion), and especially *salame*, of which Florence has some excellent varieties.

† Even its Italian name *bistecca* shows that for long beef was served generally only to those who could afford it—English-speaking visitors.

‡ Local specialities include *stracotto alla fiorentina* (veal stew), *stufatino* (veal stew in white wine sauce), *trippa alla fiorentina* (tripe cooked in tomato sauce and flavoured with marjoram), *fritto misto alla fiorentina* (calves' brains, sweet breads, chicken, artichoke hearts, and mozzarella cheese).

individually.* Except for bread, few items of food are touched by the fingers at table. Thus, an orange, apple, or pear is deftly peeled with knife and fork and enjoyed with more wine at the end of the meal.

Similarly, the espresso bar, where that unique strong coffee is made and served, opens a window on the Italian world. The espresso machine itself, whose complications remain a mystery to the foreigner, is worth observing. So also are the movements of the operator as he manipulates the valves and levers, forcing the high pressure steam through the contraption and finally coaxing the condensed brown liquid into the waiting cup.

These coffee bars are found throughout the city and form a vital part of daily life. Not only are they good places to relax for a moment during the day, but they are especially useful for breakfast, that is, an Italian breakfast of rolls and coffee. One of the chief pleasures of a visit to Florence is to settle oneself as early as possible at a convenient café, preferably at a table on the sidewalk, order the morning *colazione*, and, while occasionally glancing over the newspaper, observe the surrounding scene. One may not be quite in time to see the early risers en route to their jobs or stopping in for a quick espresso, but shortly, the shopkeepers and artisans arrive, unlocking and raising their heavy iron storefront shutters. Then come the housewives with their baskets, the students, the businessmen, the nursemaids with their charges, and the shoppers. More and more vehicles converge, and the noise and confusion increase. Finally, as the morning wears on, a sprinkling of tourists, alone or in groups, can be picked out. Mostly from northern countries, they are easily identified by their clothing, manners, haircuts, and physical differences. Well fed and prosperous looking, often larger than most Italians, at first too pale—they are soon too sunburned. There are other distinguishing features: the guide books and bulging purses, the guide himself, the ubiquitous cameras that, so often like their owners, are exposed to but do not comprehend the scene.

The annual tourist influx presents an insoluble dilemma for the Florentines. On the one hand, tourism is a vital, indeed the most important, part of the city's economy. The handicraft and

---

* Local speciality: *fagioli* (white beans), boiled and then cooked in oil with various flavorings: garlic, sage, rosemary, bay leaf, chili peppers, tomatoes.

Morning shopping scene in the Piazza di San Piero, a part of
old Florence that seems unchanged.

clothing industries are largely dependent on foreign patronage, as are many of the fine arts and antique dealers. The museums and galleries are run primarily for visitors, and housing, feeding, and transporting them requires that a major part of the best available facilities be employed for their use. On the other hand, tourism conditions the Florentines' existence and undermines their independence. In a large city such as London or Rome, visitors in such numbers are less conspicuous, but in Florence their presence becomes painfully more evident in every street and piazza as the weather warms and the season gets under way.

Since the end of World War II, and especially since the flood, much credit is due to the Florentines for their efforts to accommodate the ever-growing numbers of new residents and foreign travelers, continually improving the facilities of city life while at the same time trying not to emasculate the city's character. But some problems remain very complex and almost beyond solution. What, for example, can be done about the hordes of automobiles and especially the huge tourist buses that converge upon the town? The latter transport masses of visitors with money to spend, but their tremendous size and their increasing numbers compound the general traffic problem, which is gradually making life in the center almost unbearable. Parking is impossible, driving or walking through the streets is tortuous and tiring, the piazze are spoiled esthetically and functionally, and smog from exhaust fumes is becoming a serious matter, not only to humans, but also to the stone buildings that it attacks and ultimately ruins.*

Recently, one-way streets have been marked out almost everywhere within the central area, but, with illegally parked cars restricting the flow of traffic and with an over-all plan that often makes it impossible to proceed from one place to another without traveling blocks in the opposite direction, little improvement seems evident. Walking is therefore preferable, but even so there are hazards. Sidewalks are usually very narrow, so that it is not always possible to pass without stepping into the street, and sometimes they taper down into nothing and disappear completely. In addition, they are often unnecessarily dirty, not only

* Two types of stone are quarried in the area, the *pietra serena*, gray-green in color, and the famous *pietra forte* of golden tint. Both erode or flake away with extremes of temperature and with the action of wind, water, and pollutants.

The historic Piazza della Signoria, with (*left* to *right*) the
Palazzo Vecchio, the Uffizi, and the Loggia dei Lanzi, jammed
tight with cars and tourist buses.

with the inevitable accumulations but with the remains from
littering, spitting, and failing to curb dogs, persistent Florentine
habits. Pigeons are another source of filth, their droppings
covering not only sidewalks but hundreds of buildings and statues.
If their numbers were reduced to one tenth, there would still be
too many.

But there are larger problems that Florence must face in the
future: the outlawing of all motorized traffic in the center,
the elimination of much ugly neon lighting, the restriction of
suburban growth, flood control arrangements. These and other
questions affecting the preservation of this unique city are controversial and complicated, discussion of them tending to polarize
around opposite points of view—one side favoring traditional
values, arguing that these are the essence of Florence, and the
other wishing to modernize, arguing that Florence has always
been subject to change and must continue to do so to avoid
stagnation and artificiality.

Compromise is probably inevitable, but this is not always
satisfactory, as the new structures near the Ponte Vecchio testify.

But compromise in other cases has proved to be positive and desirable, as, for example, in preserving the exteriors of old palazzi while completely modernizing their interiors, or updating shops in a building in keeping with its essential architecture. The Loggia of the Rucellai, for instance, has been altered in both appearance and use but in such a clever way as to preserve its lines and character.

Shops, in fact, have never looked so bright and attractive as since the flood, whether a routine butcher's stall or the most elegant boutique on Via Tornabuoni, where functionalism has often been smoothly combined with the native Florentine taste in design and materials.

Throughout the city, restoration is always in process, the inevitable pile of broken stone and brick is in evidence everywhere, and though great strides have been made, the question always persists whether the patience and tenacity of the construction workers in their blue undershirts and white paper caps together with sufficient funds can win the battle against deterioration and decay. The churches, in particular, continually need repair, and many have undergone reconditioning and improvements since the flood. Adequate lighting, for instance, the lack of which was a source of frustration to visitors for years, now permits frescoes and other works of art to be seen clearly at last.

Florentines are well aware that their churches are tourist sights of the first importance, and they never seem to mind the crowds that are continually milling about inside. Nor do they expect any religious motivation or even quiet. In fact, they themselves are very casual, relaxed, and at home in church. They move about and talk, and there is none of the diffident reverence or restraint of the Anglo-Saxon who enters his church quietly in his best clothes, endures in reserved silence the service, and is somewhat relieved to depart at the end.

But recent attempts by improperly or scantily dressed tourists to gain entrance to religious buildings despite signs prohibiting the wearing of such garb in churches is understandably offensive. Current conditions have forced some relaxation of the rules, and women are now permitted inside without head covering and with bare arms, but females in shorts and males without shirts are not surprisingly asked to remain outside. It seems hardly too much to ask that sanctuaries intended for worship and escape from the pandemonium of the streets should be shown some sign of respect by those who are guests in another country.

The Florentine himself may or may not profess to believe in his religion, but he admits the church as an important fact of life. This is due to centuries of tradition and to a subconscious acceptance of Catholicism, which the current social ethics and political allegiances of the day do not preclude. The contradictions are ignored, and the church continues to work its influence in a thousand ways from cradle to grave. The rituals and ceremonies, the innumerable feast days and festivals are the outward manifestations, but the real hold is more subtle. This stems from the early molding of the thinking process through the church's intimate involvement in most aspects of life, sometimes direct, as through education or charitable institutions, sometimes indirect, through political or social influence. Reactions against this influence have taken place time and again in the past—during the Reformation, the 18th-century Enlightment, the Industrial Revolution, the Risorgimento, after both World Wars. In the past hundred years alone, decisive reforms were carried out. The pope lost his temporal dominion over sizeable areas of Italy, education was secularized to a degree, monasteries and convents were closed and confiscated, laws were passed redefining the limits between church and state. But the effects have been greater on the surface than underneath, and Italy remains a most Catholic nation, more for its approach to life than for its outward forms. The fundamental things the church has always been, the Italian state and society also are: a legal system built on theory and codification rather than on precedent and evolutionary change; a rather inflexible hierarchy of authority inherent in most social and political institutions despite the democratic façades; show and ceremony to cover up the drabness and helplessness of the daily life of the masses; the total subordination of the citizen to the system itself; the tendency publicly to voice the rules, whether God's or man's, but to adhere to them only when it is convenient.

In contrast to the pervasiveness and relative stability of the church, the continuity of which has persisted, despite superficial interruptions, Italian political institutions have been varied and often short lived. Of course, all of Europe went through the vicissitudes of the feudal phase and then experienced a shift in political power to the towns, but whereas England, France, and Spain consistently moved toward a centralization of political power while forming their nation-states, Italy remained cut up and divided until the 19th century. Almost every conceivable form of government developed on the peninsula. City-states grew up in the north, often dominated by a prince or other tyrant; Venice, in theory a republic, was ruled for centuries by a hereditary oligarchy; the pope controlled large territories as church fiefs; and in the south, where feudalism persisted, various periods saw the rule of a Holy Roman emperor or one or another royal dynasty, usually French or Spanish. Sicily was under Greek, African, Roman, Byzantine, Saracen, Norman, French, Spanish, and Austrian conquerors throughout its long history. The cities of Tuscany have had governments of nobles, merchants, oligarchs, dictatorships of tyrants and popes, republican interludes, and finally grand dukes, the pawns of foreign states. There was no consistent progress toward a single political entity or unifying political theory. Even after the Risorgimento, the system took several abrupt turns from a constitutional monarchy to a dictatorship to a republic, and there is still no general popular consensus— the political parties are unable to agree whether the nation should be republican, monarchist, socialist, communist, fascist, clerical, or anticlerical.

Tuscany's experience has been kaleidoscopic. At the end of the Middle Ages, the large feudal estates were gradually encroached upon and overcome by the towns—Florence, Siena, Pisa, Arezzo, Lucca, and others. Each expanded into a city-state with surrounding territories of its own, and each developed its own particular form of government. Eventually, these various towns came into conflict with one another, and the smaller ones were absorbed, until, by the early Renaissance, Florence dominated them all. For several centuries, the Medici family ruled, first as politically responsible private citizens, then as royal heads of state, unanswerable to anyone except the will of the larger powers. When the last Medici died in 1737, the Austrians took over. Thus Tuscany, like the rest of Italy, succumbed to external domination, unable to work out its own political destiny, and it was not until the middle of the last century that the states of the peninsula were finally able to throw out their foreign rulers and unite in one nation. Credit for this achievement generally lies elsewhere, but Tuscany too had its patriots, reformers, and idealists who sought to stir their countrymen and light the spark that would achieve the unification. Interestingly, some of these were not Italian at all but members of the Florentine foreign colony, then an important element in the social and political life of the country. This unusual group is worth considering in some detail.

Throughout the 18th century, Florence had remained one of the important cities for the educated Englishman, making the Grand Tour, to visit, but it was not until after Napoleon's time that artists and intellectuals commenced to gather here in large numbers and for long periods. Previously, only the wealthy could travel, but now, with the Industrial Revolution making itself felt, representatives of the rising middle class were appearing on the continent. Lord Byron remarked acidly in 1817 that Rome was "pestilent with English."

Among the newcomers was John Ruskin, who began in the 1840s to publish his emphatic, opinionated observations on Tuscan art, especially the works of the late medieval era that were to greatly influence the next several generations. Strangely, Ruskin did not like Florence at first and never had anything good to say about the Florentines themselves. He claimed that they were always trying to run him down with their carts and commented on the conditions in the city itself: "the noise, dirt, tobacco smoke and the spitting are intolerable."

This attitude seems to have been shared by many Englishmen and Americans who took up residence in Florence (often in a country villa), partly to pursue the arts and partly to enjoy the agreeable and inexpensive conditions of life, but always with little or no contact with the Florentines themselves, save their innkeepers, servants, or models.* Though most were English, all

* Nathaniel Hawthorne in 1858 paid $50 a month for an immense suite of rooms in town opening onto a terrace and including linen and silver. He later moved farther out to a villa at Bellosguardo, where he paid only $28 a month. Another foreigner, an English lady, paid £20 ($100) a month for a large villa of 14 well-furnished rooms, a maid, a manservant, all meals properly served, housekeeping, carriage and horses, firewood and candles.

foreigners were referred to as *Inglesi*.* These expatriates were
considered eccentric by the Florentines, who could identify them
easily by their manners and dress (Raphaelesque beret and flowing
silk cravat) and by the fact that few of them made any attempt to
learn Italian. Nevertheless, they assumed for themselves the role
of arbiter and judge of all things Florentine, past and present.
Living happily in a world of their own, forever at odds with
most of the Florentines, but dedicated, according to their imperfect knowledge, to glorifying almost everything they saw around
them, they were responsible for giving the world an oversenti-
mentalized, romanticized, unrealistic picture of the city that still
persists. In the darker recesses of almost any second-hand book-
store can be found those dusty volumes—diaries, impressions,
and descriptions—that flowed so amply from their pens and
which, though imparting a certain flavor, were often amateurish
and fanciful.

Romanticists in art and history, the Anglo-Florentines were
politically liberal, though most came from conservative back-
grounds. Aware of Italy's plight, they were intensely critical of
the nobility and contemptuous of the masses, whom they viewed
as demoralized and unprincipled. Only the small middle class,
the intellectuals and artists, were looked upon with any degree
of hope in the political struggle they foresaw and helped to
further. While some members of the foreign colony took part in
the Florentine social whirl and attended the grand duke's receptions, the more visionary, committed to Italian unity, were busy
writing newspaper articles and books and attempting to influence
opinion in support of Cavour and the House of Savoy. In the
war for independence that followed with the Austrians, the
British government's policy and diplomacy were crucial, and
public attitudes in London were in the end decisively influenced
by the literary efforts of the Anglo-Florentines.

---

* Among the prominent members were Landor, Layard, Trelawny, Jarves,
the Brownings, the Trollopes, Hillard, Howells, Clough, Hawthorne, some of
whom—Walter Savage Landor, Elizabeth Barrett Browning, Frances Trollope,
Arthur Clough—are buried in Florence. Their graves may be visited in the
English cemetery, an undisturbed, tree-covered knoll in the middle of the
Piazzale Donatello. Today it is a kind of romantic, 19th-century oasis, isolated
in time and place by the pounding traffic of the 20th century that surrounds it.

Following the unification, and after Florence became the temporary capital, the old town changed rapidly. An Englishman, Charles Weld, described the city in detail as he found it in 1866, filled with Piemontesi and other employees of the new government pushing everyone on the sidewalks and driving their horse-drawn vehicles carelessly. Prices suddenly shot up, and rooms and apartments were hard to find. Fuel was especially scarce and expensive. Weld thought the shops rivaled those of London and were full of beautiful silks and satins as well as the local handicraft specialties: inlaid marble, carved frames, straw plait, all showing an amazing dexterity of hand. His impressions of the Florentines follow the usual pattern: love of show, gossip, prying, slander and scandal, inclined to skepticism, and an unmerciful caricaturing of almost everything, especially the church. He was afraid they were too inclined to live on their past achievements and were unwilling to pay the taxes and make the other sacrifices necessary to underwrite a new and important nation. The women, he decided, were beautiful and well dressed but their voices were harsh and loud.

Another foreigner, the American William Dean Howells, who spent the winter 1882–83 in Florence, has also left his direct, unembroidered impressions, many of which are still true today. He complains of how difficult it is to make acquaintances outside of English-speaking circles, how seldom one is invited to a Florentine home, and implies that the foreign colony is still pretty well isolated from the natives. He hears more English than Italian spoken on the Via Tornabuoni and notes the alluring shops, confectioners, florists, and milliners (and high prices), the tourists and elegant passersby on that street, and even refers to the American bank, the English Pharmacy, and Doney's Cafe (all still there). He remarks how well dressed the citizens are, especially admiring their fur-lined coats. He finds the Mercato Vecchio (soon to disappear) with its crowds of peasants and donkey carts the most picturesque place in Florence but abhors the Spanish look of the Piazza San Marco. The suppression of the convents had recently taken place and he found those converted into schools on the whole to be a good thing: "young life and hope replacing the nuns who before paced up and down the corridors with downcast eyes and folded palms." His worst complaint was of the "vile,

Old photo of the palace-lined Via Tornabuoni, long a fashionable Florentine shopping street.

old, rancid stenches" which escaped from holes in the street and which made him wonder (as one does today) whether the sanitary system was functioning at all.*

No book on Florence would be complete without some mention of the world-famous art collections found there. Perhaps no city can rival Florence in this regard. But here, the very size and complexity of the subject rules out any serious review or comment. Instead, a few remarks on the nature and origins of the collections will have to suffice, and esthetic judgments and appreciations must be left to others.

Certainly the Florentines were as acquisitive as any people, and since they had the wealth, ambition, and talent to purchase or produce a vast amount of art, they long ago set the pace for other collectors. In fact, it is difficult to grasp the size of this accumulation of frescoes, paintings, mosaics, majolica, sculptures, and carvings (in marble, stone, terracotta, bronze, and ivory), gold- and silversmith's work, dispersed as it is among the city's palaces, churches, museums, and galleries. One is best advised to utilize the time available in the few principal places where the very best or at least the most famous of everything has been concentrated. For practical purposes, this means primarily the National Museum of the Bargello for sculpture and the Uffizi Gallery for painting. The Palazzo Pitti contains some of the world's greatest art treasures, but the exhibits in the other two are more strictly of Florentine origin and, being arranged according to chronology and schools, are more illustrative of the city's special contribution during the Renaissance.†

The nucleus of the principal collections stems back to Cosimo Medici the Elder (1389–1464), the first of his line to amass a fortune sufficient for the patronage of the arts on a large scale (and

---

* Actually there are no sanitary sewers in Florence, only storm sewers. Each building has its own septic tank or cesspool under the street, and when the barometer drops these exhale fumes. It is claimed, however, that they are perfectly sanitary.

† The paintings in the Pitti are arranged haphazardly. Many still hang where they were placed by the grand dukes, and most walls are covered solidly from floor to ceiling. Some people, however, prefer this esthetically rich profusion of art in its original setting to the more studied and rational approach of the Uffizi.

incidentally for the indirect control of the city). His descendants continually added to this collection until, after several hundred years, there was gathered together an unrivaled array of paintings and other objects of art. At first scattered among the various palaces and villas of the Medici family, they were gradually brought together, from the 16th century on, by the Medici grand dukes, who had those most valuable arranged for display on the top floor of the Uffizi in the long corridor or *galleria** and adjacent rooms. Over the years, the original collection, mainly of Tuscan works, continued to be enlarged by the addition of classical—mostly Roman—sculpture, paintings from the Venetian and Flemish schools, drawings, weapons, gems, coins, and other works in rare metals. Much of this was housed in the Uffizi, but a large part was used to decorate the vast interior of the Palazzo Pitti, where the grand dukes had their official residence after the middle of the 16th century.

That this private aggregation of wealth and taste has to this day remained mostly intact and accessible to the public is due largely to the last of the Medici, who in 1737 magnanimously bequeathed the whole to the city of Florence in perpetuity, on condition that it never be removed therefrom.

This mandate has been breached only twice, both times as the result of war and foreign intervention. The first occasion was during the Napoleonic period, when a number of works were shipped off to Paris, but most of these were later returned. Then, during World War II, the Nazis, a few weeks before evacuating the city, and contrary to express agreements with the Italians, hurriedly carried off some 300 paintings to several secret caches in northern Italy. The Florentines had done all they could to safeguard their art works when it became clear that the Allied advance could not be stopped south of Rome. Fixed works such as church façades, frescoes, and pulpits were covered by scaffolding and sandbags. Moveable works (paintings, sculptures, libraries) had been taken out into the country to villas and monasteries, for safekeeping. An especially large number had been accumulated at Montegufoni and Montagnana, southwest of the city, and these formed the bulk of those stolen by the Germans. Considering that they were recklessly handled by SS troops and transported

* This was the origin of the word "gallery," meaning a place to display art.

by truck over rough roads, uncrated and unprotected, it is remark-able that damage was not extensive. However, most were safely recovered by the Allies at the end of the war and returned.

Today, for purposes of convenience and organization, parts of the Uffizi collection have been transferred from there to other places of exhibition—the Etruscan and other ancient sculptures and artifacts to the Archeological Museum; the Medici jewels and religious and secular works of many kinds in porcelain, crystal, semiprecious stones, silver, and gold to the Museo degli Argenti; and the many examples of the minor arts (armor and arms, medals and coins, majolica), the small bronzes, ivories, wax works, and, most important, the Renaissance sculptures to the Bargello.

This latter group, in various mediums (stone, marble, bronze, terracotta) and in various forms (busts, statues in the round, reliefs), illustrates the whole history of Florentine sculpture from its beginnings in the 14th century through the great achievements of Donatello, Desiderio, Michelozzo, Verrocchio, and the della Robbias in the 15th century, and ending with the work of Michelangelo, Cellini, and Giambologna in the 16th.

The Uffizi has therefore been left mainly with the paintings, but these, ranging from Giotto and his followers through the Florentine, Umbrian, and North Italian schools of the following several centuries, and including many of the greatest artists of all times, represent the finest pictorial collection of the Italian Renaissance ever assembled under one roof. Here, one can study and enjoy the continuous development of the painter's art from the first breaks with the long Byzantine and religious hold over technique and approach, through the humanizing tendencies of the Renaissance period, down to Mannerism and the Baroque which grew out of it.

Certainly in the field of painting alone, if we were to disregard all other areas of achievement, the Florentine contribution to the history of Western art was second to none. From the giant step forward taken by Giotto, there followed other superior talents in regular succession whose works constitute the main theme of the Uffizi gallery; Fra Angelico, who combined the asceticism of the dying Middle Ages with the fresh, saintly spirit of St. Francis; Masaccio, the discoverer of natural light and shadow (*chiaroscuro*), rather than line, to give objects solidity and realism; Uccello, the exponent of scientific perspective; Domenico Veneziano; Andrea del Castagno; Fra Filippo Lippi; Piero della Francesca, painter-mathematician and master of abstract, formal design; Botticelli, most enigmatic and fascinating of them all, who gathered together the strands of the intellectual, spiritual, and artistic life of his times and wove them into a series of paintings of unsurpassed beauty and interest; and finally, examples of two of the greatest, most influential artists of all times, who put the capstone on the city's reputation, Leonardo and Michelangelo. The works of these men, together with others of only slightly lesser stature, provide in this pleasant setting the opportunity to contemplate the rudiments and foundations on which all Western painting has been based.

There are other places to study the art of the Renaissance, in addition to the Uffizi and the Bargello: the museum of San Marco, where most of Fra Angelico's work is found; the museum of the Opera del Duomo (works connected with the Cathedral); the museum of the Opera di Santa Croce (remnants from that church); the Galleria dell'Accademia and the Casa Buonarroti (Michelangelo).

One of the great advantages of Florence as compared with Rome, for example, is the compactness of its historical center and the ease with which a visitor may quickly become oriented. The Arno runs almost straight through the city from east to west, serving as a reliable reference point as compared to the twisting Tiber which, appearing when least expected, forever helps to confuse a stranger in Rome.

Except when arriving or leaving Florence, there is seldom need to venture into the suburbs, since almost everything of interest is concentrated within a short distance of the Piazza della Repubblica. In fact, a rectangle drawn to connect the railway station, Santa Maria del Carmine, Santa Croce, and the Church of the Annunziata would, with few exceptions, enclose everything of interest to the visitor. This area, which includes a portion on the south side of the river known as *Oltr'Arno*, can easily be covered on foot, and, indeed, this is the only way to get to know the city well.

Generally, it is best to avoid the stereotyped itineraries offered by the guide books and simply go forth with a good map and

Florence is still a center for artisans, woodworkers, painters, and, of course, shopkeepers.

ramble about enjoying the general atmosphere. Thus, *where* you go on the first day is less important than *when* you go. Without doubt, an early start will prove most rewarding, not only because it allows more time before the noon closing, but also because the activity in the streets is more interesting. This is especially true in the hot summer months, when these early morning hours can be delightful and when the middle of the day often becomes unbearable. In fact, if possible, it is best to be off the streets by 10.00 a.m. and inside the Uffizi or in the welcome coolness of one of the churches, leaving the heat and the crush of traffic outside.

Alternately, this is a good time to look into the shops, many of which are air conditioned, for merchandise of incomparable craftsmanship: inlaid marble, carvings of all kinds, ceramics, jewelry (on the Ponte Vecchio), lace, straw and leather goods, women's clothing in the latest international styles. Or, even more interesting, one can browse around the antiquarian shops, which are loaded with every conceivable form of antique furniture, objects of art, paintings, prints, and majolica, as well as numerous reproductions, some labeled so and some not, many of which are so well done as to fool the experts. In fact, there is no better way to spend an hour or two than to search out some of the dingy *botteghe* where furniture making and faking with old wood go on daily.

From 12.30 p.m. until about 4.00 p.m., almost everything closes. The clatter of iron shutters coming down in front of the shops can be heard, the churches bolt their doors, and the Florentines disappear from the streets. Traffic funnels rapidly toward the suburbs, and the hectic, noisy life of the city becomes, in a matter of minutes, an inaudible murmur. The big meal of the day is being prepared, and the siesta will follow. For the visitor, it is a good idea, especially during warm weather, to return to the hotel after lunch, and, following the example of the natives, take a nap for at least an hour. By so doing, he will have the strength to start out again when, around 4.00 p.m., traffic suddenly reappears, windows and doors are thrown open, people emerge from all directions, and the city comes back to life. The midday break has ended, and business resumes as before.

But it is around 7.00 p.m. that the high point of the day is attained and the tempo of life reaches a crescendo. Everyone is out and about, the espresso bars are packed, the stores are jammed with customers, the streets are filled with promenaders, and the excitement and energy of the Italian world overflows. It is hard to remain aloof from this contagious spirit which magically wipes away other less attractive impressions. But this hectic interval does not continue long, and by 8.00 p.m. the shops close up again and the exodus repeats itself. Relatively little night life exists in Florence as compared with other cities, and by 10.00 p.m. the restaurants are beginning to empty and a relieving quiet settles over the old town. For the tourist, there is practically nothing to do after dinner. The few night clubs are expensive and provincial, hotels are quiet, and there are no cinemas, theaters, or television programs in languages other than Italian.

But aside from the debatable advantages of contemporary Florentine life, no city has more to offer in the realm of our cultural and artistic heritage. Before it can be fully appreciated, however, even with an actual visit to Florence of adequate duration, it is vital to understand something of the city's historical development.

Fortunately, examples of most of the eras through which Florence has passed, with the exception of the very earliest times, can be found in art objects, buildings, and other structures that still exist. The basic plan of the original Roman town dating from the time of Caesar may still be seen in the key streets of the central section, particularly the Via Calimala and the Corso with their extensions and lateral connections, which were laid out in north-south, east-west directions. Substantial parts of the medieval city remain between the Duomo and the Palazzo Vecchio within an area enclosed by the Via Calzaioli and the Via del Proconsolo. All of Florence once resembled this section with its narrow streets and tall, forbidding stone structures.

Toward the end of the medieval period, the population increased considerably, causing *borghi* (suburbs) to grow up outside the then confining city walls. One of these *borghi* developed around the Franciscan church of Santa Croce and another around the Dominican church of Santa Maria Novella, both of which were originally built in open fields to the east and west, respectively. Somewhat later, with the coming of the Renaissance, new streets were laid out north of the Duomo, in what has been called the Medici quarter because of the intimate connection of that family with the area. This centers on the Via Cavour, originally called the Via Larga from its comparative breadth for the times. As the Renaissance continued and eventually in Florence (during the quattrocento and cinquecento) burned itself out, new palazzi and churches sprang up everywhere, stamping the city with the genius of its greatest architects. The Via Cavour, the Via Tornabuoni—the most elegant street in Florence—and its continuation on the other side of the river, the Via Maggio, are particularly rich in examples of town mansions of this period. Subsequent years saw numerous refinements and embellishments but no basic alterations or extensions of the city until modern times, when large-scale demolition and rebuilding around the Piazza della Repubblica, as already mentioned, provided contrasts with the older sections.

‘An especially good place to study the juxtaposition of many of these architectural and artistic creations of the past, as well as the influences of our own times, is on the steps of the Loggia dei Lanzi in the Piazza della Signoria. There, in this irregular but

Parade of sculptures in front of the Gothic Palazzo Vecchio and the Late Renaissance Uffizi. The equestrian statue honors Duke Cosimo I.

magnificent open space in the heart of the city, the eye may encompass in a few minutes a cross-section of hundreds of years of history: medieval houses and the Gothic Palazzo Vecchio (1299); the Tribunale di Mercanzia (1358); the Loggia itself, one of the earliest buildings to signify the coming of a new era (1376); the statues that mark the development of Florentine sculptural achievement through its most productive years: a copy of the *Marzocco*, or Lion of Florence, symbol of the sovereignty of the city (1438), and *Judith Decapitating Holofernes* (1460), both by Donatello; a copy of Michelangelo's famous *David* (1503), exhibiting its greatness in contrast to Bandinelli's awkward

Hercules (1534) alongside it; Cellini's masterpiece, *Perseus* (1553); Ammannati's ponderous Neptune Fountain perched above the more graceful figures of mythological marine creatures around it (1570); the *Rape of the Sabines* (1583), the equestrian statue of the great Medici grand duke Cosimo I (1595), and *Hercules Overcoming the Centaur* (1599), all three by Giambologna, the last of the famous Florentine sculptors. The Late Renaissance is also represented in the façade of the Palazzo Uguccioni on the north side of the piazza, influenced by 16th-century Roman architecture, and in the Palazzo degli Uffizi designed by Vasari in 1570. And guarding either side of the Loggia's steps are two stone lions—one of the classical age and the other, sculpted to compliment it in 1600 at the close of the Florentine Renaissance. Their presence emphasizes the great span of time between the two civilizations but also the intimate connection between them. Significantly, there is nothing to represent the years thereafter, the long period of relative stagnation lasting down to the Risorgimento. There is, however, an example of the eclecticism of the 19th century in the Palazzo delle Assicurazioni di Venezia (1871) on the west side of the piazza that combines a brittle imitation of the Gothic style with a false Renaissance cornice made of cast iron!

Less tangible than this array of monuments in stone, though equally memorable, are the many great events of Florentine history that were enacted here. The Piazza della Signoria has long been the political center of Florence from the time when the city elders, the Signoria, first took up residence in the Palazzo Vecchio, down to our own day, which finds the mayor's and other city offices still located in the same building. In the piazza took place the bloody struggles between the various political factions, the numerous popular uprisings, the lurid epilogue to the Pazzi conspiracy against the Medici, and the execution of Savonarola, the exact spot of whose funeral pyre is now marked by a bronze inscription in the pavement. Here, during the 14th and 15th centuries, when the city's fame was at its height, the populace was summoned by the ringing of the great bell to consider important public matters, or, if need be, with arms in hand, to rally in support of their hard-won liberties or to march in defense of the republic. The forbidding, rocklike solidity of the old palace is symbolic of the city's determination to rule itself as a free commune, just as the statues below of Judith liberating her people from the tyranny of Holofernes and David confronting his would-be conqueror were intended as constant reminders to the citizens of the ever-present threat to liberty, long cherished but only imperfectly realized. Unfortunately, these reminders proved inadequate, for the city's freedom and independence, so often menaced from within and without, were extinguished in 1530. In the succeeding centuries, the piazza was the scene of all sorts of public festivals, tournaments, and ceremonies held under the auspices of the grand dukes. Finally, in 1860 the results of the plebiscite were here proclaimed when Tuscany voted overwhelmingly (366,571 yes votes out of a total of 386,445) to end the old regime and to join Savoy in a united Italy. A bronze plaque commemorating this may be seen affixed to the façade of the palace.

Today the noble aspect of the piazza is somewhat diminished and its enjoyment made more difficult by the presence of so many tourist buses loading and unloading and by the unending stream of other vehicles passing through. How much more appropriate and enjoyable would be the piazza itself and the sidewalk cafés around it if motorized traffic were prohibited. Free again from their noxious fumes and distracting presence, this historic spot would resume its original purpose—a place for human beings to gather, to talk, and to be enriched by their surroundings.

Not far away lies another open square, also thronged with life and movement, which may be considered the commercial center of the city. This is the Piazza della Repubblica, so named after the last war when Italy voted to abandon the monarchy and adopt its present form of parliamentary government. Before that it was known as the Piazza Vittorio Emanuele, in honor of the first king of united Italy, and it occupies the same space that was the Mercato Vecchio and town center since Roman times. Today it is surrounded by hotels, banks, theaters, and cafés, and out of it radiate the streets with the city's best shops. Here, on summer evenings, when the heat of the day has passed, the café tables fill up while an orchestra plays and people lounge about the arcades.

A few steps farther north is the religious center of Florence, the Piazza del Duomo, where stand the Palace of the Archbishop,

The Piazza del Duomo, including (*left* to *right*) the Archbishop's palace, the Baptistery, the Cathedral, Giotto's tower, and at its base, the low silhouette of the Bigallo.

the Baptistery, the Cathedral, Giotto's bell tower, and the Loggia of the Bigallo. This interesting complex, so different from Pisa's spacious and airy cathedral group, is hemmed in on all sides by tall buildings and dense traffic. Nor does it have the architectural harmony found in Pisa. Its component parts were constructed at different times and with little attempt at synthesis. The Baptistery, the oldest surviving building in Florence, is a fine example of the Tuscan Romanesque concept, while the Cathedral and the tower, constructed over a period of many years in the 14th century, are in the Florentine Gothic style, with modifications and additions carried out still later in the spirit of the early Renaissance. The Archbishop's house was designed in the late 16th century. The flamboyant façade of the Cathedral, executed in what might be called Victorian Gothic between 1875 and 1887 by local craftsmen after it had stood desolate and bare for centuries, is impressive but lacks authenticity.

Nearby, along the Via de' Cerretani, once stood the northern rampart of the original Roman walls pierced at a point near the Baptistery by a gate from which a *borgo* or suburb extended along the street, still called Borgo San Lorenzo, which leads to the church of that name. This building we see today is one of the great masterpieces of the Renaissance (designed by Brunelleschi in 1423), but the foundation and consecration of the original church are much older, dating back to the very beginnings of Christianity in Tuscany. The present building, together with numerous other structures in this area north of the Duomo, is closely associated with the Medici, whose palace was nearby on the Via Cavour. Farther on is the monastery and church of San Marco, heavily endowed by Cosimo de' Medici, and across from it once spread the gardens of San Marco (now built over) belonging to Lorenzo the Magnificent, where Michelangelo and others who formed the first nucleus of the Accademia delle Belle Arti studied and worked. Close by is another garden, the Giardino dei Semplici, one of the oldest botanical orchards in the world, founded in 1545 by the first Medici grand dukes for the cultivation and study of exotic trees and plants.

Immediately adjacent is the academic focus of Florence, including the university and the Museum of Botany and Geology, whose collections were begun by the grand dukes. The

Accademia itself is on the Via Ricasoli in the Loggia dell'Ospedale di San Matteo, where it has been located since 1784. Its gallery contains lesser-known paintings by Tuscan artists and the famous *Prisoners* and *David* of Michelangelo.

A little to the east stands the most beautiful and harmonious piazza in Florence, that of the Santissima Annunziata designed by Brunelleschi in the quattrocento, and now, to the disgrace of the authorities, used as a parking lot. This is one place that should be seen early in the morning, before it is overrun with autos, so that its perfect proportions and its pleasing architecture, created in the full flowering of the Renaissance, can be appreciated. Here is an example of the artistic balance for which the Florentines were known: the tasteful use of classical forms with moderation, yet with decisiveness and originality.

Turning back again to the south and heading for the river, we proceed along the Via Proconsolo through an area of massive old buildings now cut up into small rented occupancies, where a dense population lives and works. The single most important

The Lungarno looking west as it appeared around the turn of the century. Except that the roadway is no longer for pedestrians, it is much the same today.

structure we pass is the Bargello, dating from 1255, whose fortress-like appearance, in contrast to the buildings on the Piazza dell' Annunziata, well illustrates the tremendous change in the life and tastes of the city during the intervening years. Continuing on, we reach the Arno, the north side of which has always been regarded as one of the choicest locations; here, many palaces, and now many hotels, are located. The Lungarno, the continuous roadway along the embankment, is not interrupted as on the south side, and this side enjoys more sun and air. Here, along the river on a beautiful day, one's eye can encompass and register in one sweep the full impact of this wonderful city—the bridges, the overhanging houses, the palaces, the towers, the domes and their warm earth-colors of ocher, tan, and terracotta shading into a hundred variations. These special ingredients contribute in sum total to an incomparable picture that fortunately still exists to impress itself on one's memory.

We then cross over to Oltrarno by way of the shop-lined Ponte Vecchio, one of the most photographed structures in the world.

Although Oltrarno is traditionally considered the poorer section, it contains the most imposing palazzo in the city, the Pitti, behind which stretch the magnificent Boboli Gardens—impressive by any standards. These were laid out in the cinque-cento and extend up the hill of San Giorgio by a series of terraces to the old city walls, most of which on the south side of the river were fortunately left standing.

A walk in the late afternoon through these gardens, past the Porta Romana, on up Viale Machiavelli and along the Via di San Leonardo, arriving at last at the highest point, the Forte di Belvedere,* is a particularly pleasant and leisurely way to ease oneself out of the 20th century by gradual stages and to adjust one's mind to an enjoyment of a past now gone but of which remnants survive. With this thought, we leave Florence as it is today and go back several millenniums to a time before man had resolved to build a town here on the banks of the Arno and the name Florence was as yet unknown.

---

* Once a fortress and now a museum, with a restaurant and bar above from which one can enjoy a sweeping view.

PART TWO

The City of Florence as History

Foundation and Early Development to A.D. 1000

Five or six centuries before the Christian era, during Etruscan times, the central valley of the River Arno, embracing the future site of Florence, presented an awesome, forbidding aspect. Thick forests covered the rolling hills on both sides of the river as it made its way from the slopes of the Apennines into the broad, marshy plain stretching toward the west. Only the Etruscan fortress-town of Fiesole, nestled on the top of a hill north of the river and girded by its defensive wall of giant stones, testified to man's presence.

Fiesole was one of a number of fortified hill towns, including places still familiar as Volterra, Arezzo, Perugia, and Orvieto, that leagued together in a lawless time to dominate the center

Remains of the Etruscan wall that once surrounded Fiesole before Florence existed.

of the Italian Peninsula. This region, now known as Tuscany, was, at that time, unsuitable for agriculture or sheep raising on any but a small scale. To the north, over the Apennines, lay the fertile fields of the Po Valley and to the south the grazing lands of Latium, both areas in contrast to the rugged, heavily timbered country in between.

There were, therefore, from the earliest times, centers of comparative wealth within reasonable distance of the Etruscan towns that provided opportunities for the exchange of goods— grain from the north, fleeces and cheese from the south. The secure transport of these cargoes, however, was subject to confiscation by rival tribes or to plunder by roving bands of marauders. The great network of Roman roads and bridges did not yet exist, and travel was confined to narrow tracks through the hill country, where soldiers and mulepack baggage trains could move in relative obscurity and safety. The Etruscans them- selves were best able to provide a safe passage for valuable cargo through their own territories and over the perilous mountain passes of the Apennines. So, from the first, capitalizing on their geographical position, they furnished the caravans and guides north and south, anticipating on a small scale the great trading activity that was later to characterize Tuscany, and particularly Florence, in the Middle Ages.

The future site of the city was, in fact, determined during those centuries. Here, directly below the fortress of Fiesole, where the Arno emerged from the last foothills of the Apennines to begin its more leisurely run to the sea, there developed a focal point of commerce. High ground on both sides confined the river with- in its banks and prevented its changing course or flooding, as was its habit, in the adjoining plain. A dry, reliable approach was therefore provided in all seasons where goods could regularly be ferried across. In addition, as the river slowed and deepened at this point, cargoes could here be transferred to barges for cheap and safe transportation downstream. For these reasons, the principal caravan trails converged at this convenient crossing.

The maintenance of a ferry and a few storehouses soon called into being the first real settlement that gradually grew up on the north bank of the river. However, nothing of much permanence or value could have been built at that time in such an exposed position, until the expanding power of Rome, imposing its rule over the Etruscans and the rest of Italy in the 3rd century B.C., brought to the peninsula a degree of internal peace and security heretofore unknown. Only then did a more stable and extensive agricultural life become feasible, together with the opportunity to exchange goods on a larger scale. Under these more favorable conditions, the small colony by the Arno, supported by the inhabitants of Fiesole, attained a more permanent character, particularly after the building of new Roman roads suitable for wheeled traffic. One of these coming from Rome, and still known as the Via Cassia, led to the foot of the hill of San Giorgio on the south bank, where the Romans, for the first time, probably in the 2nd century B.C., spanned the Arno with a bridge, thereby greatly increasing the value of the crossing and the importance of the colony that served it. No trace remains, however, of this ancient settlement, and the records show that it was completely destroyed in 82 B.C. during the Roman civil wars.

However, the need for and advantage of a bridgehead at this crossing of the road and river and the convenience there of a storage and marketing center had become obvious. Therefore, it was not long before a new and larger town arose on the north bank, peopled this time, not only by natives of the area, but also by retired veterans from Caesar's legions who laid out the streets in the orderly form of a Roman camp, surrounded it by what historians call the *primo cerchio*, or first circle of walls, and gave it the name Florentia. Thus were laid the foundations of the present city, and after two millenniums the imprint of the original plan still survives clearly in the street pattern of the city's center. Little other physical evidence of the Roman town remains. Excavations have revealed a few Roman substructures and mosaic pavements, but it is the street layout that to this day most clearly marks ancient Florentia.*

A glance at a map of the city reveals the outline of the Roman walls, long since gone, in the form of a rectangle still traced by the

---

* The derivation of the name is uncertain; speculation has connected it to the Latin for the "flowery" meadow on which the city was built and to the "flowing" waters of the Arno. More likely, however, it is derived from the augural name *florens*, meaning to flourish. Later in the Middle Ages, it became Fiorenza (after the Italian *fiorente*) and then Firenze.

Via del Proconsolo, the Via de Cerretani, the Via Tornabuoni, and the Borgo Santi Apostoli surrounding a grid of relatively straight streets within. In the approximate center lay the forum, later to become the Mercato Vecchio (Old Market) and, in our own day, the more spacious Piazza della Repubblica.

Several other street names remind us of the Roman beginnings, such as the Via Campidoglio, where a great temple stood, and the Via delle Terme, location of the *thermae* (baths). The Via Porta Rossa (Red Gate) and the Via Por (for Porta) Santa Maria indicate the position of two of the ancient gates in the original walls. Outside, to the east, an interesting landmark survives in the Via Torta (Curved Street) and its extensions, which delineate the circular perimeter of the Roman amphitheater built outside the walls for gladiatorial games in the days of the Roman Empire, and on the ruins of which were later constructed the medieval houses we see today.

So little in the way of documentary evidence has survived with respect to this Roman period and to the succeeding centuries of the Dark Ages, that it can only be concluded that Florence was little more than one among many Italian provincial centers and of no outstanding importance. An occasional light gleams in the darkness, but only faintly. We hear of the martyrdom of a Greek named Minias (afterward San Miniato) during the Christian persecutions of A.D. 250, indicating that, even at that early date, Florence harbored a colony of Christianized Hellenes. Later, in 393, after the triumph of the new religion throughout the empire, we read of the dedication of the church of San Lorenzo (then outside the city walls) as the episcopal seat, and the consecration there of one of the city's first bishops, Zenobius.*

It was during the latter's term of office that the city suffered its first siege by the Goths, in 405; and, though they were driven off, other invaders followed periodically. With the collapse of the Roman authority, anarchy spread throughout Italy and orderly trade and communication became impossible. A long period of

---

* Also a Greek name. Throughout its history, Florence was often to be influenced by the Greeks. It was they who first brought the Christian religion to Florence as well as the city's first patron saint, Santa Reparata. The earliest tombstones have Greek letters. Later, contacts with Byzantium sparked much artistic and literary effort.

slow disintegration commenced. Political chaos and economic depression forced an exodus of the population from the cities to the countryside, where individual landlords, guarding their properties from fortified strong points, could provide a degree of security and employment.

Within Florence, many buildings were abandoned, and in the surrounding fields, the elaborate drainage systems installed by the Romans ceased to function. Reclaimed land returned to bog and marsh. Epidemics of malaria reduced the population, and, at times, the city was practically uninhabited. Over the years the principal structures of the Roman town collapsed and crumbled away or were pulled down by the survivors for use in rebuilding and adapting their miserable dwellings to the necessities of the times.

In this derelict condition, Florence entered the latter part of the 6th century, at which time a fresh series of invasions from across the Alps into Italy began. The newcomers, Teutonic tribesmen, were called Lombards. Their conquests proved to be the most far-reaching and durable of the many waves of barbarian invasions, for they came not only to plunder but also to stay. They had first conquered the plain of the Po Valley (which is still known as Lombardy) and afterward penetrated the Apennines to sweep away the remnants of the land-owning classes in Tuscany, appropriating their estates and serfs. For decades, the Lombards kept the peninsula in a continual turmoil, incessantly warring with the Romans to the south and their allies, the Byzantines, who together still controlled what was left of the empire. Eventually, Lombard rule extended over most of northern and central Italy, and, by the end of the 7th century, finally settled into a more permanent and peaceful phase. Only then did the fortunes of the many decayed towns, Florence among them, commence slowly to revive.

It is this period of subjugation by the Lombards, lasting for some two centuries, that marks the transition of Italy into the relative stability of the Middle Ages and the creation of the medieval Italian from a fusion of the conquerors and the conquered. The customs and usages for land tenure, agricultural production, and military service evolved during this time into the system we call feudalism, while the process of Italianizing the Lombards occurred apace. Ruling from their fortified hilltops throughout the country, the Lombards soon adapted their clothing and their habits to the Mediterranean climate. They became bilingual and later gave up entirely their Teutonic tongue for the more expressive local idiom, the vulgarized Latin, which was already forming itself into the several dialects of the Italian language. And, most important, they gradually adopted the Catholic religion in its Italian form and accepted its ecclesiastical organization, including the supremacy of the Pope.

During this period, the city of Florence, ruled over by a series of Lombard dukes and serving its masters primarily as a military outpost and marketing center, continued to present a disorderly appearance within its already ancient Roman walls. The streets remained unpaved and poorly drained, and sanitation was nonexistent. Most buildings, whether of stone or wood, were constructed in a ramshackle fashion and have long since disappeared. A massive watchtower (which is known to have existed), erected by the Lombards to overlook the approaches to the east, has vanished without a trace. Even the churches—and some of Florence's earliest religious foundations date from this period— were later completely rebuilt or modified beyond recognition. Practically nothing, therefore, remains to identify this period. Life continued bleak and precarious amid the squalor of the town, as Florence, along with the rest of Europe, struggled slowly out of the Dark Ages. Only in the monasteries were the vestiges of classical scholarship and learning preserved, awaiting the day when they could be again employed to illuminate men's lives.

No great change occurred with the coming of the Franks, another Teutonic people, who, on the invitation of the pope, had crossed over the Alps into Italy to overthrow the Lombard regime. Charlemagne, the greatest of the Frankish leaders, decisively crushed all resistance in Italy by the year 777 and imposed his will on the Lombard nobles through his agents called *conti* (counts), one of whom, taking up residence in Florence, ruled the town and its surrounding district—henceforth known as its *contado* (county). The high point of Charlemagne's effort was reached in the year 800, when, proclaimed the effective restorer of the Western Empire, he was crowned emperor by the Pope in Rome.

But following his death in 814, Europe saw the gradual undoing of his work and the weakening of the imperial domain, which, despite the efforts of his German successors, never again enjoyed the same political cohesion. It was too vast and unwieldy to be effectively held together in that primitive age after the magic of Charlemagne's personality had become only a memory. During his lifetime, the empire had enjoyed a complementary and peaceful relationship with that other great medieval institution, the Roman Catholic church, but the subsequent growth of papal ambitions and the extension of clerical authority into the temporal sphere, combined with the natural tendency for feudal allegiances to shift back and forth, led to a gradual repudiation of the emperor's prerogatives and eventually to the decline of the imperial system itself.

Another phenomenon also contributing to this end was the slow revival of trade in the 10th and 11th centuries with its consequent stimulation of town growth and independence. This, perhaps more than anything else, sealed the fate of the empire, and though its moral force was never wholly lost, particularly in Italy, and it continued to serve as the theoretical source of ultimate temporal authority and the official apex of the feudal system, the emperor's effective political power over most of his subjects gave way to the new aggressive forces that centered in the towns.

Nowhere was the increase in commerce and communal autonomy felt earlier than in central Italy. This was partly due to the appearance in the 10th century of a dignitary known as the margrave of Tuscany, a feudal noble who was able to secure the allegiance and loyalty of the other *conti* within that relatively large and homogeneous territory and to bring it under his personal rule. Though technically he owed fealty to his liege, the emperor, he in practice achieved a high degree of independence and authority, and was accordingly able to maintain a greater measure of peace and security within his jurisdiction than generally existed elsewhere. It followed that, as conditions for the orderly production and safe exchange of goods improved with the stabilizing rule of the margraves, an increase in commerce in Tuscany was experienced, and the revival of the towns commenced.

Florence, in particular, benefited, for a number of reasons. In the first place, after 1057, the city was used at various times by the margraves as the center of their Tuscan administration, thereby increasing its political importance. Secondly, goods moving north and south always had to pass over the Apennines, preferably by the shortest possible routes, and several of these, as we have seen, converged on Florence. Controlling the river crossing and several of the key roads, the Florentines were able not only to regulate and tax this traffic but also to take an active part in the carrying trade itself. Finally, the surrounding hills enclosing the upper reaches of the Arno had not, at that time, been deforested, and rain water feeding its tributaries was released in a more gradual and regular manner than today. The river bed below Florence, therefore, had not yet been silted up and was still navigable to the sea in most seasons, making possible the easy trans-shipment there of cargoes bound for more distant parts.

The Later Middle Ages: 1000 to 1200

As a focal point for an increased trade in several directions on road and river, Florence experienced a surge of new life. For the first time in many centuries, opportunities for employment stimulated a growth of the population. More and better dwellings were required, and, as the space available within the walls was limited, taller and more permanent buildings of stone began to arise. Freed, to a degree, from the interference of the surrounding *conti*, the Florentines, rediscovering their civic spirit, stirred themselves to new efforts. A modest increase in wealth took place, and the city began to take on the appearance it was to assume throughout the later Middle Ages.

The clergy, meanwhile, pursuing an ever larger role in the secular affairs of the peninsula, found it increasingly difficult to remain aloof from the corrupting influences that accompanied the acquisition of wealth and political power. The townspeople themselves were partly responsible for this, since they regularly enlisted the support of the church in their struggle to exclude the *conti* from town affairs and, later, to extend their influence into the adjoining territories. Thus as the religious hierarchy became more intimately involved in worldly concerns, it seemed to forget its spiritual mission. Bribery, simony, and a degrading materialistic attitude became only the most obvious signs of corruption, particularly among the great land-owning abbots and bishops. At last, these practices grew so flagrant as to stir among the mass of the people of all classes a strong reaction, which, culminating in the 11th century, provoked one of the most fervent of those periodic religious renewals that have swept over Italy.

In Florence, this expressed itself in a purging of the priesthood, a rededication to Christian principles, and the building or re-building of a number of monasteries and churches. It is from this moment in our story, when a general improvement in the city's welfare combined with a desire to purify and exalt the church, that there survives some important, tangible evidence to look upon today. By far the most significant among such remains, and the oldest structure within the city to come down to us intact, is the Battistero di San Giovanni (Baptistery of St. John), located near the northern perimeter of the old Roman wall. Scholars do not know exactly how long a building has stood there. Tradition once ascribed its origin to the Romans in the form of a temple to Mars, but recent excavations have proved that this was not so and that the structure's base and core were built after Christianity had established itself firmly in Italy, probably sometime in the 6th or 7th century. But although the foundation and plan of the building pre-date the period of the religious revival, it is believed that, under the stimulus of the reform movement, extensive restoration and rebuilding took place, giving it the distinctive appearance it has today. For this reason, we may assign its consequence to the 11th century.

The persistent legend that the Baptistery was founded by the Romans emphasizes the old Florentine longing to connect the city's history with the Roman heritage. Though it was built long after the demise of the empire, the early Christians responsible for its basic plan drew heavily on classical architecture, utilized numerous ancient columns and capitals salvaged from abandoned temples, and laid out the building on the cardinal points of the compass according to a Roman scheme. But whereas, in the classical period, the peristyle usually surrounded the walls, the Christian builders inverted this feature, constructing the walls to enclose the columns inside. In addition, the use of an octagonal rather than a strictly circular plan and of superimposed interior galleries points to a break with the older pagan architecture of the temples.

It is not known in what pattern (if at all) marble was used originally to decorate the outside of the Baptistery. It is thought, however, that its present most characteristic and distinguishing feature, the encrustation of its exterior in green and white marble, is 11th-century work carried out around the time of the religious revival. It is here, in the decoration of the surfaces, that the Florentines made their earliest and most original artistic contribution. It differs essentially from contemporaneous work at Pisa and Lucca, where the decorative effect is achieved, in addition to the many complicated little columns and arches, by the use of alternating black and white building blocks as a part of the structure itself. In Florence, flat marble slabs were applied as an envelope or surface treatment, independent of, but coordinated with, the structural lines of the building. It has been suggested that this idea may have come from the east, but this is unlikely as Florence did not yet have strong contacts with Byzantium, and it was still Rome that provided the medieval city with its heritage and its legends. More probably, Florence remained faithful to the old classical tradition, taking its several forms—capitals, columns, moldings, cornices, architraves, arcades—refining and rearranging them in a new concept, and thus producing a new architectural style generally known as Tuscan Romanesque. In common with other European building of the time, it is characterized by round-headed arches, small narrow windows, and an over-all heaviness, but it gains its distinction in the elaborate, geometric marble exteriors peculiar to Florence and the surrounding area.

Also during this period, the raised attic and pyramidal roof of the Baptistery were largely rebuilt in their present state. Subsequently, other changes were effected, modifying somewhat its original concept—for example, the addition of the alternating stone courses at each exterior angle; the rectangular apse or tribune on the west side; and the little lantern at the top which replaced an opening in the roof and seems too small. Still later, the level of the surrounding piazza was raised, when a number of ancient marble sarcophagi were removed from around the base of the building to promote the flow of traffic. This has had the effect of reducing its height, leaving it with a certain heaviness, but did not significantly alter its character.

The perceptive observer will not give the Battistero di San Giovanni a hurried and uncritical glance. On the one hand, he should try to visualize the building as it was in the Middle Ages, its elegant geometric patterns of marble contrasting sharply with the crude, drab buildings that crowded around it. On the other, he should compare its simple dignity with the overpowering bulk of the more recent Duomo standing across the street and the intricacies of its façade which, despite the consummate skill of its many parts, is too ornate and bewildering to the eye. On turning back to the older building, a sense of order appears and the mind achieves a tranquility and an awareness of proportion and strength. Here, the architectural forms from classical and pagan Rome have been ingeniously adapted to Christian purposes and, in the process, have created a new style and tradition, uniquely Florentine. Filled with symbolism, the building embodies much of what the city was and is. Countless thousands of children have been

The Baptistery of San Giovanni, the oldest surviving building in Florence, exhibits the strength and elegance of the Tuscan Romanesque style.

baptized under its roof. Untold numbers of other religious ceremonies have been celebrated there. For centuries, it has been a hub of social activity, of festivals, and the chief object of concern and pride for all Florentines. Architects through the ages have analyzed its structural techniques, proportions, and decorative details, painters have studied its mosaics, and sculptors, its doors. Much of the inspiration that produced the Renaissance may justly be said to have stemmed from the esthetics bound up in this small Christian building. In short, it symbolizes the essence of the city— as indestructible as the faith it was built to honor and as enduring as the architectural principles it embodies.

Several other structures in and near Florence contemporary with the reconstruction of the Baptistery have come down to us. On the side of a hill north of Florence, just below Fiesole and overlooking the Mugnone Stream, stands, imbedded in the rough stone of an ancient wall, part of a façade of colored marbles similar in style to that of the Baptistery. This is all that remains of La Badia Fiesolana, an abbey built by the Benedictines shortly after 1028. Standing on ground used as a cemetery since the earliest days of Christianity, when burial was always made outside the city walls, it is significant because of its beauty and age.

Even more interesting is another ancient place of worship and interment, also high up in the surrounding hills but on the opposite side of the river, known as San Miniato al Monte. Here, according to legend, one of the first Florentine martyrs, a Greek named Minias or Miniato, was beheaded and buried. Sacred ever after to his memory, the cemetery became a place of pilgrimage. It was taken over in 1018 by the Benedictines, who, later in the century, rebuilt the entire complex, including what we admire today as the Basilica of San Miniato, perhaps the most perfect example of Tuscan Romanesque style.

The interior, with its choir raised on ancient columns above a crypt containing the bones of the Saint, reflects an arrangement common to earlier basilica–churches found in Rome and else-where.* The structure in its over-all conception represents an ambitious effort for the time, straining the meager resources of its

* The basilican type derives its form and name from the rectangular Roman courts of justice with their lofty central hall (nave), lower side aisles, and semicircular apse at one end.

(*left*) The façade of the Badia (Abbey) of Fiesole is all that remains of this 11th-century Benedictine monastry. (*right*) One of the medieval towers (the Corbizi) as it looked around 1900. (Compare the same piazza in the recent photo on page 58). (*below*) The façade of the church of San Miniato reflects, especially in its lower half, the essence of the Tuscan Romanesque style.

sponsors. Marble is, of course, expensive in any age, and much of what we see here was skillfully faked by the builders or was added at a later date. The columns in the nave, for example, though they look genuine, are, in reality, blocks of stone covered with a coat of marbled stucco. Only the columns and arches of the choir and crypt, the encrustation of the interior of the apse, and the rhythmical arches forming the lower half of the façade appear to be original and genuine marble work completed near the end of the 11th century. The limitations thus imposed by lack of resources are here obvious. The upper, more complex encrustation of the façade, the altar, choir screen, pulpit, and beautiful floor, as well as the mosaics over the altar and in the façade executed in the archaic manner, are all work of a century or so later when resources were more abundant, and show Byzantine influence. Almost everything else within the basilica is of the Renaissance.

Another 11th-century church, although legend takes its original foundation back to Charlemagne's time, is that of Santi Apostoli situated close by the Arno and, like so many ancient establishments, outside the perimeter of the old Roman wall. The public baths of the Roman town had been located near here (on the Via delle Terme), from which came some of the building materials for the church, including several of the wonderful columns of dark stone standing in the nave. The interior, with its narrow little windows in the clerestory and its raftered roof, still retains, despite the later Baroque chapels along the sides, much of its early Romanesque feeling—simple, intimate, solemn. In this and other similar places of worship, the faithful gathered in a primitive age when life for most was exceedingly hard, punctuated by periodic misfortune, and tempered only by faith and hope, whose symbol and custodian these churches were.

Before leaving Santi Apostoli, it is worth noting the small open space in front called the Piazzetta del Limbo, which was hallowed ground, reserved over an ancient cemetery for unbaptized children. This little area was typical of others adjoining small parish churches, providing a breathing space among the jumble of medieval dwellings that grew up and pushed upon one another in ever more crowded conditions, both inside and outside the walls. These openings served not only to dignify the approach to

Santi Apostoli, typical of medieval Romanesque parish churches,
has survived basically unchanged.

a place of worship, but also to provide a place for neighbors to
meet and talk. Here, the immediate problems of community life—
the repair of the church or the maintenance of the drainage
system—were discussed and a course of action was agreed upon.
It is, in fact, from these local parish assemblies that the beginnings
of town government may be traced.

During this period, it became common practice for representatives from the several parishes to meet periodically to discuss and
rule on matters involving the city as a whole. Known later as
consuls, these town spokesmen gradually encroached on the
authority of the margrave and his local *conti*, not at first in the
wider issues of peace and war, but certainly in other vital matters
directly concerning the city. Usually these men were chosen

from among the older established, local families, the lower nobility, who owned houses in town and land in the *contado* and who, because of their aristocratic and martial attitudes, were often looked up to by citizens for leadership and protection.

But, while these men were sometimes able to act in concert for the good of the city, more often than not they were involved in quarrels and fighting among themselves. In fact, the history of these centuries is, in large measure, the story of the interminable violent feuds that erupted continually between these proud families, no less in Florence than in other Italian towns.

A few material manifestations of this exaggerated family pride and pugnacity still remain scattered about Florence in the form of those singular architectural remnants, the medieval stone towers. Now unfortunately truncated, they survive as reminders of the insecurity that pervaded all human existence in those times. In fact, the idea of the tower became so marked a part of the life of the town nobility, so essential for their defense and so symbolic of their attitudes, that their owners were known collectively as the Società delle Torri. During the 11th and 12th centuries, almost two hundred of these towers appeared in Florence alone. At first only three or four stories in height, many eventually rose to over one hundred feet with the need of each family as it grew in numbers, importance, and wealth both to secure itself and its property against the physical threats of the period and to increase its prestige.

The architectural evolution of the tower followed a definite pattern dictated by use and convenience. The lower floor at street level contained one or two large rooms enclosed overhead by a massive stone vaulting through which a hole gave access to the rooms above. This lower area had one or two heavy exterior doors wide enough for a loaded beast to pass through and was generally used for storage of country produce or as a place of business. Above the vaulting, the remainder of the tower, where the family took refuge, was divided on the inside into successive floors by wooden beams and planks. Outside and high above the street, provision was made, by means of stone footings and sockets, to prop up moveable wooden balconies one above the other. These provided an escape from the close dark confinement of the crowded upper rooms and, on feast days, a means for displaying the colorful banners and rugs of the household. In times of trouble, these galleries could be quickly removed, leaving, if need be, only the one near the top, safely out of reach of the enemy, from which missiles could be hurled down. As the years passed, a large family or a group of related families might maintain in close proximity several or a whole series of these towers capable, if danger threatened, of being linked together by a system of wooden catwalks. Thus, with doors and windows securely barred, such a network of fortified houses could withstand even an extended siege.

Possibly the grouping of these towers in rectangular blocks around a central open space established the pattern for the distinctive, cubelike shape, peculiar to the Florentine palaces that were built in the following centuries. Certainly the crenelated parapet, jutting out on stone corbels high atop the walls, a most characteristic feature of the many fortified towers and palaces that followed, evolved directly from the earlier wooden galleries resting on wooden struts.

A number of these old towers (reduced in height) can still be seen in Florence, though most have disappeared or have been morticed into later buildings. One of the best preserved is that of the Foresi on Via Porta Rossa, while others still line the Via delle Terme and the Via dei Cerchi.

Until well into the 11th century, few Italian towns had much of a corporate existence of their own, separate and independent of the feudal system that surrounded them. In theory, at least, the townspeople were looked upon in the same light as their country brethren—all equally subject to the will of the *conti* and other great nobles, and ultimately of the emperor himself. But gradually a change of great importance took place, growing out of a division of interests between the town dwellers and the feudal élite: land was being challenged by commerce as the only important source of wealth. The existing system of agricultural production, with its attendant feudal arrangements firmly established by long tradition, had no room to accommodate a new class of wage earners or their ambitious employers. The towns had been looked on primarily as market centers for food or local handicrafts, not as safe places to harbor new industries or as focal points for an increased volume of foreign trade. This unwelcome development, it was seen by the *conti*, would lead to an exodus of workers from the countryside, the growth of the towns in population, wealth, and power, and their inevitable claim for greater freedom and independence.

The imperfect administration of the central authority, whether in the person of the margrave or emperor, had long been a characteristic of the times and had enabled the townsmen to appropriate for themselves many purely local functions, but now they were making novel requests and even demands. As it happened, the townsmen were decisively aided in their assertion of independence by a protracted struggle that had developed in the last half of the 11th century between the pope and the emperor. This epic contest, growing out of the question of which power would appoint and hence control the bishops and abbots throughout western Christendom, set the pattern for Italian politics for generations. Each side, seeking to attract support, found itself forced to grant unprecedented privileges and immunities to the growing young communes. Evidence of this is seen in the early town charters, wrung from reluctant church and lay lords during this period, which formally bestow important new rights.

Florence sided with the pope, partly because of the religious reform movement that had swept the town, and partly to secure further political and economic concessions from the margrave of the day, the Contessa Matilda, colorful figure beloved by the Florentines, who also favored the papal cause.* By the turn of the century (1100), the city had obtained a large measure of independence, including the right to impose its jurisdiction and collect taxes in the surrounding *coutado* and the right to regulate its own commerce in and out of the city.

* Called *la gran contessa*, Matilda, the last of her line, acceded to the margraviate in 1069 and reigned for almost half a century. It was at her ancestral castle stronghold of Canossa that the famous confrontation occurred in January 1077 between her guest and ally Pope Gregory VII and his adversary, Emperor Henry IV, who, bereft of support, had come to seek a reconciliation and was kept waiting outside the gates in the snow for three anxious days. The emperor's humiliation was only temporary, however, for the struggle over the question of lay investiture continued thereafter between them and their successors for many decades.

As the trade routes multiplied and the volume of traffic increased, it was inevitable that conflicts should arise with the great landowners through whose estates these goods must pass. The traditional way-tolls and taxes for the use of roads, rivers, bridges, and landings, the restraints and regulations became ever more obnoxious and provided a convenient excuse for the ambitious townsmen, bent on expanding their jurisdiction, to sound a call to arms and to mount an expedition against one or another of their feudal antagonists. In fact, the history of Florence during the 12th century is, in large part, a series of battles and sieges against the great neighboring feudatories, in particular the Conti Guidi and the Conti Alberti, two vast families of Teutonic lineage, who owned scores of castles throughout Tuscany, Even before Matilda died in 1115, the vigorous young commune had acquired sufficient authority to wage war on its own account. With no interference from the margrave, one of the earliest chroniclers tells us, Florence attacked and destroyed two strongpoints belonging to the Alberti in the valley of the Arno about eight miles to the west of the city.* Presumably the trading interests of Florence had come into conflict with the landed interests of the Alberti.

For similar reasons, the city also found itself at war with a number of its neighboring towns, which, like Florence, were attempting to acquire freedom of action and to extend their jurisdiction outward. Accordingly, we read of the early subjection of Prato nearby on the plain (1107) and of Fiesole on the adjacent hill (1125). The first wars with Pistoia and Siena were recorded at this time; and later Figline, up the Arno, and Empoli, down stream, were forced to submit in 1168 and 1182 respectively. Of Florence's neighbors, only Pisa remained friendly—primarily because of a mutually advantageous trading agreement involving the shipment of goods down the river to Pisa and hence to other Mediterranean ports. Two ancient porphyry columns, gifts from the Pisans and symbols of this period of cooperation with the city at the mouth of the Arno, still may be seen standing on either side of the eastern doors of the Baptistery.

The success of this aggressive Florentine policy throughout the 12th century may be laid in part to this treaty with Pisa and in

---

* The castles of Monte Gualandi and Monte Cascioli, destroyed in 1107 and 1114 respectively, both of which lay near the existing village of Lastra.

part to the fact that, following the death of Matilda (1115), no successor to the margraviate ever again secured effective control of Tuscany. Nor were a long line of emperors, preoccupied in trying to control their own German subjects, capable of exacting allegiance from those towns south of the Alps that were prepared to withhold it. Even the great Emperor Frederick I (known as Barbarossa), despite several expeditions into Italy, could not prevail and, after the epic battle of Legnano in 1176, was forced formally to confirm and extend the independence and privileges of the Italian communes. Florence, in particular, always resisted the imperial authority, remaining generally faithful to the pope, a policy that was to prove advantageous for many years.

It should be noted that, within this political framework, the actual military successes achieved by Florence, whereby the neighboring towns were forced to succumb and the great landowners to surrender parts of their estates as well as the control over cargoes passing through them, were accomplished largely through the cooperation and military capacities of the lesser nobility. These men, who owned smaller landed properties close by in the *contado* and chafed under the yoke of their more powerful overlords, had by a combination of pressure and self-interest gradually aligned themselves on the side of the townsmen. Many of them lived within the city for at least part of the year, often serving as consuls, and, when not fighting among themselves, were willing to employ their weapons and their retainers on behalf of the commune. Handsomely mounted and clad in armor, they led into battle the town cavalry, augmented now from the ranks of the city merchants, who were well able to afford war horses and their equipage. Close behind, on foot, came the mass of the citizenry, organized by the parishes in which they lived and patriotically supporting the campaigns. A new spirit and energy animated and united the people and their leaders. For a time, the town nobility even put aside their feuds to concentrate on the enemy outside the walls, or so it seemed to the great poet Dante, who looked back on this era as one of Florence's finest periods. Certainly, as the city's jurisdiction spread out and its power and security increased, the conditions developed under which industry and commerce could flourish. Employment opportunities attracted peasants from the fields, and the population expanded. Besides the common wage laborers, the number of shopkeepers, artisans, and other businessmen doubled and tripled. Long *borghi* (suburbs) began to form along the roads outside the town gates, as many street names still attest: Borgo San Lorenzo, Borgo degli Albizzi, Borgo dei Greci, Borgo San Jacopo. Soon, so many houses and workshops were outside the old Roman walls, it became imperative to tear them down and build a new circuit, completed by 1176, enclosing a larger area and extending to the opposite bank of the river. Thus, at last, were brought within the city proper, in addition to the various suburbs, a number of ancient churches: San Lorenzo, Santa Trinita, Santi Apostoli, Santa Felicità.

Unfortunately, however, other than the truncated towers, very little remains to mark this important period in the growth of the city. Civic buildings did not yet exist, and the second circuit of walls has long since disappeared. What new church construction may have taken place has not survived. Only some decorative marble designs and carvings can be definitely attributed to the 12th century. These, the earliest in existence after the marble façades already mentioned, are therefore important not only because of their age, but also because they serve to illustrate the very beginnings of Florentine art, which can be traced back to the practice of the simpler crafts by humble, unknown artisans. It was natural that the churches, crude and on a modest scale, should first provide the need and inspiration for artistic effort: articles for use in the service of the altar table—chalices, candlesticks, reliquaries—and then more ambitious undertakings in stone and marble—the elaboration of the altars themselves with intarsia (inlay work) and carving of the altar rails, pulpits, floors, and tombs.

Of surviving examples, first in point of time is the tomb of a Bishop Rainaldus (1113), found in a wall of the Baptistery, to the right of the apse, which has around it a border of lozenges or diamonds similar to those earlier designs seen in the apse of San Miniato. Of the same period is the altar in the latter church with its beautiful panels of intarsia designs. Slightly later comes the altar in the Baptistery which retains much of the simplicity of San Miniato's earlier one but incorporates certain classical details in the colonettes and the entablature. This represents a

Marble patterns in the apse (11th century) and altar (12th century) of San Miniato and the mosaic in the Byzantine style above (13th century).

Mid-12th-century altar in the Baptistery.

transition to the somewhat later choir screen and pulpit in San Miniato, which are magnificent examples of late 12th-century work. Here, the earlier flat encrustation with simple geometric patterns becomes more complicated. Intarsia in geometrical forms still predominate, but the moldings are more richly carved; more naturalistic plant forms are used, and designs from oriental textiles appear. Now, for the first time, can be detected that combination of influences from Rome and from the eastern Mediterranean that, ultimately, merged with the native genius to create the art forms of the Renaissance. And also, for the first time, there appears on the pulpit an example of the human figure, one of the earliest such carvings from the hand of a Florentine.

Slightly later is another remarkable pulpit, from which, tradition says, Dante often spoke. It is located in the little church of San Leonardo in Arcetri near San Miniato in the hills just south of the city. This pulpit, probably carved around 1200, is similar to the one in San Miniato, but each panel includes figure reliefs representing the Nativity, the Adoration, the Presentation, the Baptism, and the Deposition superimposed on the intarsia of the background—an advance over the earlier, purely decorative and abstract tradition.

Late 12th-century choir screen and pulpit, with carved symbols of the evangelists, in San Miniato.

Two carved panels showing Byzantine influence (the Baptism and the Deposition) from an early pulpit (about 1200) in the church of San Leonardo in Arcetri.

Europe in Transition: 1200 to 1300

But, as yet, the arts were of relatively minor importance, and the main energies of the Florentines (as well as of other Italian townsmen) were bent on the acquisition and control of as great a surrounding territory as possible in order to further their economic interests and enhance their prestige. By the turn of the century (1200), this somewhat unbridled spirit for expansion led Florence into more serious, prolonged conflicts with some of its neighbors—Siena, Pistoia, and Arezzo—over boundaries and trading privileges. Finally, quarrels erupted even with its old ally, Pisa, over the use of the coastal ports, which had become increasingly important as the volume of trade widened throughout the Mediterranean.

The same contentious attitude seems to have prevailed in domestic matters, as there is evidence of the feuds and vendettas among the nobles taking on a more organized and permanent nature. One of the main sources of such friction had become the annual election of the 'consuls', particularly when one faction had been able to dominate the government over a period of years. In an attempt to solve this problem, recourse was had to the appointment of a disinterested and impartial official called the *podestà*, invariably a foreigner, who, replacing the consuls, was to try to administer the city government with the aid of advisory bodies but without yeilding unduly to one side or the other.

Another cause for division was created by a situation from across the Alps that disturbed the peace of all Europe: an open struggle for the emperor's crown between two venerable German families, the Hohenstaufens and the Guelphs. In Florence, the upper class quickly divided itself into two rival camps, one headed by the haughty, aristocratic Uberti clan, who sided with the Hohenstaufen claimant, Frederick, and the other led by the Buondelmonte, supporting Otto of the Guelph family. The old Società delle Torri was finally and irrevocably rent in two. Each side assumed the name of its respective champion, becoming the Parte del Guelfo and the Parte del Ghibellino, the latter title an Italian corruption of Waiblingen, the ancestral castle home of the Hohenstaufens. Otto's death, the triumph of the Hohenstaufen champion (1215), and his subsequent descent into Italy as the Emperor Frederick II forced the Guelphs into the arms of the pope, who was at odds with the new emperor on a dozen scores, religious and political. Only the institution of the *podestà* managed to restrain the parties in Florence from armed conflict but the pattern was thereby set for years to come, the Ghibellines siding with the emperor and the Guelphs with the pope.

It is clear, however, that neither faction in Florence (or elsewhere, for that matter) was primarily concerned with which man wore the emperor's crown or even with the principles involved in the struggle with the pope. Rather, each side aided its ally on the condition that it would receive support for the purpose of capturing political control of the city itself.

Frederick II proved to be an exceptionally strong, dynamic leader and commanded a considerable army, but his rival, the pope, was not without the means to resist. Besides his own military resources and those of his allies, the pope also possessed an arsenal of less tangible but even more persuasive weapons.

These were the time-honoured penalties or sanctions the church's chief spokesman could impose at will, particularly a pronouncement of excommunication or the severing of all ties with the religious establishment and hence with God, the threat of which alone had a terrifying effect in those days; or the laying on of an interdict whereby the offender's property was subject to confiscation and his debtors released from their financial obligations. In addition, the pope was free to declare sweeping annulments of all titles and prerogatives held by those who aided the emperor, and even on occasion went so far as to proclaim his struggle with Frederick a holy crusade and to tithe all Christendom for the purpose.

Among the members of the vast ecclesiastical structure called upon to resist Frederick and his allies were two recently formed organizations of dedicated religious men directly under papal control who proved to be especially useful. These were the mendicant orders of the Dominicans and Franciscans. Both had achieved rapid and widespread recognition, due largely to the magnetic, though differing, personalities of their founders, each of whom was to have a profound effect on the events of the age. The one, a Spaniard named Dominic (Domingo de Guzmán), had organized a brotherhood of preaching friars to combat certain heretical sects. He sought to impose orthodoxy by means of persuasion and teaching but also, if necessary, by the sword. The other, a very different man, Francis (Francesco) of Assisi, emphasized the spiritual side of Christianity, the sentiments and aspirations growing out of the love of God. Gathering a company of humble followers around him, Francis did not rely upon argument or force to communicate his message. Nor did he seek the solitude of remote places in which to study, meditate, and worship, as was the custom of the older monastic orders such as the Benedictines. Rather, he sought to influence the world by example, and to do so he sent out his missionaries to mix with the common people, tending the sick, helping the poor, and extending charity to all. Less militant than the Dominicans, the poor brothers of St. Francis were even more effective. As the years passed, however, the two orders became more alike and indeed competitive, the Franciscans also preaching and pursuing scholarly matters, and the Dominicans doing good works. Both had been founded

Terracotta lunette by Andrea della Robbia commemorating the supposed meeting in Florence (1219) between St. Francis and St. Dominic.

on the principle of obedience to authority and of poverty for themselves, being careful to distinguish that such privation did not extend to the institution of the church or to the pope himself. The willing instruments, thus, of the papal will, the two orders helped considerably, throughout the 13th century, not only in strengthening the church but also in mustering lay support in the struggle against the emperor.

It appears that Dominic visited Florence only once (in 1219), but that was sufficient to call into being a Dominican community outside the second circuit of walls around a small church, later to be rebuilt as Santa Maria Novella. Nearby, in a street, can be seen a memorial column, the Croce al Trebbio, marking the spot where a particularly bloody clash occurred (1244) between the Dominican brothers and a group of heretics.

Francis was many times in the city on the Arno, but it was not until after his death in 1228 that a Franciscan community was established on the opposite side of the town, also outside the new walls, at the place where the church of Santa Croce was later to arise.

Meanwhile, in addition to the opposing forces of pope and emperor, of Guelph and Ghibelline, of religious orthodoxy and heresy, of the new commerce and the old feudalism, the subtle but growing influence of Byzantium was felt in Italy. Cut off from practical communication with the eastern Mediterranean for so many centuries, Europe had gradually begun to re-establish contact in the previous century (the 12th) as the result of the early Crusades, those idealistic but generally futile expeditions against the infidel, the last fruition of the religious revival.

Now, new trading arrangements made possible a fresh flow of oriental refinements and ideas, which were to have widespread economic and artistic influence. Articles of carved ivory, gold-smiths' work, spices, silks, and lace were now imported in mean-ingful quantities. Byzantine craftsmen in mosaic, ornamental glass, enamel painting, and fresco, venturing forth into the western world through the port of Venice, brought their secrets to the cities of Europe, stirring a new interest in artistic expression. The best surviving examples of their work in 13th-century Florence, apart from the many small objects that are to be found in museums, may be seen today in the lacy patterns and zodiacal symbolism of the marble intarsia pavements laid down at that time in the Baptistery and in San Miniato.

But other, more practical artistic innovations were also being introduced from the east. These had to do with the techniques of dyeing and dressing cloth, the importance of which may be illustrated in the history of a venerable and wealthy Florentine family named Rucellai. The founder of their fortunes was a crusader who returned from the Holy Land with the knowledge of a secret oriental dyeing process by which could be created the most brilliant and lasting colors. The new method, applied by his descendants in the workshops of Florence with great skill to woolen stuffs and later to silks, produced very beautiful fabrics, which came into great demand throughout Europe. One distinc-tive hue of red, long used for ceremonial costumes of state and particularly for cardinals' robes, is especially identified with the Rucellai. Their name, in fact, derives from the plant used to

(*left*) Detail of marble pavement in the Baptistery. (*right*) Interior remains of the old Romanesque façade of Santa Trinita to which was added in 1250 the present Gothic church.

make the dye—the oricella—and their emblem—a sail, full-blown before a favorable wind (from the east, no doubt)—can still be seen on several buildings within the city.

In general, commerce over the western European trade routes in luxury goods from the east came to be dominated by the Italians because of their geographical location and trading acumen. From the beginning, these foreign traders functioned in groups, called *compagni* (companies), for only by teamwork could they operate over vast distances. Likewise, profitable transactions were possible, particularly on a credit basis, only if customers could deal at long range with confidence. The *compagni* therefore bound themselves and their fortunes, without limit of liability, to cover their business dealings as well as the acts of their associates. In so doing, they established what we recognize today as the fundamentals of partnership operations. Mutual trust thus being essential, most *compagni* started out as family affairs.

Florentine merchants appear to have been especially active in the buying and selling of woolen cloth, one of the basic forms of wealth at that time. Their customary practice seems to have been to buy up large quantities of rough cloth from scattered sources, particularly in France, England, and Spain, ship it to Florence for dressing and dyeing, and then re-export it to markets all over Europe.

Eventually, due largely to a combination of shrewd management and the maintenance of a high quality of craftsmanship in the cloth finishing process, the Florentine *compagni* were able to control a great part of this trade. To impose standards, they early subordinated themselves to a guild organization, which came to be known as the Calimala, from the street of that name where their offices and warehouses were situated.* The statutes of the guild clearly set forth its purpose by laying down the conditions of apprenticeship and membership, conduct and discipline, as well as the requirements for buying and selling and for maintaining a high standard of workmanship. Prices were partially regulated, and in general the conduct of the business was supervised, through the guilds.

The actual work of processing the imported cloth was not carried out by the merchants of the Calimala but by independent operatives under their strict supervision. These were the artisans and laborers responsible for achieving the attractive colors, designs, and textures that caught the fancy of the world: the *tintori*, who dyed the cloth, the *tagliatori*, who cut and shaped it, the *compitori*, who smoothed and corrected the surface with heated rollers, and the *piegatori*, who carefully folded and packed it for shipment. Of these, the *tintori* were the most important. Only pure vegetable or plant parasite dyes were used, most imported from the eastern Mediterranean, of which the oricella became the most valued. To maintain their lead, the Calimala absolutely forbade the emigration of skilled workers or the export of vital raw materials. Alum, a chemical vital to insure the fastness and vibrancy of the dyes, was stockpiled in large quantities and new sources were constantly sought, while the secrets of the dyeing process and the substances used were jealously guarded. By the end of the duecento, Florentines were the chief traders of woolen goods in Paris, Marseilles, Arles, Avignon, Bruges,

---

* The derivation of the word is thought to come from *calle mayor*, as it had always been the principal north-south street since Roman times.

London, Rhodes, and many other large market centers. Ultimately, they achieved a virtual monopoly of the output of the very best quality cloth obtainable, that from the looms of England and Scotland, which, after passing through the workshops of Florence, arrived on the markets of the world unsurpassed in excellence.

The importance to the Calimala of this product is underlined by the fact that the guild's coat-of-arms features a replica of a bale of woolen cloth—*torsello** in Italian—on which stands a rampant bird of prey. The names of the leading families engaged in this activity have come down to us on the rolls of the Calimala: the Cavalcanti (whose house became the guild headquarters), the Cerrchi, Pozzi, Frescobaldi, Nerli, and especially the Bardi and Peruzzi.

Concurrent with these developments, early in the duecento, another religious brotherhood from the north, less well known than the two famous mendicant orders but destined to greatly influence the fortunes of Florence, was establishing itself along the Arno—the Fratri Umilati, who, while wearing the white robes of penitents, were less interested in religion than in their principal occupation, the weaving of wool. This craft had, of course, long been practiced in Tuscany, but the Umilati brought with them a better technique, better looms, and a new organization for efficient large-scale production. One by one, their mills and workshops were set up outside the second circuit of walls in the area immediately adjacent to the present Via dei Fossi—the street of the ditches—so named from the many trenches dug here to carry the water from the Mugnone, a stream, to the mills for washing the wool and turning the paddle wheels.

Encouraged by the Florentine government, the Umilati set the pattern in their own organization for the subsequent expansion of the city's weaving industry, which had already formed a guild of its own known as the Arte della Lana.

As the demand for finished Florentine cloth increased throughout Europe, more and more raw wool was needed by the local weavers of the Lana. To supply it, the services of the Calimala companies with their purchasing agents north of the Alps were

* A typical *torsello* contained ten or twelve bolts of cloth wrapped in canvas and corded, several of which could be hung over the back of a mule.

called upon for the purpose of acquiring and shipping, in addition to the usual foreign cloth, foreign fleeces, especially the high quality staple from England. Consequently, throughout the 13th century, with ever-increasing regularity, the loaded baggage trains converged on the city.

In order to clearly define the limits within which the two wool guilds could operate without infringing upon the rights of the other, a series of agreements was worked out between them. For the protection of the Lana, no raw wool was to be exported from Florence but must be woven into cloth there. In addition, the Calimala could not sell garments made of imported cloth within the city but must re-export all such finished goods. In return, the Lana agreed not to deal in—that is, not to buy or sell—foreign-made cloth, leaving this exclusively to the Calimala. It is interesting to note that the Florentines followed an exactly opposite policy from that of most other Italian wool centers, which often prohibited the importation of foreign wool or the dressing of foreign cloth in order to protect their local growers and weavers. This restrictive policy of so many towns only served to make available to the Florentines the best grades of wool in Europe in greater quantity and at a lower price.

At the same time, the separate operations needed to transform the raw wool into finished cloth were more clearly delineated and restricted to specific trades, one of the earliest examples of the division of labor, so important to the efficient production of wealth.

On arrival in the city, the fleeces passed into the custody of the masters of the Lana, on whose premises they were washed, dried, cut, combed, and oiled. Next came the spinning of the yarn and the weaving itself, also under the supervision of the wool companies. Thereafter, the rough cloth passed temporarily out of the hands of the Lana into those of various independent operatives: the *qualchieri* (fullers), the *tiratori* (stretchers), the *rammendatori* (those who mended faults), the *cardatori* (those who raised the pile high), and the *affettatori* (those who clipped and trimmed). Finally, as in the case of foreign cloth, it passed on to the trades that dyed and finished it.

More and more, as the number of weaving mills increased, all these various operatives fell under the influence of the Lana, which came to wield the greatest influence over the workers, while the Calimala gradually became less concerned with the details of processing and more with the importation of raw wool and the selling of finished cloth; that is, with foreign markets, routes, and prices.

As more jobs were created, the influx of people from the farms continued, until, near the end of the 13th century, over 100,000 people were crowded together within the city. Outside the recently completed walls, which were already too confining, new *borghi* sprang up; while inside, whole streets were taken over by the workshops of the woolen industry from whose windows hung countless long hanks of spun wool or woven cloth to stretch or dry. Many of the street names still attest to this: Via dei Cimatori (Street of the Shearers), Via delle Caldai (cauldrons), Corso dei Tintori (Dyers). To handle the increased traffic, it became necessary to construct a second bridge over the Arno (1218), soon called the Ponte alla Carraia, from the great number of carts laden with wool that used it, and then a third one, named the Ponte Rubaconte (now alle Grazie), after the *podestà* who commissioned it (1237).

The Fratri Umilati continued to prosper, and about the middle of the 13th century, they acquired a piece of land where they built their monastery and church dedicated to *Ognissanti* (All Saints), which still stands today, though much altered, on the piazza of that name. This open space, extending to the river bank, was officially reserved for the use and enjoyment of the brotherhood in a deed dated 1279 "to be forever free of any structures." In the meantime, around this piazza in several directions and centering on the principal thoroughfare, the Borgo Ognissanti, there developed a sizeable suburb of mills, shops, and workers' houses.

Parallel with the growth of the two wool guilds, other trades and professions prospered, expanded, and formed associations for self-protection. Two were made up of merchants—the guild of the silk mercers and the guild of the furriers. Two others— the guild of the bankers and the guild of the judges—were closely involved with the business community. These six, together with the guild of physicians and apothecaries, came to be known as the *arti maggiori*, while those of lesser stature were collectively known as the *arti minori*. The more important of the *arti minori* were the butchers, blacksmiths, builders (or masters of stone and wood, which included the sculptors and architects), shoemakers and leather workers, *rigattieri* (dealers in household goods), innkeepers, wine merchants, tanners, armorers, and bakers.

The makeup of the various guilds was generally more complex than their names would indicate, since numerous other occupational groups, often only remotely related, were attached to them. For instance, linked to the doctors and apothecaries were dealers in oriental spices and cosmetics, dressers of parchments, manuscript copyists and illustrators, wood and copper engravers, and the small but later notable group of *dipintori* (painters), who were dependent on the guild for the importation of their pigments. Similarly, the minor guild of the *rigattieri* included tailors, linen drapers, and dealers in bedding, canvas, hemp, and raw flax.

While the guilds were mainly economic in nature, they also acquired a social function, assuming the role of fraternal organizations with chivalric and religious overtones. It is interesting to note that all seven of the major guilds were to some degree involved in foreign trade. The two wool guilds, of course, were almost wholly dependent on sources of supply and markets outside Tuscany, as were the silk mercers. The furriers obtained their skins and pelts for dressing from distant places, while the bankers conducted many of their operations in other European cities. Even the physicians and apothecaries had foreign contacts, since the ingredients for their medicines and drugs usually came from abroad, as did the raw materials for the painters, cosmetic dealers, and others who attached themselves to the guild.

Finally, the judges and notaries were also embroiled in all this foreign commercial activity, traveled widely, and resolved disputes between parties from different lands. In an age when a merchant's goods and chattels located abroad or in transit were subject to arbitrary confiscation by foreigners, it would have been impossible to conduct business unless guidelines for fair treatment had been agreed upon. It was therefore one of the primary responsibilities of the legal profession to negotiate the trade treaties and commercial agreements with their opposite numbers in other cities which would permit the *compagni* to operate without interference. Tangible evidence has come down to us in a body of laws worked out at that time, known in English as the law-merchant, which came to be adopted by most European countries side by side with their existing national legal systems to regulate the conduct of foreign trade. Later, with the coming of the Renaissance and the rediscovery of the older Roman law, which had placed more emphasis on the rights of individuals as opposed to hereditary family rights and to move-able property as opposed to land, the legal tools were thus already at hand with which the judges could assist European society in moving from a feudal to a commercial economy.

The prestige of the Florentine judges, in particular, was widely acknowledged and many of them ended their careers as ambas-sadors or ministers of state with their own or other governments. Their guild in Florence, which probably existed even before the 13th century, was always accorded the highest respect, and its head official, Il Proconsolo, who was maintained in a house on the street of that name, always held precedence of place in all public ceremonies over the heads of the other guilds.

The notaries, more numerous than the judges, also became indispensable members of the community. In their capacity as lawyers, they were required to investigate and plead cases, to draw up wills, and to reduce commercial and political arrange-ments to writing. As advisors, they were attached to the treasuries of the guild and of the city and to foreign embassies and business houses. In addition, various clerical duties devolved upon them: they were required to maintain accounting records and to carry on correspondence in an age when most citizens were illiterate.

But ultimately, of all the businesses to evolve out of the com-mercial activity of the period, none were to surpass in wealth, reputation, of influence those that dealt, not in merchandise, but in money. Known collectively as the Arte del Cambio, the bankers had their origin in the service of providing a market in coins of diverse issue—that is, money changing, or what we today would call foreign exchange. This became a particularly special-ized profession at a time when countless authorities—communes, princes, feudal lords—were all free to issue what coinage they pleased and were equally free to debase it, whenever it became advantageous to do so. Throughout the Middle Ages, practically

the only coins issued were silver pennies—*denari*, in Italian—
which were minted in great variety and regularly debased with
copper when the occasion demanded. This naturally resulted in
a constant depreciation of the coinage and a continually changing
relationship of one coin to another. The resulting confusion
created the necessity for the orderly establishment of the relative
value of all these coins, plus a facility for exchanging them upon
payment of a fee, which were the earliest functions of the *cambiatori* (money changers).

Later as the volume of trade and its value increased, a need was
felt for coins of a larger denomination. These were first effectively
supplied by the Florentines, who in violation of imperial prerog-
ative, issued in 1235 the silver *soldo* worth 12 *denari* and in 1252
the gold *lira* (the famous *fiorino d'oro* or golden florin) worth 20
soldi or the equivalent of a *libbra* (pound) of silver.* Anyone who
took to the mint 240 *denari* or a pound of silver could have a
golden florin, or vice versa. These innovations, though soon
copied by others, gave the Florentines a head start in the complicated business of trading in money. In the course of time, their
golden florin, which was never debased and was always maintained at full value by the members of the Arte del Cambio,
became and remained for several centuries the standard of value
in which prices were quoted and to which other currencies were
related throughout Europe, much like the dollar or the pound
sterling today.

We should picture these *cambiatori* as they would have appeared
in the Mercato Nuovo, which was reserved for them, sitting
behind their *banchi* (benches) covered by a green cloth with a bowl
full of mixed coins, their ledgers before them and a bag of golden
florins at their feet.†

Their subsequent history is closely bound up with the Calimala,
for, as capital began to accumulate in the hands of the merchants,
excess funds were entrusted to the *cambiatori* for safekeeping

---

* This monetary relationship of 20:12:1 existed until recently in the English
pound, shilling, and pence, the symbols for which (£ s d) stood for the Italian
libbra, *soldo*, and *denaro*.

† This space called the New Market, to distinguish it from the Mercato
Vecchio and later roofed over by a Renaissance loggia, is now the straw
market.

and loaning out at very profitable interest rates, running at times as high as 20 or 30 per cent, indicative both of the scarcity of money capital and of the high risk. Technically, the charging of interest was forbidden by the church, but there were innumerable ways of getting around the prohibition. Financial transfers and loans in foreign commerce were specifically exempt, since exchange of currencies was usually involved for which fees could legitimately be charged. But even interest charges in local transactions could easily be camouflaged by calling them fines, gifts, or fees, or by the device of making the lender a temporary participant in the business enterprise.

It was not long before the merchants of the Calimala, noting the tremendous profits to be made by dealing in money as well as in wool, emulated the *cambiatori* by establishing banking facilities in their foreign branches to convert currencies, lend money at interest, and finance the purchase of raw wool and the sale of finished cloth for themselves and others. Thus, they became bankers as well as traders, carrying on both functions concurrently. To these men we owe the invention, or at least the perfection, of an invaluable banking device, the exchanging of cash values against paper. It was early recognized that the transportation of large amounts of money over long distances was cumbersome and risky. It was also expensive and unnecessary if reliable transactions could be effected on paper. Thus, a system was devised that employed bills of exchange and letters of credit by which foreign trade could be financed without the actual transfer of money. This saved time as well as carrying costs. Bullion took twelve days, for example, to reach Genoa or Rome from Florence, while a courier for a Calimala agent could make the trip in four. For London, the figures were about fifty days as opposed to seventeen.

With these and other financial innovations, the Florentines were thus among the first to discover the key to the control of commerce between the nations. As greater amounts of capital were required, the larger and better organized houses, such as the Mozzi, Bardi, Acciaiuoli, Frescobaldi, and Peruzzi, tended to capture the lion's share of foreign banking operations. The Bardi became perhaps the largest and most famous in the 13th century, with agents scattered throughout France, Flanders, England, Spain, Italy, and the eastern Mediterranean. The French, in particular, were very good customers, and this fact largely explains the efforts made by the Florentines to keep on good terms with Paris.

Their other principal ally, the pope, also became one of their chief clients and contributed immeasurably to the growth of their banking operations. The struggle between him and the emperor that continued unabated through much of the 13th century required an ever larger number of soldiers, whose maintenance was costly. The pope was seeking not only to resist the expansion of German influence in Italy but also to consolidate his hold over the territory known as the Papal States, which stretched across the peninsula from Rome to Ravenna. All this required money, and the burden of supplying it fell on the whole Christian community. As canon law forbade the church's direct participation in financial enterprise, the pope naturally looked to his Guelph friends, with their offices and agents throughout Europe, to assist in the collection of funds. Italian merchants had often been called upon in the past to help in the gathering of church revenues, Peter's Pence, and other offerings and forwarding of them to Rome. Florentines had competed with Sienese, Pisans, and merchants from other Italian cities for this privilege. Now, at lucrative fees, they were employed to collect the tithe monies repeatedly demanded by the pope, and, incidentally, allowed to provide the loans—at high interest, of course—to all those in need of ready cash to cover the papal assessments.

The great landed proprietors—the church and lay lords in the country—were often those most in need of money loans and apparently seldom able to pay them back. In fact, it has been concluded that during the 12th and 13th centuries a great deal of the landed wealth of the Florentine *contado* passed gradually by the process of foreclosure from the old feudal estates into the hands of the traders and bankers.

As can be appreciated, this business became increasingly intolerable to the Ghibelline nobles, and sporadic fighting between the two parties erupted throughout Italy. In Florence, the situation came to a head in 1248, when the Ghibelline contingent there, encouraged by the military power of Frederick II, made the fateful decision to attack and overwhelm their rivals within the city. So suddenly did they strike that their success was immediate, if short lived. The Guelph merchants and their supporters fled in panic to the countryside, leaving their goods and houses, as well as control of the city, to the mercy of their enemies.

The split between the two sides was now complete. The Guelphs, however, did not have to wait long for revenge, as the unexpected death of Frederick two years later signaled the break-up of his personal military following and the temporary collapse of imperial pretensions. Seizing the opportunity, the common people of Florence—the shopkeepers, artisans, and laborers—generally sympathizing with the Guelph cause and seeing their chance to obtain some concessions, unexpectedly rose up in arms to the cry of *"Viva il popolo"* and drove the Ghibelline nobles out, killing those that resisted. Shortly, the Guelph merchants were invited to return to the city and to re-establish the prosperity on which all were dependent, but with the understanding that henceforth the people were to have a voice in all important matters. A new official, the *capitano del popolo*, with whom the *podestà* was required to consult, was elected to represent them. And to mark the beginning of a new era, the ancient banner of Florence, the white lily, or fleur-de-lis, set upon a red field—the origin of which may have been connected to the city's old name Fiorenza but which had become increasingly the symbol of the Ghibelline nobles—was henceforth transformed by simply reversing the color schemes.

Thus began an energetic though brief period (1250–60), known as *il primo popolo* (the first democracy), marked by affluence and expansion within a framework of political accommodation and compromise. The common people, though at first jealous of their new-won privileges, were soon content to conform to the rulings of the *podestà*, who, in turn, was manipulated by the merchants. Foreign policy, in particular, was dictated by them, and, taking advantage of the empire's feebleness following Frederick's death, the city aggressively challenged its rival neighbors. Almost immediately, the smaller Tuscan towns of San Gimignano, Volterra, and Poggibonsi were compelled to submit and accept a Florentine *podestà*. Pistoia was overcome in 1254. Even Siena was forced to surrender certain disputed areas, and Pisa had to open its port to unrestricted Florentine commerce.

The Florentine flag, now the red lily emblazoned on a white field, after a few short years flew over a larger territory than ever before.

Within the walls, the appearance of the city underwent a change. In the first flush of power, the people, seeking to humiliate the nobles of both parties, forced through a new law requiring the ancient towers to be reduced to a maximum height of about 70 feet. Some, belonging to the most hated of the Ghibellines, were completely razed to the ground, including a group belonging to the Uberti that stood in a part of the present Piazza della Signoria. The Piazza, in fact, did not exist before this time and thus owes its origin to the destruction of these buildings.

In 1252, work was begun on a fourth bridge across the Arno, called the Ponte Santa Trinita, after the church of that name at its northern end. At the same time, the church itself was completely rebuilt in a new style which had not been seen before in Florence and which the Italians called Gothic. Its introduction south of the Alps was due to the monks of the Cistercian order, a religions brotherhood from Burgundy, who were among the first to employ the improved structural principles of this style of architecture.

The original Santa Trinita was a Romanesque construction with a crypt and raised choir similar to San Miniato, but its only remains that can still be seen are the interior frontal walls—the rough stonework to the sides of the main door—revealing the width of the original nave, and the bases of several columns which have been disclosed on either side of the stairs leading down to the crypt. The new church was laid out on a more generous scale in the shape of a T by the Cistercians and reconstructed in the Gothic style, using ribbed vaulting, pointed arches, and buttresses, thereby establishing the pattern for the much larger Florentine churches that followed later in the century. For the most part, Santa Trinita remains relatively unchanged, somber and monkish, except for the altars, tombs, and other embellishments of a later age, including the Baroque façade facing the little piazza.

But the most ambitious undertaking of that decade was the construction of the city's first great civic building, the Palazzo del Popolo, which was intended not only as the residence of the *capitano del popolo* but as the symbol of the triumph of the people and the commune over the Ghibellines and the empire. Started in 1255 and incorporating some older structures, including the existing tower at the corner, the work was carried forward in several stages. The oldest part, along the Via del Proconsolo, completed within a year or two and containing the heavily vaulted entrance hall, which still shows traces of the original fresco decoration, appears to have been carried up only about two-thirds of the way and faced with the large, finely hewn blocks of stone that can be seen today. At that time, it probably had a wooden roof. Subsequently, the walls and tower were raised to their present height in a coarser stone, the great assembly hall above was vaulted over, and the battlements were set out on their projecting stone corbels.

The builders were, of course, well aware that it was merely a question of time before the enemies of the new regime, both within and without, would resume their attack. A building capable of defense was therefore the primary consideration, as its architecture confirms, but for all its fortresslike character, the Palazzo del Popolo did not prove to be the impregnable bulwark or, even for long, the headquarters of the popular cause, as within a few years all practical power had passed again into the hands of the merchants, and the building became the residence of the *podestà*. It was progressively enlarged to the east, and its outstanding feature, the magnificent courtyard, was completed. Here, by the open stairway and the loggia above, with their pleasing proportions, hang the coats-of-arms in stone and terra-cotta of the various *podeste* who ruled here continuously through the next two centuries. During this time, it was known as the Palazzo del Podestá, until the rule of the grand dukes in the 16th century, when it came to be called the Bargello, as it is today, after the police official who occupied it.

From the beginning, a large part of the building was given over to dungeons and cells, and instruments of torture were kept and employed there. Executions for treason and other crimes took place in the courtyard, on which occasions the great bell in the tower rang out, a practice that lasted until as late as 1848. All evidence of its grisly past, however, was completely removed following the departure of the grand dukes in the 19th century, when the structure was restored and converted into the National Museum.

Old photo of the Bargello, which houses the National Museum of Sculpture.

Stairway and loggia of the Bargello and coats-of-arms of the
various *podeste* who ruled the city from here.

(*left*) The assembly hall of the Bargello where the greatest sculptors of the Renaissance are now represented. (*right*) The Palazzo Spini, an example of a 13th-century fortified town house.

As indicated, the productive though precarious balance of power between the various classes was not destined to continue long, and in 1260 the Ghibellines again upset the status quo. Allying themselves with the Sienese and the imperial troops of the Hohenstaufens, they were able to achieve a victory that year over the Guelphs at the Battle of Montaperti in central Tuscany, in which the Florentine cavalry was routed and the infantry was overrun and slaughtered. Thousands were killed or imprisoned in Siena's dungeons, and the surviving Guelphs were forced to flee for their lives. So ended *Il primo popolo*. Again, Florence and its dependent towns fell into the hands of the Ghibellines, and Tuscany came under the sway of the empire.

In this emergency, the Guelphs turned to the pope and through him to the French king for assistance, which was soon supplied, for a price, in the person of Count Charles of Anjou, who descended into Italy in 1265 at the head of a large army. The French liberator, of course, was in continual need of papal monies to sustain his expensive expedition, which the pope strove to supply with the assistance of the Guelph trading houses. In the past, some of this business emanting from the papal court had been carried on by Sienese and Pisan companies, but when most of them shortsightedly joined the Ghibelline cause, their Florentine Guelph rivals, though for the moment in exile from their native town, secured a virtual monopoly in the collection and transmission of church revenues.

As it turned out, the imperial triumph was short-lived. Within a few years (by 1268), a series of battles, waged vigorously by Charles of Anjou, who commanded some 30,000 soldiers in addition to a strong contingent of Florentine Guelphs, ended with the death of the Hohenstaufen claimants and the defeat of their army in Italy, again reversing the situation. For the second and last time, the Ghibelline nobles were expelled from Florence and its dependencies, and their power thereafter suffered a protracted eclipse throughout central Italy. Count Charles assumed the crown of Naples and Sicily, and, at the invitation of the Florentine Guelphs, selected their new *podestà*, who installed himself in the palace of the *capitano*. At the same time, the triumphant Guelphs, seeking permanently to prevent a resurgence of their rivals, systematically confiscated every remnant of their estates within and outside the town. So it was that, after a brief interruption, Florence resumed its Guelph identity and its prosperous pursuit of business.

What was the city like during the latter half of the 13th century, on the threshold of the Renaissance, as its population and its fame grew so rapidly? Fortunately, a number of documents and drawings have survived to enable us to picture the life of that remarkable period. We may begin by trying to visualize, from some vantage point high above the city, the crazy pattern of hundreds of tile roofs, jumbled together at every angle, through which snaked a maze of narrow streets. Some of these were newly paved with hard, flat stones, though most were still cobbled, and all were choked with carts and wagons jostling for passageway.

At the approximate center of the old town was a relatively large, open space marked today by the northern half of the Piazza della Repubblica. This was the Mercato Vecchio, into which poured a torrent of humanity from the surrounding streets. Hundreds of farmers' carts heaped with local produce gathered here, while, all around, the bales of cloth and other goods passed in and out of the many shops and warehouses. The Mercato Vecchio opened each day at dawn at the ringing of a bell set upon a marble column, a copy of which may still be seen standing in the piazza on the same historic spot, which since Roman times has marked the crossing of the two principal streets of the town. People from all classes gathered here to bargain, talk, and argue. Fights and riots were not uncommon, and the presence of a thief in the crowd was announced by the loud sounding of the bell. Market porters, working under set regulations and fees, loaded and unloaded. Local wine from the *contado* was sold here in the cask by the wine merchants or by the mug in one of the many taverns that grew up in and around the square. Imported wines, however, were by custom handled only in the *alberghi* (inns), which were, by this time, well established in the vicinity of this piazza to accommodate the growing number of commercial travelers from abroad. A few of these inns and taverns are still commemorated in the names of streets nearby: La Spada, Il Inferno, Il Purgatorio.

On the north side of the piazza stood the most impressive private house in the city at that time, the ancient and famous Palazzo de Tosinghi, which has long since vanished, though a street behind still preserves the name. Something of its imposing scale can be imagined by comparing two surviving palaces from the same period—the Palazzo Spini and the Palazzo Gianfigliazzi —which still stand opposite one another on the Via Tornabuoni guarding the approach to the old Santa Trinita bridge. These well illustrate the fortresslike appearance of the dwellings of the time, which were no more than enlargements and lateral extensions of the older, truncated towers.

The Palazzo Spini in particular seems to have been continually added to over the years. The side facing the river once rose straight from the bed of the Arno, and the street now known as the Lungarno Accialuoli passed under the palace by a long arched tunnel. This portion of the building was torn down in the 19th century and the façade pushed back to where we see it today. Also, a number of extensive restorations increasing the size and number of its windows and ground floor openings have altered somewhat its earlier, more rugged, less ordered appearance.

Also in the Mercato Vecchio stood some of the city's oldest parish churches, all since gone: San Pierino, where the post office is today; San Tommaso, on the site of the Savoy Hotel; and Santa Maria in Campidoglio, near the northwest corner of the piazza.

In the neighbouring streets were located the many shops and warehouses loaded with stocks of merchandise of great value. Though the buildings were largely of stone, fire was still a constant concern, since the wooden floors and fittings, and the windows covered by oiled linen, to say nothing of the stock themselves, were all highly inflammable. We read of periodic conflagrations, ignited by carelessness or riot, which consumed vast quantities of goods and gutted the buildings.

The small street at the end of the present Via Porta Rossa leading to the Via Calzaiuoli (Street of the Stocking Makers) was called Via Baccano (Rowdy Row), because of the frequent fights that broke out there. In fact, Florence was anything but a quiet place even after the worst of the quarrelsome nobles had passed from the scene. With an increase in wealth came a spirit of definace and profligacy. Irreverent pranksters and scoffers challenged the order of things, often rebelling against the social prohibitions and restraints of the day as laid down by the authorities. We read of animals driven into the churches, ink poured into the holy water basins, foul smelling chemicals mixed with the incense stocks in the sacristies. Groups of young scoundrels rushed through the streets, houses were broken into, and violence and robbery occurred almost daily. To control the criminal element, executions were commonplace, the bodies sometimes being dragged through the streets afterward. The authorities struggled to suppress these outbursts, but, generally, a citizen had to look out for himself. From diaries and other sources we get a glimpse of the everyday precautions required of those who would safeguard their lives and property. For example, one is admonished to check bolts and locks at all windows and doors carefully at sunset. If a trip out at night was unavoidable, a companion, a weapon, and a good lantern were essential. And though it was customary to arise early, before dawn, few would venture outside until the opening of the neighborhood shops could be heard, and then only after saying a prayer on the doorstep and making the sign of the cross.

Despite the comparative well-being of the times, it was also advisable to keep a good supply of oil and grain on hand against the occurrence of shortages or famine. The number of inhabitants of the city had, in fact, so increased that the Florentine *contado* could scarcely supply half the grain necessary to feed the population and periodic food crises developed when imported stocks could not be had in sufficient quantity.

Clocks were nonexistent in 13th-century Florence, but scores of church bells rang out intermittently to signal the time. Work always began early but ceased well before dark to allow workers who lived outside the walls to leave the city before the gates were closed at dusk. Holidays and feast days multiplied with prosperity, until, by one estimate, there were fewer than 275 work days annually at the end of the 13th century. On the most important festival, that of the city's patron saint, San Giovanni Battista, an elaborate procession with many banners and ornamented carts paraded through the streets and converged on the Via Calimala, where the wool companies had their offices and warehouses and which was covered over from end to end on that occasion by a blue awning of the finest material sprinkled with golden fleur-de-lis. On such days, the real essence of the passing Middle Ages came alive as religious ritual in the city's churches combined with pagan celebrations, tournaments, and horse races in the streets.

Such was the aspect and flavor of the city when, toward the end of the century, from about 1280 on, the *arti maggiori* (greater guilds), which had hitherto manipulated the government indirectly in the background, now with the consent and support of the *arti minori* (lesser guilds), assumed direct, unconcealed control. A new executive body, the priorate, made up of seven members, chosen exclusively from the *priori* (priors or leaders of the guilds) was formally established, a system which was to last thereafter, in form at least, for some two hundred years. One of the seven was designated as the gonfalonier, whose function it was to carry out the orders of the government. Again the *podestà* was retained, but he became more and more simply the tool of the priorate.

In the meantime, the class position formerly occupied by the older families of nobles, the exiled Ghibellines, had been replaced by a new group of landed *signori*. These men considered business beneath them and instead emulated the feudal ways of their predecessors by practicing horsemanship and arms and by seeking honors and titles of nobility. Many of them, though officially Guelph, had intermarried with the remnants of the old Ghibelline families, whose lands in the *contado* they had often acquired. While their services in the cavalry were occasionally useful—they helped win the Battle of Campaldino against Arezzo in 1289 and they took part in the first campaigns against Pisa—the guild leaders did not trust them and opposed their sharing in the government of the city. Steps were therefore taken to curtail permanently the influence of the *grandi*, as this new landed class came to be called. First, a law was passed in 1289 freeing all the serfs in the *contado*—that is, all those still bound by the traditions of the feudal system to the manorial estates—with the obvious purpose of weakening the hold of the *grandi* on their servants and retainers. More important, a second enactment, promulgated shortly thereafter (1293) and known as the Ordinances of Justice, decisively terminated whatever political power they might have enjoyed. This law, in addition to laying down certain rules of conduct, flatly excluded the *grandi* from eligibility for guild offices or for the priorate itself. The effects of these disabilities, rigorously enforced in the following years, resulted in many of the *grandi* being forced into exile like the Ghibellines before them. Thereafter, throughout the brightest period in the city's history, the destinies of Florence were exclusively controlled by men from the middle class—by merchants with a practical, businesslike turn of mind—and not by the landed gentry.

With the undisguised assumption of power by the *arti maggiori*, the guild leaders turned to the long-considered need to enhance the beauty of the city's two oldest and most important, yet unfinished, religious buildings—the Baptistery and San Miniato. For this purpose, mosaic workers from Venice and Byzantium were commissioned in the last decades of the 13th century to cover vast surfaces in these churches with their glittering stones for the glory of God and the edification of the Florentines. Today, their work may still be seen illuminating the cupola of the Baptistery and the apse of San Miniato unchanged and undiminished by time. The former depicts Christ the Judge, some 26 feet in height, separating the Saved from the Damned; the latter shows Christ, in the act of blessing, between the Madonna and the Saint, intercessors for the Florentines, and records in Roman numerals the exact year it was completed—1297. From these prototypes in the Byzantine style, carefully studied by Giotto (1266?–1337) and his successors, came the inspiration that was progressively to refine and humanize the figurative art that Florence so profoundly influenced later.

At the same time, plans on a grand scale for a number of new buildings were conceived and carried forward. Florence's three largest churches were then undertaken as a joint effort by the city, the guilds, and the monastic orders. First to be commenced (in 1280) was the Dominican church of Santa Maria Novella, an enlargement of a small pre-existing one, followed soon after by Santa Croce (1294) and the new cathedral, Santa Maria del Fiore (1296). All three structures were decisively influenced by the new Gothic style imported from the north, which had been employed a few decades earlier in the rebuilding of Santa Trinita. In viewing these magnificent buildings today, we must keep in mind that over the years many modifications of dubious value have been effected, but, happily, the basic architectural elements of all three remain much as they were planned and built almost seven centuries ago.

Gothic forms, as revealed in Florentine churches, differ considerably from those of northern Europe, where the pointed arch, a variety of buttresses, soaring vaults, wide expanses of stained glass, and wealth of decorative detail achieved their highest expression. The new building techniques that prompted this style, however, were fully exploited in Florence as elsewhere, primarily to overcome the disadvantages inherent in Romanesque construction methods when applied to buildings of larger proportion. Experience had shown that the interior spaciousness, height of the vaulting, and amount of window light were all limited by the older system. Widening the nave or raising the walls higher invariably meant increasing their thickness and mass in order to sustain the greater weight and lateral thrust of the

Late 13th-century mosaic of the Last Judgment in the cupola of the Baptistery.

vaulting. This, in turn, often caused them to sink into the ground or settle unevenly of their own heaviness. It also necessitated smaller rather than larger window openings, which together with the ponderous nature of the supporting walls created a crowded and oppressive effect.

The solution was found in the Gothic system, by which the downward push and lateral pressure of the roof were offset, not by opposing them with heavy, static masses of stone, but by a new type of cross-vaulting that concentrated and channeled these forces earthward through a system of buttresses. By this device, stresses were carried out over the side aisles of the building and dispersed over a more extensive area on a series of exterior piers. The weight therefore was much less concentrated. Thrust and counterthrust were ingeniously made to balance, so that it was possible to utilize more slender columns to support wider arches and vaults. These latter, in turn, formerly rounded, were now pointed, further increasing their stability by reducing their side-ward push and lifting the roof ever higher. At the same time, the walls, no longer the principal supporting members, were reduced in thickness and were pierced with much larger windows, thus creating a spaciousness and lightness never before achieved.

The effect of these innovations is not so apparent in the great Florentine basilicas, as it was never the intention of the Italian church builders to create the mysticism and exaltation or the inspiring sweep upward that humbles the worshipper in northern cathedrals. Windows, too, though larger than in their Roman-esque predecessors, were of comparatively modest proportions, though adequate enough for the bright southern sun. The emphasis instead was on wider and more open interiors, on spaciousness to accommodate vast numbers, and on vaultings lower than their northern counterparts so as to dispense with the need of flying buttresses, considered by Italians as barbaric. Missing are the articulated vertical shafts and columns, the complicated tracery, the unfolding decor, the intricate ribbed vaults that carry the eye aloft and that seem, to us, the essence of the Gothic style.

Nevertheless, these three buildings are impressive, not the least because of their vast size. Santa Maria Novella, the smallest, measures more than 300 feet from end to end and further gives the impression of great length inside by the fact that the distance between the columns diminishes as they march forward from the façade. It was planned and carried out by architects selected from among the Dominican brotherhood and is a good example of the blending of simple Gothic principles with the older Romanesque tradition. The persistence of the latter style can clearly be seen in the bell tower and the cloisters which followed the construction of the church itself. If the interior seems somewhat bare, we must remember that originally the walls of the church, and of the cloisters too, were covered with frescoes illustrating stories from the Bible for the multitude who could not read. These were later whitewashed over, hidden by altars, or otherwise destroyed, though fragments may be seen here and there. Similarly, the wonderful carved tomb slabs, which once covered much of the floor, have mostly disappeared. Of the façade of the church, only the bottom half containing the recessed tombs is contemporaneous work, but it is interesting as revealing another example of the blending of Gothic with Romanesque forms: the pointed arches of black and white stone over the tombs and the decorative marble slabs under round arches above.

The sober Gothic style of the Dominican church of Santa Maria Novella, commenced in 1280.

A little later, on the opposite side of the city, the Franciscans, too, commenced the complete rebuilding of another small church known as Santa Croce together with its monastic buildings. Though it boasts the same open feeling as the Dominican church, achieved by slender, widely separated columns, larger windows, and an even greater length, it differs in one major respect, since it is roofed over, not by a ribbed vaulting, but by a painted beam ceiling common to the older Tuscan churches. It is probable that this feature was planned from the start, as the width of the nave and the size of the piers would not have permitted a heavy roof of stone. Here again is an example of a reluctance to exploit fully all the possibilities of the Gothic style.

Within, the church suffered the same alterations as Santa Maria Novella and lost most of its tombstones and frescoes. The floor was raised, windows were closed up, and a great number of incongruous altars, tombs, and monuments were erected along the sides. Traditionally many of the chapels and altars pertain to private families who, by contributing to the costs of construction and decoration of the building, received this right and privilege.

The light and airy Franciscan church of Santa Croce (begun 1294), where many great Florentines were buried.

Burial at Santa Croce was eagerly sought after in the early centuries by those who wished to shelter under the protection of the great saint and founder of the church, whose influence might speed the passage to a heavenly reward, and it therefore became a kind of pantheon where many famous Florentines have been laid to rest. Here in Santa Croce were later consecrated the tombs of Machiavelli, Michelangelo, and Galileo, as well as Dante's cenotaph (empty tomb or sepulchral monument). *

Two names, in particular, stand out in connection with the building and decoration of Santa Croce. The one, Arnolfo di Cambio (1232–1301), the foremost architect of his day, planned the church and adjoining cloister and commenced the construction; and, though he did not live to see its completion, the work was carried out according to his designs. The other, Giotto (1266?–1337), regarded as the greatest innovator in painting of the age, here left some of his most famous frescoes. Executed about 1320 on the walls of the Bardi and Peruzzi chapels, dedicated to those two important banking families, these frescoes, by their radical departure from the earlier Byzantine stylization and by their new pictorial realism, were to have a profound influence on the development of painting. Parts of the paintings were destroyed and the remainder were covered by a layer of plaster during the Renaissance, when the church was redecorated. They were not rediscovered until the 19th century, at which time they were partially and unsatisfactorily repainted. Only recently have they been restored to something of their original appearance. Unfortunately, the colors have long since faded and much detail has disappeared, but enough remains of the compositions and the solidity of the figures to testify to Giotto's great stride forward. Looking back from our vantage point in time, his work at first may seem primitive and crude, but when compared with the abstract symbolism of his contemporaries, a new quality and dimension appear. For the first time a painter not only carefully studied the human figure and countenance from life but succeeded in expressing, though perhaps imperfectly, the essential feelings and drama of the scenes depicted. In fact, Giotto's representation

* Dante died and was buried while in exile at Ravenna, and, despite innumerable official pleas by the Florentines for the return of his body, the citizens of Ravenna will not give it up.

of three dimensional, solid looking forms arranged in space, and his expression of human emotion in these murals, the counterpart of St. Francis's sermons, prescribed the objectives of Western painting until modern times.

Just before the turn of the century, plans were drawn up, also under Arnolfo's supervision, for rebuilding the old cathedral church of Santa Reparata, which had stood for many years opposite the Baptistery.* Rechristened Santa Maria del Fiore, but customarily referred to as Il Duomo, the new cathedral, designed to accommodate some 30,000 people, was to be one of the largest in Europe.† The cost was to be borne partly by the city treasury, partly by special taxes, and partly by contributions from the faithful. The work progressed rapidly for a time, but the tremendous expense of the undertaking plus the diversion of money for military purposes periodically exhausted the funds available. Progress several times came to a halt, finally prompting the city to assign the relatively stable income from the forests in the Casentino to the Opera del Duomo (Cathedral Works Office), but even so the construction of the building required more than a century to complete.‡

Similar inside to Santa Maria Novella, but much larger, the structure is built along Gothic lines, but, in spite of its great height, does not seem to soar skyward. The arches, though pointed, are wide, the columns are stout and firmly planted, a number of horizontal architectural elements carry the eye forward, not upward, and there is a sparsity of furnishings—a few memorials, a few frescoes—in the great echoing, barnlike nave, all of which in the dim light, though impressive, give an austere and somber feeling. Its greatest merit is its honesty. Nothing stands between the worshipper and the building itself, whose essential structural anatomy stands out in a clear architectural statement.

---

* The foundations of Santa Reparta under the floor of the present cathedral have recently been exposed to view.

† Duomo, from the Latin *Domus Dei* (house of God).

‡ The Casentino, an area east of Florence, near the headwaters of the Arno, was acquired from Arezzo after the Battle of Campaldino in 1289. It was then still heavily forested, and the sale of its timber contributed substantial sums to the building and upkeep of the Duomo for several centuries.

(left) The cavernous nave of the Duomo, Santa Maria del Fiore, commenced in 1296. *(right)* The San Niccolò gate, the only one in the third circuit of walls to retain its original height.

Though Arnolfo's models and plans have since been lost, we know that, before he died in 1301, he was personally responsible for pulling down several buildings on the site, fixing the width of the church, laying the solid foundations of the nave, and raising up the walls themselves. It is sad that the great façade he designed and partially completed was long ago destroyed, the more so because it represented a new departure from the customary Florentine approach. Arnolfo had been trained in the Pisan schools, which, more influenced by the Gothic tradition, viewed sculpture as a complementary adjunct to architecture, especially in the design of church façades. In contrast, therefore, to the flat, abstract, geometrical forms adorning the earlier Florentine buildings, he introduced a scheme (drawings of which are extant) employing alcoved arches, niches, and other recesses to accommodate sculptures. Several of those that formed part of the façade he carved himself, including representations of Santa Reparata, Zenobius, Pope Boniface VIII, and an enthroned Madonna, which, weatherbeaten and worn, can be seen today in the Cathedral museum. Lacking drama or emotion, but monumental and imposing, they have a quality of expressive three-dimensional volume unequaled by most of his more famous successors and not fully rediscovered again until Michelangelo.

At the same time, aware that the new façade might not correlate with that of the adjacent Baptistery, Arnolfo cleverly added the alternating black and white stone blocks at each corner of the older building to match similar work in the Duomo façade. Nothing now remains of the latter, but the magnitude of his over-all conception endures in the fabric of the building itself, which, disproportionately large for the size of the city then and even now, attests to Arnolfo's and the Florentines' remarkable ambition and boundless faith in the future.

Finally, to the architectural genius of Arnolfo is due another landmark of the age—the Palazzo dei Priori, or Palazzo della Signoria—now called the Palazzo Vecchio (Old Palace). From the beginning (1299), its purpose was to house in a secure, impressive manner the newly constituted government of the city —the gonfalonier and the *priori* (priors), who were collectively known as the Signoria.* These men, having only recently trimmed the power of the *grandi*, were anxious not only to provide themselves with a safe headquarters, but also to erect a symbol to the authority they had acquired and the permanence to which they aspired.

Unlike the aforementioned churches, whose construction spread over several generations, the new building, or at least the original part forming the solid cube that faces the piazza, was brought rapidly to completion at the turn of the century in only a few years time. Enclosed by soaring, battlemented ramparts and crowned by a magnificent tower, it has long been recognized as one of the most remarkable monuments of the later Middle Ages.

Apparently Arnolfo was required to incorporate some older structures already on the site into the new building, which is supposed to account for its irregular arrangement inside and the eccentricity of the tower. The main exterior wall, pierced with

* The word *Signoria* refers to these men as a group, or rather to "their honors," since, being of an exalted stature, their persons were not presumptuously referred to directly.

The Palazzo Vecchio, hub of Florentine civic affairs for more than six and a half centuries.

two rows of mullioned Gothic windows, and the corbeled, battlemented gallery above, are its most distinctive features. It is interesting to note how this latter architectural element is repeated in another gallery high up on the tower, which itself is boldly resting part of its weight on the projecting support of the one below. Thus the west face of the gallery of the tower is actually jutting out on its corbels some ten feet in midair from the line of support of the walls far below, which sustain this massive and precarious pile without the aid of concrete or steel.

The stone corbels of the main gallery and their connecting arches, which bear up all this masonry, greatly enhance the looks of the façade, but they also served a military purpose, having trap doors between them from which missiles and burning oil could be dropped on unfriendly persons attempting to gain entrance below. High above, surmounting the gallery of the tower, four stout columns of stone support the uppermost terrace. Here hung the bells that, throughout the tempestuous centuries that followed, were frequently sounded to call the citizens together whenever danger threatened the life of the city. And at the apex, crowning all, was placed a lion rampant, symbol of the sovereignty of the commune.

Inside, the priors took up their residence for the term of their office, which was generally limited to two months in order that power might not be concentrated too long in the same hands. During this time, they were not permitted to leave the building except on vital business affecting the city. They could carry on no private conversations with anyone outside. All business was conducted by the priors as a group, and aside from state visitors or official messengers, they saw no one except the monks who were assigned to prepare their meals and administer their devotions. Thus insulated from temptation, they were charged with maintaining the liberty of the citizens and the integrity of the commune, and in general they succeeded. While their rooms inside the palazzo have been considerably altered from their original state and the building has been progressively enlarged to the east, the exterior remains faithful to Arnolfo's plan—a worthy monument to the lofty aspirations of the Florentines of that age.

In the meantime, work had been started on the construction of yet another new surrounding wall—a third circuit designed to greatly enlarge the area of the city, taking in the numerous *borghi* and monastic settlements that had grown up outside. Begun near the end of the 13th century (little more than one hundred years after the second circuit) and not completed until about 1328, the project constituted a tremendous undertaking at enormous expense. It finally attained a length of some five miles on both sides of the river, stood about forty feet high, and included fifteen massive gate towers. A part of this rampart surrounding Oltrarno survives today, but, north of the river, broad *viali* (boulevards) have taken its place, leaving only a few of the gate towers, minus their upper stories, to remind us of the city's former boundaries. Only the Porta San Niccolò, standing in lonely isolation at what was once one of the busiest entrances to the city from the east, preserves its original forbidding height and dignity.

The Early Renaissance: 1300 to 1400

All these ambitious undertakings were not lost on the many visitors from afar to the city on the Arno, whose already great reputation was further enlarged. Neither did the brilliant exploits of its merchants and bankers pass unnoticed. By the end of the 13th century, there was hardly a country in Europe where the Florentines were not the chief traders. Agents of the most important houses, as well as of the Calimala itself, were regularly stationed in all the wool-producing and cloth-manufacturing centers. The astute and practiced minds of these men of affairs were highly valued, and many were sought after by foreign states for service as advisors or diplomats. In fact, so many appeared in Rome as the official representatives of various potentates and princes at the first great jubilee in the year 1300, as to cause Pope Boniface VIII to remark that "Florence must indeed be the greatest of cities as she appears to govern us all" and that "the Florentines themselves are, together with air, water, earth, and fire, in truth, the fifth element of the universe."

Charles II of Anjou, King of Naples, employed Florentines in many capacities—as judges, retainers, court bankers—and provided their fellow countrymen with a virtual monopoly of the commerce passing through his capital city and port. For example, the grain trade, the single most important export of this southern kingdom, once carried on only by Pisan and Venetian merchants, became the exclusive preserve of the Florentine *compagni*, who also brought into the country most of the manufactured goods imported. The mints of London, Naples, and other cities were periodically under the supervision of men from Florence, and the golden florin itself was widely imitated by the French, Flemish, Spanish, Hungarian, and Bohemian rulers.

But, in spite of these achievements, there remained a strong tendency for feuding and division among the upper orders of Florentine society. The wealthy traders who gained control were no more immune from wrangling among themselves than were the nobles before them, and soon (by 1301) had split into two antagonistic factions known as the Bianchi and the Neri (whose history is too complicated to recount in detail here). One group within months emerged triumphant and, exploiting their opportunity to the full, ordered the gonfalonier to arrest all those of the opposition who dared remain in the city. Most, however, were able to escape, and they thus formed another band of bitter exiles. Following in the footsteps of those banished earlier, they congregated in the traditionally Ghibelline centers of Pisa and Arezzo, or attached themselves to the feudal lords remaining in the more remote areas of the Apennines. The great poet Dante Alighieri (1265–1321), having sided with the losing faction, was among their number. Alienated forever from the Guelph cause, he and his companions were obsessed with the desire to revenge themselves on their antagonists and to regain their lost positions and property by any means available. Unfortunately, the institutions on which they pinned their hopes—the empire and the feudal system—had spent their force. Though from time to time, one German emperor or another, persuaded by his Italian adherents, attempted to reassert his sovereignty in Tuscany, the effort was always in vain. One emperor, Henry VII, actually laid siege to Florence (1312), but his army, wracked with disease and unable to provision itself in the unfriendly countryside, had to give up and seek refuge within the walls of Pisa. Near there he died and was buried (his tomb may still be seen in the Pisa

Cathedral), and the imperial threat, along with his army, again dissolved in defeat. Florence and the Guelph communes, supported by the pope and the kings of France and Naples, were now too strong a combination to be overcome or even restrained.

Looking back over the centuries, we recognize the Florentine, Dante, as the spokesman, not only for the cause of the exiles, but, generally, for the passing order of things. For him, the search for an ideal view of life had ended with Thomas Aquinas, the greatest of the medieval philosophers, who produced that masterful synthesis of faith and reason, the *Summa Theologica*. Therein all doubts were forever resolved, all worldly matters relegated to their proper place, and salvation reconfirmed as the overriding concern of man. This, the culminating achievement in medieval theology, formed a part of the inspiration and philosophical background for Dante's great poem *The Divine Comedy*, one of the loftiest literary works of all time. Prompted by the sufferings and injustices he was forced to endure at the hands of his fellow citizens who had banished him forever, the poet tells of his imaginary journeys and observations as he passes through the world after death—Hell, Purgatory, and Paradise—and describes the punishments and agony of those he finds there who failed to live up to the standards of a Christian life. In doing so, he attempts to provide conviction beyond any doubt that only in closer adherence to the precepts of the church fathers and the vainness of pursuing more mundane goals was there any hope or point to human existence. A painting executed in the century following Dante's death, which can still be seen in the nave of the Duomo, shows the poet explaining his work to the Florentines, a copy of his masterpiece in hand. Behind him to the right is the old city of Florence within its walls and on the left a representation of Hell, Purgatory, and Heaven.

But Dante and his fellow exiles were out of step with the leaders of the Guelph middle class, who, proud of their new and vital urban life, their widening commerce, and their effective self-government, lost interest in the abstract philosophical disputations of the clergy and the schoolmen. As the conditions of material well-being filtered down from the top, laymen with new-found time to think and study, stimulated by the opportunities to travel and to exchange talk and ideas, became skeptical of the traditional view of the world. Preoccupied instead with the engrossing concerns of business life, their attention had been diverted primarily to the study of man's material wants and his immediate earthly surroundings. This, in turn, was to lead to an awakening of interest in past accumulations of secular knowledge as embodied in Roman and Greek literature, which, for the most part, had remained locked away and forgotten since classical times. Thus, after many centuries, intellectual matters no longer remained the exclusive preserve of the church. Rather, the active curiosity of the urban laity motivated thought in a new direction, the essence of which came to be called humanism and which, combined with the rediscovery of the western world's cultural heritage, ushered in a new epoch, the Renaissance.

The man who was to sound the first clear call for this break with the past and become the acknowledged master of a new generation of scholars exploiting the "rebirth" of classical literature and thought was Petrarch (Francesco Petrarca, 1304-74), who has been called the "Father of the Renaissance." Though he spent most of his life traveling around Italy and France, he was born of Florentine parents and maintained close contact with the leaders of that city's cultural life. Florence therefore claims him, even as it does Dante, whom it exiled. Thus Dante, the last and greatest voice of the passing Middle Ages, and Petrarch, the first conscious advocate and interpreter of the revival of classical learning—the two brightest stars in the firmament of Italian literature—were decisively, though differently, influenced by the slow eclipse of their familiar world by a new era, which, embracing earthly pursuits as valid ends in themselves, evolved out of the urban centers of Italy, especially their ancestral town of Florence.

Also to be affected by this change of direction and new intellectual climate were the universities, already formed or forming in many Italian towns. Until now, mostly informal and transitory conglomerations of teachers and scholars, they assumed a more permanent character. In Florence, the government, somewhat belatedly (1321), extended official recognition to its university, which later in the century added to the curriculum, besides the traditional disciplines of philosophy, law, and medicine, a chair for the study of classical literature. Still, as its resources were meager and books were an expensive rarity, the Florentine institution had practically no physical facilities, not even a library. What book collections existed were in the hands of the church or a few wealthy merchants—scholars themselves or patrons of scholars—who were to play an important role in the intellectual ferment of the times.

The revolutionary new concept of man's true nature and role provoked bitter differences of opinion between segments within a city and between cities themselves about the place of the church, the monasteries, the empire, and the feudal system in society, all of which did nothing to moderate the already contentious and discordant Italian situation. In the circumstances, a long period of general warfare was inevitable.

In Tuscany, Florence became the main center of controversy. Its merchants, unlike many of their rivals, having rid themselves completely of the reactionary elements in the population, were relatively free to pursue their own best interests. It was, therefore, not only the scheming and plotting of the exiles that brought Florence into conflict with its neighbors, but also the acquisitiveness and ambition of its citizens. Florence, in fact, became the chief local threat to those still tied to the party of the emperor, as nothing less than undisputed ascendancy in all of Tuscany began to form as the political objective of the Florentine government. Among others, the once friendly Pisa stood in the way, not only because it was traditionally Ghibelline and supported the imperial cause, but also because it controlled the mouth of the Arno and the coastal ports. A number of conflicts had already broken out between the two cities, but after 1314 an almost continual state of warfare ensued, the immediate object of which was the control of the greatest possible area from Florence to the sea, including the two smaller towns of Pistoia and Lucca in between. Battles were won and lost on both sides, and the war dragged on inconclusively until 1328, when Florence managed to establish final control over Pistoia and to enlarge, somewhat, its territorial jurisdiction to the west.

During this period, for the first time, there is evidence that neither side relied for its fighting force entirely on its own citizen manpower but resorted instead to hired foreign soldiery. In Florence, this expedient became almost a necessity, as the ranks of the *grandi*, who heretofore had provided the military leadership, had been generally alienated and reduced in number by banishment. At the same time, though the old cavalry units were still maintained, many prosperous individuals had neither the desire nor the ability to fight. Instead, their military obligation could now be satisfied by supplying a mounted substitute or simply by making a money payment, an alternative the Florentine merchants were, of course, well able to afford. Coincidentally, the mass of foot soldiers drawn from shop and farm, who had previously been adequate for short campaigns in the immediate vicinity of the town, were found to be less effective for protracted and wide ranging warfare. For these reasons, professional mercenaries, usually disbanded soldiers from the north, first singly and then in bands, under their respective *condottieri* (leaders), gradually assumed the burden of military operations. The age of the feudal levy and of the citizen army was almost over.

The recapture of Pistoia in 1328 marks what historians believe to be the beginning of one of the most prosperous decades ever enjoyed by the Florentines. Proof of their energies and productive capacity is found, for example, in the rapid recovery they made following one of the worst and most destructive floods of the Arno in the city's history—that of 1333—which carried away large sections of the surrounding wall and substantial parts of all four bridges. Contemporary accounts state that the cost to the city of making good the damage to the walls and bridges alone amounted to 150,000 gold florins, but the work was speedily carried on and completed within a few years time. The most venerable of the bridges, the Ponte Vecchio, badly damaged by the flood, was considerably redesigned, its piers enlarged, its arches reduced in number from nine to three, and their spans accordingly lengthened. The roadway itself was doubled in width to permit a greater flow of traffic and more space was provided for its traditional shops, which, previously of wood, were now reconstructed in stone. This is the bridge that still stands today, having survived war, flood, and time.

It has been estimated that by this time the population of the city had grown to at least 120,000 people, making it one of the largest cities in Europe, and probably the richest. There were some

100 churches, including those outside the walls, 30 hospitals supported primarily by the guilds, 100 operating pharmacies, 80 banks, and over 200 wool workshops, employing as many as 30,000 workers at peak periods. One account lists 80 judges, 600 notaries, and 60 physicians registered on the guild rolls. Public spirit ran high. Work was resumed on the cathedral, after several decades of inactivity, under the general supervision of the great Giotto, who, at the same time (1334), was commissioned to plan and commence the building of the adjacent campanile, forever after known as Giotto's tower. This he carried up to the first main cornice before he died in 1337, and though others took over the work to complete it later in the century, its final appearance, with a few modifications, follows generally Giotto's original conception. Though utilizing a number of conventional Gothic features, it nevertheless resembles no other campanile previously built. At first glance, it does not seem characteristically Florentine, with its rather colorful and elegant marble façade and its ornate, mullioned windows (both suggestive of Venice), but on further consideration, the essentials of the structure—its grace and pro-portion, its weightlessness and openness in spite of its great bulk—reflect the artistic ideals that were just then beginning to form in the Florentine environment.

Before he died, Giotto also found time to execute the designs for many of the hexagonal tiles that stud the lowest band of the tower, the most important of which are found on the west, south, and east sides. They were actually carved by Andrea Pisano, a sculptor of exceptional ability. As his name suggests, he was associated with the city of Pisa, where a school of sculpture had existed for some time, but his carvings, under Giotto's guidance, signify a departure from his native tradition. Compared with the restless, overcrowded reliefs of his Pisan teachers, Andrea pro-duced simple, clear sculptures, the counterpart of Giotto's work in fresco. The aforementioned tiles, displaying various biblical figures and symbolic human achievements, and forming a cycle of man's life on earth following the expulsion from Paradise through the various stages by which he overcomes and adjusts to his earthly environment, are early and good examples of man's new approach to art and life. These, together with the first set of bronze doors for the Baptistery, consisting of twenty

Hexagonal tiles from the Cathedral's Campanile executed by Andrea Pisano from designs by Giotto: the Creation of Woman, the Promulgation of the Law, the Penalty of Work, the Art of Weaving.

Andrea Pisano's bronze doors (completed 1336) for the Baptistery, the first monumental work in that medium commissioned in Florence.

One of the quatrefoil panels of Pisano's doors—the Interrogation
of the Baptist in prison.

panels illustrating the story of San Giovanni, also completed about this time (1336) by Andrea (and now hanging at the south entrance), differ substantially from Arnolfo's solemn, hieratic, statuesque approach. Andrea's work instead, deriving from the lyrical nature of the Gothic style—fluid, dramatic, refined—set Florentine sculpture on a different path.

Another structure also brought to completion during the 1330s was the belltower of the Badia (Abbey) of the Benedictines, one of the oldest foundations in Florence, dating from the 10th century. The church and the adjoining buildings have been rebuilt periodically over the centuries and belong to no particular era, but the campanile's slender silhouette, part Romanesque and part Gothic, has long been one of the key features of the city's skyline.

During this period of unparalleled prosperity, we begin to hear more and more of another guild destined ultimately to surpass in importance most of the others. This was the Arte della Seta (Silk Mercer's Guild) or, as it was more commonly known, the Arte di Por Santa Maria because its coat-of-arms contained a representation of St. Mary's gate near which its headquarters were located. The trecento palace that housed them can still be seen on the Via Capaccio with the guild's crest set in the wall above the front entrance. Many of the techniques connected with the weaving of silk fabrics—velvets, satins, brocades, damasks, taffetas—as well as the dyeing methods, were learned originally from the east, but were subsequently exploited to the full by the Florentines. As with the other guilds, subsidiary crafts attached themselves to the Seta, a prominent one being that of the gold- and silversmiths who, though they pursued an independent artistic development in other fields, also fashioned the metallic threads that enhanced the beauty of so many Florentine silks.

To the care of this enterprising guild was entrusted, about this time, the erection of one of the most interesting buildings in the city, known as Or San Michele (written by the Florentines Orsanmichele), Originally used for commercial purposes and later also as a church and as a frame for art, thus combining the three most vital elements in the life of Renaissance Florence, it stands solidly in the center of town, a square pile of weathered stone, warmly colorful in the sunlight. The recorded history of the site goes back to Lombard times, when there stood on the spot a small church dedicated to the archangel and surrounded by a vegetable garden (*orto* in Italian, contracted to *or'*). The original church was destroyed sometime in the 13th century and the space thereafter was reserved for use as a grain market. Apparently, an open loggia of brick and wood was built there to shelter the traders, and attached to one of its supporting pilasters was a painting of the Madonna, which came to be highly venerated for its miracle-working wonders. The loggia seems to have burned down early in the 14th century in the course of one of the many fires that periodically devastated parts of the medieval town, though the picture itself was saved. It was accordingly resolved in 1337 to rebuild the loggia in a more substantial manner and to provide two great spacious floors above for the storage of grain, made more imperative by the increase in population and the recurrent need for reserves in times of shortage or siege. And so the present building was speedily erected. The arches opening onto the ground floor were not filled in as we see today but were left open for the easy movement of the traders and

The south east corner of Orsanmichele, unique combination of church, market center, and focal point of art.

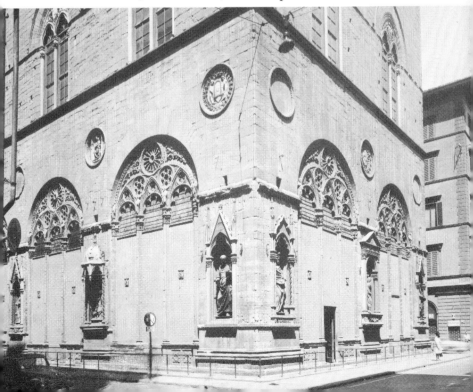

their wares. Several features still remain to indicate the structure's original purpose. For example, high up in the vaulting may be seen an aperture leading to the floor above, through which sacks of grain were raised for storage. Just below, a replica of the grain measures used at that time is carved in stone, while nearby, in one of the pilasters, is a chute outlet from which distribution was made to the populace.

As it happened, the need for such a building to safeguard emergency stores was not long in manifesting itself, for within a few years there followed, one upon another, a series of disasters, natural and man-made, that not only almost ruined the town financially, but drastically reduced its population and slowed its development for decades thereafter. The extent to which these events were connected is not known, but to the Florentine citizen of that day they seemed like a continuous series of interdependent misfortunes decreed by divine providence in its displeasure with the world and, in particular, with the new-found wealth of such cities as the prosperous commune on the Arno.

No doubt the inability of the merchants to invest the new accumulation of capital wisely and the temptation to employ it in risky adventures was partly responsible for the first disaster—the financial debacle of the 1340s. So also was the municipal government, whose enlarged scope of civic improvement, combined with the demands of an aggressive foreign policy involving war with Pisa, created an escalating drain on public funds.

At first, sufficient city revenue had been obtained by simply increasing the traditional *gabelle* (tolls), such as those on roads, river rafts, and certain commodities (salt, wine, grain, and meat) entering the gates. When these proved inadequate, new taxes were imposed on such routine activities as the slaughtering of cattle in the market and the grinding of grain into flour. Later, each house, even those in the *contado*, was assessed and taxed and those having special luxuries or additions, such as a loggia or corbeled projections over the streets, at a higher rate. Still later, the priors were forced to resort to a form of general property tax wherein each citizen made an accounting of his wealth (*estimo*) and paid proportionately. This was, of course, not popular with the merchants and was ultimately abandoned in favor of large-scale borowing at interest from the bankers. These loans, secured by the various sources of public revenue, were soon employed to excess in order to meet the ever-increasing demands of the treasury, until before long, the municipal debt, aptly dubbed by the populace *il monte* (the mountain), far exceeded the means of repayment.

In addition, not content with extravagance on a large scale at home, the leading Florentine banking houses, particularly the Frescobaldi, Acciaiuoli, Peruzzi, and Bardi, had been busy for many years making larger and ever larger loans to numerous foreign powers in need of ready cash—the pope, the Flemish, the kings of England, France, and Naples. In England, the Bardi and Peruzzi enjoyed a practical monopoly in the British wool trade, in return for which new advances were continually being demanded to fill the seemingly bottomless royal coffers of Edward III and his immediate predecessors. In fact, Edward's financial needs were so pressing in his attempt to conquer France that, to obtain the necessary funds, he gave the Florentines—foreigners!—the privilege of handling large parts of the English customs and even of superintending the royal revenues.

All this came to a dramatic climax in 1339, when, owing to military failure and financial ruin, Edward was forced to repudiate his debts. It has been calculated that, with this default, the Bardi and Peruzzi alone lost more than one million gold florins. This was followed by a similar repudiation from the king of Naples and others. When the news reached the Florentines, they were thrown into a panic, and a run on the banks was precipitated, prompting the priorate to declare a moratorium. Shops shut down, business came to a virtual standstill, tax revenues suddenly dried up. The bankers called for repayment of their loans, but the city treasury could not begin to meet its obligations. Without work, the mass of the people seethed with discontent, and catastrophe impended. To meet the situation, the merchants, in agreement with the remnants of the *grandi*, turned in alarm away from a democratic solution to an authoritative one, inviting one of their *condottiere*, whom they thought they could control, to take over the government (1342). The man they selected, Count Walter of Brienne, a Frenchman connected with the House of Anjou and known by one of his titles as the duke of Athens, was fairly successful for a time, continuing the bank moratorium and bringing the war to a temporary cessation. But gradually, as he gained the support of the common people, he alienated the merchants. With each month in power, the duke seemed to rule more despotically. Finally, when he was forced to suspend all payments on the city's debts and reactive the *estimo* tax, the breach was complete. Almost at once, he became a symbol of tyranny to the commercial class, and for one of the few times in its history, Florence felt the iron fist of the despot. Plots and counterplots were soon astir, and, before a year had passed, a combination formed that was strong enough to force his abdication and expulsion from the city. Partly responsible for this turn of events, the lesser guilds were now given genuine representation on the priorate, sharing power with the *arti maggiore*. New measures were again taken to exclude the *grandi*, who, as usual, .were considered sympathetic with tyranny. But the new government was equally incapable of dealing with the financial crisis, and a terrible collapse ensued. One by one, the great trading companies and banks went into bankruptcy, dragging the smaller ones after them.* The woolen mills closed down, and widespread unemployment followed.

In the meantime, similar difficulties were taking place throughout Europe, as a general economic depression developed and trade slowed to a trickle. A shortage of food, never in adequate supply, quickly occurred, particularly in the towns that had not the means to grow or import it. Serious as all this seemed, it was as nothing compared to the arrival of the next catastrophe, which followed on the heels of the first. An epidemic of bubonic plague from the Orient, known as the Black Death, swept over the land. Reaching its climax about 1348, it proved to be the worst of its kind ever let loose in Europe and completely rent the fabric of urban society. In some cities, the population was almost exterminated. Florence is believed to have lost over half of its people in the space of a few years' time. Contemporary accounts of this episode make tragic reading. No one knew how the disease was transmitted or where

---

* The word *bankruptcy* comes from the Italian *banca rotta*, meaning broken bench, as it was the custom from early times for merchants who had to go out of business to break up the benches over which they dealt.

it would strike next. There were no means by which to avoid it or to treat it. Whole families were wiped out, and sometimes there were not enough living to bury the dead.

Those few who had lands in the *contado* sought to escape the worst of the epidemic by fleeing into the countryside. We have been left an account of such, although imaginary, in the stories of the *Decameron*, by Giovanni Boccaccio (1313–75), which concern a few lucky survivors of the pestilence who retreated to the safety of a villa a short distance from Florence. Rebelling against the accepted medieval ideals of chivalry and the church, Boccaccio, who became one of Florence's most gifted writers, irreverently and sarcastically wrote down his tales in a cynical though lucid prose, reflective of the new bourgeois mentality. For the vast majority of the citizens, however, there was no alternative but to remain in their homes and pray for deliverance. Of those who stayed behind and managed to live through the ordeal, a small group took it upon themselves to assist the all but helpless city government with emergency tasks, including the transporting in litters of the sick to hospitals and of the dead to burial. These volunteers carried on under the most terrible conditions, daily risking their lives by contagion. Later, bound together by their common sacrifices and sense of duty to their city, the group formed itself into an institution known as the Confraternità della Misericordia (Lay Brotherhood of Mercy), one of the earliest beneficent societies of its kind in the world and one which has had a continuous existence to this day. Robed anonymously in black from head to toe, the members may still be seen in Florence aiding the sick and the aged, their only reward being found in the phrase of their ritual, "God give you merit for it."

In 1352, after the ravages of the plague had spent themselves and the town again began to reorder its life, the Fraternity of the Misericordia helped sponsor the building of a small head-quarters across from the Baptistery. Known as the Loggia del Bigallo, this little example of Florentine Gothic architecture, with its interesting protruding eaves and its elegant windows and arches, has been used for centuries for charitable purposes, including the sheltering of abandoned children. Now seldom visited, it still stands in silent dignified tribute to its worthy sponsors.

During this same period of recovery following the plague, the miraculous painting of the *Madonna of the Pilaster*, which had been left standing within the new building of Orsanmichele, began to attract so many worshippers that the place, more and more, took on the aspect of a shrine, hampering the conduct of business. The need therefore developed to separate the activities of the tradesmen from the devotions of the supplicants, so it was decided by the guild leaders, in grateful appreciation for the city's deliverance, first from the tyrannical yoke of the duke of Athens and later from the scourge of the pestilence, to dedicate the ground floor of the building as a church in honor of the Virgin and her mother, St. Anne. The miraculous painting of the pilaster was therefore ordered to be enclosed in a new tabernacle by the versatile artist Orcagna (1308–68), who created here one of the most elaborate, marvelous works of the age. An infinite profusion of statues and pinnacles, reliefs and mosaics, precious stones and rich marbles, it was patiently assembled over a number of years, piece by piece, without the use of cement, like some great interlocking puzzle. While the tabernacle's purpose was to serve as a frame for a painting of the Madonna by a follower of Giotto, similar in spirit to the older one of the pilaster enclosed inside, its main significance is as an outstanding example of the fusion of artistic styles and of the various crafts themselves. Here, in one momentous ensemble, are combined the older mosaic traditions from Byzantium and the mystery and decorativeness of Gothic architectural motifs with the humanized narrative statement and carving skills pioneered by Giotto and Andrea Pisano. Florentine art has here taken on a new dimension.

Rather complicated and somewhat crowded under the vaulting, Orcagna's masterpiece is not easy to appreciate in the dim lighting. But for those who take the trouble to study its parts, particularly the large relief on the back representing the death and assumption of the Virgin, where the artist has left his likeness, his signature, and the date of completion (1359), the magnitude of the achievement emerges.

At the same time, the grain traders were cleared from the building and the openings under the arches were closed up with light walls of Gothic tracery to dignify and protect the interior. Outside, twelve tabernacles or niches were set into the masonry

Orcagna's celebrated tabernacle to the Madonna in Orsanmichele, completed 1359.

and one each was assigned to the more important guilds, with the understanding that each would supply a statue and would proceed and worship there on its particular saint's day. None of the original sculptures remain, however, and those we see today are works of the next century.

Adjoining Orsanmichele by a curved, overhead passageway to the west is another building from the same era, the Palazzo dell'Arte della Lana—the headquarters of the wool guild— partly restored at the end of the 19th century. At one corner of the building may be seen a Gothic tabernacle of carved stone, the Oratorio di Santa Maria della Tromba (St. Mary of the Bugle), also dating from the 1300s, enclosing a painting of the Madonna by a contemporary of Giotto's. This small, canopied structure, supported on delicate, twisted columns, once stood at the southeast corner of the Mercato Vecchio and was reassembled here when the old center was destroyed in the 19th century. According to tradition, prisoners condemned to death were brought to this

(*left*) The tabernacle of the Madonna della Tromba, one of the many street shrines in Florence. (*right*) The courtyard of the Palazzo Davanzati.

shrine to say their last prayers on their way to the executioner. It is typical of the many street shrines in Florence—the custom of building such shrines was introduced by the Dominicans to remind and inspire the faithful. Most of these tabernacles are dedicated to the Madonna, who was regarded by the Florentines as their special advocate with the Redeemer.

The same year (1359) that Orcagna finished the tabernacle in Orsanmichele, construction started in the Piazza della Signoria on the Tribunale di Mercanzia (Mercantile Court), where disputes affecting commercial transactions were thereafter settled. High up on its front walls can be seen the heraldic coats-of-arms of the various guilds. Also, at the church of Santa Maria Novella, the year 1359 saw the completion of the Chiostro Verde (Green Cloister) and the adjoining chapter house, famous for the frescoes that soon adorned its walls. These paintings are an excellent example of the method used to summarize and expound the medieval role of the church in society as guardian of spiritual values and teacher of truth. Here, on the left side wall, amid religious themes and characters, the artist has set forth the triumph of divine (as opposed to worldly) wisdom, which, flowing in the form of light from the Holy Spirit (the celestial dove in the vaulting above), spreads out through the apostles, prophets, and saints, shown grouped around the enthroned likeness of St. Thomas Aquinas, the supreme spokesman for that divine wisdom (and for the Dominican order), to guide all worthwhile human activities, symbolized by fourteen female figures representing the arts and sciences.

On the opposite wall is the allegory of the church itself. Pictured are the two main pillars of society, spiritual and temporal —the pope and the emperor—the former on a throne slightly higher. Each, accompanied by his hierarchy, presides over flocks of the faithful shown as sheep, who in turn are protected from marauding wolves (heretics) by black and white dogs (the Dominicans), while the three principal saints of the order—Dominic, Peter Martyr, and Thomas—strive to instruct and shield the people from sin and heresy and lead them to the celestial kingdom. All this, in the lower half of the fresco, illustrates the church militant, while in the upper part, symbolizing the church triumphant, is seen the medieval concept of Paradise, the objective of

A detail from the fresco, completed 1359, in the Chiostro Verde illustrating the church militant and triumphant, showing the pope and emperor with their adherents ranged in front of Florence's projected cathedral.

all earthly strivings, with St. Peter and the heavenly host gathered together under Christ in glory.

Of interest in this latter fresco is the building depicted on the left—a conception of the yet-unfinished cathedral as it was finally expected to look. Arnolfo's scheme had apparently been enlarged by the addition of a fourth bay to the east and by increasing the height of the walls. But of more interest is the shape of the crossing which appears here for the first time as an octagon. The fresco, however, reveals no plan for a raised base or drum below the dome, as the projected cupola is shown springing directly from the roof level. It seems rather heavy and squat, an error that was later corrected in the construction of the actual dome.

The long series of business failures, famines, and other disasters that fell on Florence during the 1340s shook the prestige and undermined the power of the merchant and banker oligarchy, which for half a century had controlled the government. As a result, the major guilds were forced to admit to the priorate members of the lesser guilds of shopkeepers and artisans whose participation theretofore had been relatively minor. This was a step in the direction of a more democratic system, but it had no beneficial effect on the great mass of the *popolo minuto* (proletariat), consisting mostly of carders, spinners, dyers, weavers, and other textile workers known as the *ciompi*. They did not qualify for membership in the lesser guilds and were not permitted, under penalty of death, to form any guilds or other labor associations of their own. They were, of course, excluded from any share in the government. For this reason, with the revival of some of the bankrupted business houses and the formation of new ones, and with the renewed growth of the wool business in the 1350s, the *popolo minuto*, living on subsistance wages, were as helpless as ever to enlarge their share of the attendant prosperity or to improve their generally miserable lot.*

That prosperity returned is well illustrated by the financial success of Niccolò Acciaiuoli, important Florentine merchant-banker, who achieved a position of power in the Angevin kingdom of Naples second only to the ruler himself and obtained for his house and for other Florentines a virtual monopoly on the banking and commercial business of that southern country. He became, in fact, one of the wealthiest men in Europe and, before his death in 1365, so as to perpetuate his name and fame within his native city, commenced and largely completed with his own funds the entire complex of the Certosa of Galluzzo, the Carthusian monastery and church just south of Florence on the Via Senese. Though altered in some respects over the years, the vast structure, resembling a walled town more than a religious establishment, still retains most of its original character, the scale of which testifies to the financial resources required. In the subterranean chapels, perfectly preserved are the tombs of Niccolò

* Among the new and revived business houses were the Albizzi, Corsini, Pazzi, Strozzi, Soderini, Rucellai, Peruzzi, Bardi, Acciaiuoli, Ricci, Alberti, Medici, Capponi, and Salviati.

The Certosa of Galluzo built in the mid-trecento by the Acciaiuoli
family on the city's southern outskirts.

and others of his family, carved by followers of the great
Orcagna.

A number of town houses typical of the era, also built by the
Acciaiuoli, can still be seen in the Borgo Santi Apostoli. Number
8, though modified in later centuries, is a good example of the
way older towers (at the right-hand corner) were grafted onto
other structures to form a palazzo, still austerely medieval in
appearance and function; number 9, across the street, has frontal
stone work that reveals periodic restoration.

Another immense family fortune built up after the plague was
that of Niccolo' degli Alberti, who, when he died in 1377, was
said to have left 340,000 gold florins, an enormous sum.

But though Florence had again become one of the wealthiest
cities in Europe, tensions had developed as usual within the
guild leadership, which had been sharing the responsibility of

government since midcentury. Among the greater guildsmen two factions developed. On the one side were the older families of established merchants and bankers, sometimes allied by marriage or interest with the remnants of the *grandi*. Many had retired from active business and invested their wealth in safer directions, mainly land and the public debt. Conservative and closely allied to the papacy and to traditional Guelphism, they were contemptuous and jealous of their opponents, ambitious products of a generation or two of success in the wool, silk, or banking business, whom they called the *gente nuova* (new men). The guild records of 1349–56 indicate several hundred new family names enrolled with the Lana, Calimala, Cambio, and Seta. At the same time, these two groups were in turn alienated on many questions, especially taxes, from the lesser guildsmen, who lived in continual apprehension of losing their position in the government. For some three decades, however, a delicate constitutional balance was maintained, though no clear underlying agreement had ever emerged defining the exact distribution of powers within the state. Executive authority continued to lie with the Signoria, but legislative authority increasingly was shared with several other larger bodies or councils.

To further complicate the situation, there existed a quasi-independent political body—the Parte Guelfa—which infringed upon the sovereignty of the commune. The Parte was an institutional outgrowth of the 13th century during the time when the Florentine leadership had firmly established itself with the church against the empire and had banished their opponents of Ghibelline persuasion. It long remained the repository of Guelphism and symbol of Florentine independence. It was also the recipient of the confiscated Ghibelline properties and hence very wealthy. Gradually the Parte Guelfa grew into an extremely conservative body, dominated by the older families, especially those opposed to sharing the government with the *gente nuova* and the lesser guildsmen. At the same time, always virtually autonomous, it was often able to dictate policy by eliminating its opponents one by one from the lists of those eligible for office. This was accomplished through its exclusive privilege of labeling them, with or without evidence, as Ghibelline, even though Ghibellinism as such had long ceased to be a serious threat. So branded, neither the victim nor members of his family could hold any political position. In addition, those accused lost certain legal protections, were liable to discriminatory taxation, and were socially ostracized. As a consequence, the Parte was increasingly feared and detested by a majority of the citizens, but not until 1378, when a serious difference of opinion arose over Florence's relationship with the papacy, did the situation become untenable. The Parte Guelfa precipitated the crisis by attempting arbitrarily and sweepingly to remove from the councils a large number of the *gente nuova* by declaring them Ghibellines. The latter, realizing a showdown was imminent, organized a revolt and called upon the populace for support. However, as soon as the *popolo minuto* were aware that the government was divided and helpless, matters got out of hand, and a city-wide rebellion, known as the Rising of the Ciompi, materialized overnight. Houses of the key members of the Parte were burned and the mob forced its way into the Palazzo Vecchio, where it demanded the right to organize and to participate in the government. The guildsmen, unprepared for this display of force, had no choice, and the workers were forthwith permitted to form three guilds of their own and to share in the communal offices.

But this experiment in democracy, which lasted several years, proved to be a period of continuous agitation and crisis. *Parlamento* after *parlamento* was summoned in the Piazza della Signoria.* Plots, counterplots, uprisings, and executions followed one after the other until the resulting chaos prepared the ground for the only well organized and economically strong group— the major guilds and especially the *gente nuova*—to re-exert their power and again acquire the dominant role. Once in command of the situation (1382), they promptly disbanded the *ciompi* guilds, reduced the participation of the lesser guilds, and re-established the oligarchy that seems to have been the most workable form of government for Florence.

* The custom of the *parlamento* (parliament)—an assemblage of the adult male citizens—dates back to the 12th century during the time of the consuls. In theory, it was the ultimate source of political power within the city, but in practice it was seldom called together except in emergency situations or when the ruling faction reached an impasse. In later years, it became a means for the controlling group to rally mass support on emotional issues or to lend a constitutional authenticity for reform of the government.

The Parte Guelfa, however, though it continued to exist as an organization, was henceforth subjected to the will of the communal government and was never again permitted to exercise political power. The palace of the Parte, which was structurally completed just before the revolt of the *ciompi*, may be seen today in the Piazza di Parte Guelfa. The side and back of the building were remodelled in the quattrocento in Renaissance style, but the part facing the piazza has been restored to its original trecento Gothic façade and battlements.

During this period of the so-called Second Democracy (1378–1382), when the many parliaments were called in the Piazza della Signoria and attention was repeatedly focused on the priorate of the moment, the need became evident for a more impressive civic rostrum, raised above the piazza and suitably protected, from which important officials could preside and speak and where official receptions could be held. For this purpose, some old buildings were cleared from the area just to the west of the Palazzo Vecchio and an imposing new covered structure was erected. Designed by the artists then working on the Duomo, the Loggia della Signoria, completed in 1382, combines Gothic elements (the piers and the vaults) with something reminiscent of ancient Roman buildings (the three wide, open, round arches), foretelling to a small degree the coming of Renaissance architecture. The stone used was cut smooth and the capitals of the piers were intricately carved in contrast to the rugged, fortress like façade of the old palace adjacent, implying a transition from a cruder to a more civilized era. Much later, the rostrum came to be known, as it is today, as the Loggia dei Lanzi, after the grand duke's *lanzi* (lancers), bodyguards who were stationed under its protective vaulting. It is only in modern times that the building has been used as a shelter for the display of sculpture.

Also dating from the late trecento, there survives nearby an excellent example, recently well restored, of a private habitation of the period, which may be considered as representative of the next major step in the evolution of the Florentine town house. This is the Palazzo Davanzati on the Via Porta Rossa. Though its functional use remained unchanged—the wealthy merchant who built it still had his business there, requiring storage, workshop, and office space, as well as residential quarters above—

The Loggia dei Lanzi, completed 1382, in the Piazza della Signoria, originally a rostrum for political business, now shelters an array of sculpture, including Cellini's *Perseus* and Giambologna's *Rape of the Sabines*.

The Palazzo Davanzati (late 1300s) illustrates the transition of the Florentine town house from crude fortress to more civilized architecture.

for the first time a Florentine building now assumes a slightly more peaceful and civilized aspect. The need for defense still existed, of course, as the massive walls and barred doors testify, but no longer dominates every feature. The old nobility had been expelled, the guilds were more or less in effective control, and prosperity had returned. Conditions thus allowed for a better designed, more open structure, in contrast to the ponderous, forbidding traditional buildings. Most obvious, the battlements at the top have disappeared, replaced by an open loggia with slender columns, and the windows and rooms are now arranged after a definite architectural plan. In the stonework of the façade, irons of various kinds are imbedded: rings to tether horses, sconces for torches, and higher up, brackets and hooks to hold the wooden poles on which draperies and tapestries were displayed during festive occasions.

The courtyard inside is still narrow and confining, but there are columns with carved capitals and architecturally more sophisticated stone stairways leading up to the floors above. Opening off the courtyard on the ground floor were the stables and storerooms, while the large room across the front, with its customary large doorways and vaulted ceiling, was the owner's place of business. Immediately above is the great hall, which also spans the width of the building and is of a new, generous proportion. In fact, all the rooms have become more spacious. Many open out onto the courtyard. Their interior walls are decorated with intricate, colorful frescoes and their wooden ceilings are beautifully carved and painted. Here on the *piano nobile* (first floor above the street), the owner and his wife had their bedrooms, wardrobe, and chapel away from the noise and dirt below but still easily accessible. On the floors above lived the rest of the family, servants, and retainers, while high at the top, cooled by the gentle breezes, stands the open loggia with its wide protecting eaves, a place of refuge in hot weather.

Today the house has been opened as a museum and furnished in the style of the trecento and quattrocento. The simplicity of Dante's time was beginning to give way to more comfort and refinement. Windows are larger, and fireplaces, seldom found in older palaces, appear in many of the rooms, some with carved mantelpieces. Tapestries and framed pictures hang from the walls,

The great hall of the Palazzo Davanzati partially restored to its original condition.

and furniture has a less crude look. The owner's large double bed, for instance, is set on a raised platform and covered by a generous canopy. There were few chairs, but a number of large chests, tables, and other amenities attest to a certain improvement in domestic life.

The Flowering of the Florentine Renaissance: 1400 to 1500

Throughout the latter part of the trecento, four or five important Italian cities increasingly came to dominate their immediate neighbors. In the north, Milan and Venice pushed out their boundaries, absorbing many of the smaller cities within the Lombard plain. Farther south, the pope in Rome continued the attempt to bring the State of the Church under his effective authority, while the kingdom of Naples consolidated its domination of southern Italy. At the same time, in the heart of the peninsula, Florence, aspiring to comparable status, strained to extend its power throughout Tuscany. Conflict was inevitable, of course, not only with the smaller cities taken over but also between the

greater states themselves. Thus began, toward the end of the century, a long series of wars and counter wars, alliances and counter
alliances, victories and defeats, the details of which are hopelessly
complicated. It is enough to say that near at home, Pisa, and
farther afield, Milan, ruled by the aggressive Visconti, were
Florence's chief and formidable antagonists. But by a fortunate
combination of money, determination, and luck, Florence—
assisted by the military sagacity of a number of superior *condottieri*
—was able to hold off Milanese expansion at the Apennines,
consolidate its territories at home, and finally, once and for all,
defeat and occupy Pisa (1406).* This latter achievement culminated the long Florentine attempt to control the mouth
of the Arno and the immediate coastline. It also permitted Florence to acquire title to the Pisan fleet and the many Pisan commercial enclaves scattered along the Mediterranean coast. More
conquests followed, Cortona being captured in 1411 and Leghorn
in 1421.

During this period of confused and unending warfare, Florence,
unlike most of its rival cities, did not succumb to the rule of a
single tyrant but continued to function, even in long periods of
crisis, under its traditional institutions. These, of course, did not
permit active participation by the lower classes, and it would be
naive to suppose that there was no great inequality of status. On
the contrary, the leaders of the major guilds continued to dominate the government, and, over the decades, certain names appeared
repeatedly on the roles of the priorate and the advisory councils.
Moreover, power was often consolidated behind the scenes in
the hands of a few key individuals who were able to influence the
elections. In the early 1400s, for example, several men exercised
a disproportionate influence: Maso degli Albizzi (died 1417),
Gino Capponi (died 1421), and especially Niccolò da Uzzano
(died 1433).† They, together with their sons and immediate

* One of the most famous *condottieri*, an Englishman named John Hawkwood,
was employed by Florence from 1382 to the year of his death (1394). More
loyal and successful than most, Hawkwood was honoured with Florentine
citizenship, a life pension, exemption from taxes, and a commemorative
fresco on the wall of the cathedral showing him armed and mounted on a
charger.

† Niccolo da Uzzano's portrait bust in painted terracotta, one of Donatello's
most realistic works, is in the Bargello.

adherents, effectively secured a large degree of control long before the Medici family, who have repeatedly been accused of upsetting the city's traditional constitution, assumed the leading role. The Medici were not, however, unimportant or obscure during those years, the name of Giovanni di Bicci de'Medici (died 1429) several times appearing as a member of the priorate, but he and his father before him had concentrated primarily on building up their banking business, at which they were exceedingly successful, and they never played paramount political roles.

However, guild membership and hence government office were open to a wide segment of the population, so that opportunities existed for men of relatively humble birth to rise to the highest positions. This was a far cry from an hereditary nobility or the arbitrary rule of one man. Other Italian cities had enjoyed varying degrees of freedom and self-government but almost without exception had lost them. Perhaps they lacked the tenacious grip on their traditional constitutions that characterized Florence, and the respect and admiration for Republican Rome to which the Florentines considered themselves heir.

Throughout the last decades of the trecento, Florentine humanists had been busy carrying on the work of Petrarch, diligently searching the monasteries of Europe to find the lost works of Latin authors, many of which had lain forgotten and moldering since the Dark Ages. Hundreds of ancient manuscripts were thus discovered on almost as many subjects: poetry, drama, agriculture, astronomy, cooking, architecture, education, medicine, and especially Roman history and politics. In the course of studying and translating these texts, scholars revived the political and philosophical ideals of the Roman period and many of the educated class were introduced to the pleasures of classical research and the collecting of books and antiquities.

The importance attached to these matters is apparent in the choice of the city's chancellors, the officials responsible for the day-to-day running of the government and for diplomatic contacts abroad, all of whom from this time on were humanists and scholars of the highest caliber. Two were especially brilliant and influential: Coluccio Salutati (1331–1406) and Leonardo Bruni (1369–1444), who between them held their posts for a total of more than sixty years during the long series of wars with Milan and the repeated threat to the continued independence of their city. In addition to possessing a practical talent for administering city business and dealing with foreign ambassadors, both men were serious scholars and highly eloquent in their speeches and writings. Salutati discovered long-lost works by Cicero, the contents of which revealed much of the reality of the ancient world, so consistently misrepresented by church scholars. Bruni, the son of an obscure grain dealer, studied and wrote history, poetry, and political tracts and conducted an immense, vital correspondence with the leaders of other states. Both made ingenious use of their researches into the classical texts as propaganda weapons to attract allies and support in the long wars against the Visconti of Milan. Salutati especially likened Florence to the Roman Republic—defender of freedom, resister of tyrants—drawing his arguments from Cicero, Virgil, Ovid, and other early Roman writers. The moral persuasion they extended in the name of liberty and freedom from tyranny and for the ideals of the classical age did much to stem the tide of aggression and make Florence not only the apparent guardian of republican institutions but also the hub of humanistic studies.

At the same time, the closer the Florentines studied the Latin writers the more they realized how much the Romans owed the Greeks. Neither Petrarch nor any other Florentine of the mid trecento could read or write Greek, but so rapidly did interest develop that by 1397 Salutati was able to persuade the Signoria to establish a chair of Greek studies in the university. Moreover, once the extant body of Greek literature—histories, plays, poetry, philosophy, oratory—had been rediscovered, the Florentines realized what a gulf divided their own achievements from those of the classical world.

One of the most important concepts learned from the Greek authors was the idea of will or will power, the ability of man to realize his own capabilities—the innate power to achieve—with or without God's help, called by the Italians *virtù*. It was this concept of man refusing to resign himself to a destiny not of his choosing that later created a conflict with traditional Christianity and the resulting attempt to reconcile the two positions. Many conventional values and institutions were therefore laid open to question. Could medieval political systems, for example, stand comparison with those of the Greek city-states or the Roman Republic? Would the Tuscan vernacular, soon to become accepted as the Italian language, be improved by the study of classical languages? Should religious taboos stand in the way of the study of anatomy? Salutati was one of the first to argue boldly and publicly against the church's prohibition of reading pagan literature. For one thing, he felt that only there could his contemporaries read anything worthwhile on the subject of statecraft. Further, he asserted, the style of the Roman writers was more fluid and correct than the medieval Latin used by clerics. Bruni, among other scholars, fell more under the spell of Greek literature. He found time to translate Plato, Demosthenes, and Aristotle.

It was in this context that the traditional practices associated with architecture and sculpture were also called into question. Could the older methods and objectives be improved upon? Should buildings, for instance, be improvised and added to piecemeal or planned as a whole from the start? Should churches and chapels perhaps be constructed on a more human, rational scheme? Should columns and round arches replace piers and pointed arches? Should sculpture follow the classical models that were then being unearthed?

The answers to these questions were not forthcoming during the last decades of the trecento although they were no doubt in incubation, for a number of artists were born and matured during those years whose studies of the remnants of classical civilization would soon radically change the course of Western art: Filippo Brunelleschi (1377–1446), Lorenzo Ghiberti (1378–1455), Donatello (1386–1466), and Masaccio (1401–28). These men, all Florentines, were truly great innovators and the precursors of the flood of art work that was to follow in the next several centuries. The first two, who started out as goldsmiths and sculptors, were almost exact contemporaries but temperamentally and artistically quite different. Ghiberti's work serves more as a link between the Gothic age and the rebirth of classical ideals, while Brunelleschi, abandoning sculpture for architecture, more decisively left the immediate past behind, and taking the elements of the Roman heritage, translated them into the new Renaissance idiom. Donatello, slightly younger and a student and associate of both, became the major spirit in the development of Florentine sculpture, introducing in his work a new understanding of realism and the classical ideals of form and subject matter. The last, Masaccio, was to achieve in painting what Brunelleschi and Donatello had pioneered in the other two branches of the fine arts.

The earliest event to command attention, and one that literally ushered in the Florentine quattrocento, was the decision in 1400 of the Signoria, in concert with the Calimala guild, to order a competition for the second set of bronze doors for the Baptistery. Many artists were considered, but the field was narrowed to six, who were requested to design, cast, and submit within one year a single bronze panel representing in relief the Sacrifice of Isaac. The subject matter was prescribed in some detail—a medieval quatrefoil frame, the number of figures, the exact size, etc. Of the six trial pieces presented, those of Ghiberti and Brunelleschi were considered superior, with the final judgement going to Ghiberti's. By good fortune, both may be seen today on display in the Bargello. Both artists, under the influence of the humanists and believing, as did all Florentines, that the Baptistery was of Roman origin, attempted a classical interpretation, especially in the modeling of the figures, but in fact the panels, still predominately Gothic, represent a transitional stage.

Each, however, worked out a different over-all solution. The consensus has always been that the judges made the correct decision, Ghiberti's plaque being more rhythmically sophisticated, more finished in realistic detail, and of a better compositional unity. His figures also seem to come alive and escape the posed feeling of earlier work, and appear to be arranged pictorially in spatial depth, an accomplishment heretofore achieved only by the late Gothic painters. Some critics, however, consider Brunelleschi's more agitated and dramatic arangement, though less coordinated and less pictorial, perhaps sculpturally more monumental and forceful. In any case, the decision discouraged Brunelleschi, who thereupon gave up sculpture, and put the seal of approval on Ghiberti's approach. The doors were not actually finished and installed until 1424, but, in the interim, Ghiberti's workshop became the principal training ground for many younger talents: Donatello, Nanni di Banco, Michelozzo, Uccello, Gozzoli, Antonio Pollaiuolo. It has therefore been argued, for good or bad, that the outcome of the competition for the doors

Ghiberti's (*left*) and Brunelleschi's trial bronze reliefs in the competition (1401) for the Baptistery's second set of doors.

decisively influenced the artists who followed and set Florentine sculpture on the road to an ever more perfect representation of man and nature, real or ideal.

But whatever sculpture may have lost by Brunelleschi's departure, architecture more than gained. He left Florence and went to Rome for several years where he dedicated himself to studying, sketching, and measuring the ruins of antiquity, not only to grasp the essence of the classical style, but also to deduce the building techniques that had been used. He diligently combed the Roman Forums, sometimes having the accumulated debris of centuries dug away to expose the lower parts of structures. Here was the first conscious effort in the field of architecture, inspired by humanist sentiment, to challenge all of the building concepts and methods of the Middle Ages and to consider building again with elegant columns and pilasters, with finely carved capitals, with friezes, cornices, and pediments in the Greek and Roman manner.

Brunelleschi was accompanied at Rome for part of the time by his friend Donatello, who, though equally interested in the antique, concentrated his studies on sculpture rather than architecture. The two returned to Florence some time before 1407, and Donatello soon set to work on several commissions that were to make his reputation and to place sculpture once again on a plane comparable to that of the ancients. The forward step he made can be seen in the two statues he carved for exterior niches in the church of Orsanmichele: the *St. Mark*, relaxed and meditative (finished about 1411), and the *St. George*, tense, alert, yet quizzical (1415). In each of these can be marked Donatello's concern with the psychology and personality of the man portrayed. In addition, the figures suddenly take on a lifelike existence under their clothing and seem capable of movement. Each has a feeling of self-sustaining balance and independence from the architectural settings which embrace them. For the first time since antiquity, sculpture assumes an end in itself and ceases to be, as in medieval work, merely an accessory to architecture.

Equally important, below the *St. George*, Donatello has carved a shallow marble panel showing the saint slaying the dragon

(*left*) Donatello's *St. Mark* (1411), at Orsanmichele, has been called the earliest unequivocal Renaissance sculpture. (*right*) His *St. George* (1415). The original at Orsanmichele has been replaced by a copy and transferred to the Bargello.

(*left*) Nanni di Banco's *Quattro Coronati* and (*right*) Ghiberti's *St. John the Baptist* (1414), both at Orsanmichele.

wherein the rules of linear perspective recently rediscovered and worked out by Brunelleschi are tentatively indicated in the columns and trees that form the background, an innovation in the illusion of spatial depth never before attempted by a sculptor.

Other sculptors, too, were working at Orsanmichele about the same time at the behest of the various guilds, each of which was made responsible for one of the niches. One of these sculptors was Nanni di Banco, who executed three of the statues there between 1410 and 1415: the *St. Eligius*, the *St. Philip*, and the *Quattro Coronati* (Four Saints). He, too, has managed to escape the confines of the Gothic approach and has mastered something of the Roman qualities of mass and form, but he never quite infuses his figures with an independent life of their own or achieves the realism found in ancient sculpture and rediscovered by Donatello.

Ghiberti is also represented here and, befitting his reputation, was commissioned by the three wealthiest guilds to supply statues of their patron saints: *St. John the Baptist* for the Calimala (1414), *St. Matthew* for the Cambio (1420), and *St. Stephen* for the Lana (1428). But as in his reliefs for the Baptistery, Ghiberti's figures, stylized and rhythmical, continue for the most part to restate in ever more polished form his link to the Gothic tradition, with the exception of *St. Matthew*, in which he appears to have followed the lead of Donatello and produced a figure whose posture, gestures, and expression stem more from the Roman concept. In general, it can be said that while both Ghiberti and Donatello were inspired by the idealized human figure of classical art, Ghiberti's work reflects also the serenity and idealism of his immediate artistic heritage, while Donatello's more original approach exploits the possibilities, previously overlooked, for drama and realism. And around one or the other of these two talents the younger artists grouped themselves.

Meanwhile, the single most important project facing the city, and by far the most forbidding, was that of finally attacking the problem of the dome of the Cathedral, the solution to which had been repeatedly put off and never seriously attempted. The facts of the situation were awesome. Here stood a gigantic opening almost 140 feet across in the difficult shape of an octagon and with a drum or base for the dome already raised up on too-thin walls 180 feet in the air. No precedent existed within memory or documentation. True, the ancients had built domes—but how? Even the Pisans and others had done so in recent times, but these domes were convenionally round, adequately buttressed, lower in height, and much smaller in diameter. In other words, they had been built by the usual methods of constructing wooden centering from the ground up, on which tight-fitting stones were placed in a series of horizontal rings or crowns and the centering removed. A stone dome is no more than a stone arch rotated on its axis and built up crown by crown until the final keystone at the exact center or the topmost ring locks the whole system.

But how could this be done in the Florentine Duomo? No trees could be found that would possibly reach the heights or span the distances required, and even if they existed they would have broken under their own weight before any stone was added. All kinds of preposterous and expensive schemes were proposed; one was to raise up from the floor tremendous stone columns to support the dome; another, that it be made of wood; and another that the area of the crossing be heaped up with a massive pile of earth to support a shorter scaffolding, the dirt to be mixed with coins to provide an incentive for the citizens to later dig it away.

The Opera del Duomo (Cathedral Works) was under the immediate supervision of the Arte dei Maestri di Pietra e Legname (Minor Guild of the Masters of Stone and Wood) and under the financial patronage of the Lana. The responsibility for proceeding had been placed on the officers of these guilds, who, fearing ridicule for failure, were desperate for a solution. For a number of years, Brunelleschi, Ghiberti, and other architects were consulted for a plan of approach, and discussions went on. Finally, in 1417, Brunelleschi submitted a definite proposal wherein he stated he would build a cupola of an eight-sided shape to harmonize with the sides, entirely of stone and brick and without the use of either framework or centering. It was this latter boast that created the greatest furor, and though he supplied drawings and descriptions he would not submit his models or tell how he proposed to do it. From the accounts of these proceedings, Brunelleschi emerges as one of the most interesting Florentines of all time. He apparently exuded self-confidence and had complete faith in his own ability. He was also extremely stubborn and wary, and no doubt for good reason. The Florence of his day had become highly competitive. Projects of all kinds were under discussion and the rivalry among the artists was fierce. What if he disclosed his method without having received the commission? On the other hand, why should the *maestri* accept his plan without knowing whether the technique was feasible? An impasse was reached. For several years, the arguments continued, and neither side would give in. Finally, however, lacking any better alternative, and not knowing where else to turn, the guild officers accepted Brunelleschi's plan on condition that he present a model and explain his approach in a general way.

Now Brunelleschi was the only builder who had taken the trouble to study in detail the domes of the Pantheon in Rome and of the Florentine Baptistery. Neither could give him any direct answers, but they provided certain clues. The Pantheon's dome was comparable in size, though not in height above the ground. Nor was it an eight-sided shape but circular, and had somehow been cast in one tremendous, monolithic pouring of concrete, the secret of which had been lost with time, so that its weight pressed down evenly on the supporting walls with no lateral thrusts whatsoever.

Brunelleschi had a different problem. He had to build his dome of stone and brick and had to support the weight of an exceedingly heavy central lantern. This fact alone required the most careful planning, for the total weight of the upper half of the dome and lantern together could never be allowed to exceed a certain relationship to the weight and binding power of the supporting material below. Otherwise the lower section of the dome would be forced open in a bursting effect and the whole structure would collapse. During Brunelleschi's time, the mathematical formulas for this did not exist, but he understood the principle. Moreover, the solution had been complicated by the raising of the walls of the octagon into what is called the drum of the cupola. This feature, with its *occhi* (or eyelike windows), greatly enhanced the beauty of the whole building, raising its silhouette higher and eliminating any squatness, but also deprived the masonry above it of the buttressing effect or lateral counterthrust that otherwise would have been provided by the structure of the nave, the transepts, and the radiating choir chapels with their half-domes. He had therefore strictly to control and minimize the lateral thrust outward that would be imposed by the great weight of his dome. At the same time, it must soar heavenward, must dominate the city and be visible for miles around. Consequently, he discarded the idea of a hemispherical dome in the shape of the Pantheon, the classical form of which he might have preferred, because in that shape the dome would have exerted too great a force outward on the supporting walls. In addition, it would have been esthetically out of keeping with the rest of the building's architecture. Instead, he proposed a dome of a more pointed shape to minimize the outward thrust caused by the weight above and against which any kind of buttresses would have been visually unacceptable and out of the question.

It was in overcoming these problems that Brunelleschi came up with his most original solutions. Instead of constructing his cupola in one solid mass of material, the customary procedure, he

The Cathedral's great dome and crowning lantern, both designed by Brunelleschi, with Giotto's tower (*left*), as seen from the east.

proposed building two concentric shells, an inner shell of about 7 feet in thickness, and an outer of about 3 feet with an air space of about 4 feet in between. This would create a thicker dome wall and a corresponding increase in its stability, since the two shells would be interconnected by a common ribbing and thus be structurally one, but without the additional weight of the material in between. Brunelleschi was the first to conceive of this concentric shell system, and after him all large domes (for example, St. Peter's, Rome, and St. Paul's, London) were built on this principle.

Without modern engineering formulas or data as to the strength of his materials, Brunelleschi had no independent way to confirm the adequacy of his scheme or measurements, but modern mathematical proofs have shown that his specifications were more than adequate to insure the dome's stability. As an example, a graphing of the points of pressure set up by the successive crowns of masonry shows that the resultant line of pressure lies wholly within the shells so that one of the greatest dangers, that of excessive weight bursting the dome, was carefully avoided.

At the same time, Brunelleschi exploited the Gothic building technique of concentrating pressures at specific strong points, namely, the eight massive corner ribs. Each shell was therefore to carry only part of its own weight while the remainder was transferred to the ribs, which acted as a kind of skeleton for the rest.

Finally, the outer shell had the additional purpose of serving as a protective umbrella to the inner shell so that moisture would not penetrate through to the inner surfaces, which were later to be frescoed. Thus, his system, comprising a double interconnected dome keyed to its eight main corner ribs, ingeniously solved in one stroke the most important problems of excessive weight, lateral thrust and concentration of forces. At the same time, no compromise was made with the esthetic need to dispense with buttressing.

But the cupola still had to be actually built, and the most awesome difficulty was its tremendous height above the ground. Brunelleschi had stated he would build the dome without the use of centering, and this he proceeded to do by raising the structure in brief horizontal crowns or courses. Each stage was bonded to the one immediately below and temporarily supported in such a way as to sustain its own weight until the complete circle had been closed and bound together with ties and hence fixed in place. Each piece pressed against the next and so was able to hold the row to follow above.

Work started in 1420, and a tremendous pile of materials—cut stone from the quarries near Settignano, marble from Carrara, lime, timbers, bricks—was assembled in the piazza, until one citizen remarked that it seemed as though "Filippo was going to build a city up in the sky" and that "Arnolfo's church would be crushed beneath it." Every detail was under Brunelleschi's personal supervision, from the firing of the brick to the instructions to the masons. A contemporary describes how the master masons would come to him on the job asking his advice—how to cut a stone or cast a brick so as to dovetail into its neighbour—and Brunelleschi would thereupon take his knife and cut a model using anything at hand—sometimes a turnip. He devised new kinds of cranes for

(*left*) Access stairs between the inner and outer shells of the Duomo's cupola as they begin to curve in over the opening. (*right*) Herringbone brickwork of the intertied ribbing, high inside the cupola.

hoisting materials, a special type of barge for hauling marble up the Arno from Pisa. One of the most difficult problems was the erection of flying scaffolds on which the workmen and material could stand, and these he invented while the work proceeded. As the dome continued to rise upward and inward over the opening, the hazards increased, and many of the workmen refused to continue or went on strike for long periods. However, in spite of all the problems, Brunelleschi's methods were one by one vindicated and the opening was finally closed in 1434. Only then did he reveal his detailed plans, which disclosed the tremendous amount of original thought that had gone into the cupola. Many things had been planned for: stairways and guide rails between the two shells, openings to let in the light, other apertures to break the force of the wind blowing against the outer surfaces, intricate gutters to carry off rain water, irons on the underside of the inner dome for the fixing of scaffolds for the workmen who would later paint the frescoes; "and when the people considered what he had done in dovetailing, inlaying, joining, and binding the stones, it filled them with awe and trembling to think that one man could achieve what Filippo had done." A statue of Brunelleschi and one of Arnolfo have been placed in the piazza to the south of the Duomo looking up at the building they created, while nearby is the so-called Sasso (or stone) of Dante where the great poet is supposed to have sat while watching the early construction of the cathedral.

Another competition was then held for the design of the crowning ornament, the marble lantern, which again Brunelleschi won with a wonderful plan, part classical and part Gothic, perfectly complementing the cupola itself. Its size, over 50 feet high, and tremendous weight, gave rise to repeated warnings that it was too heavy and that the key stones of the dome would not prevent it from all falling in; but to the end (he died before it was finished), Brunelleschi kept urging the masons on and insisting that the heavier it was the better it would fix the stones in a firm and permanent bond, pressing them ever tighter together.

No effort is more worthwhile than to climb the steps up into the interior of the drum where the magnitude of the whole construction and the immensity of the space over the choir become apparent. Human figures below, moving about in the dimness of the church, appear unreal. Then one should continue on up between the two shells of the dome itself by a series of stairs, coming out on top at the base of the lantern some 300 feet above the ground, to comprehend the marvel of the architectural feat. It is almost impossible to believe that all that mass of stone and brick is hanging there in mid-air over such a vast space. As a contemporary of Brunelleschi's said, "It is for certain that the ancients never went so high with their buildings and never took so great a risk as to wish to do combat with the heavens."

No such dome had been built since the Pantheon, and even it cannot compare esthetically, for Brunelleschi's cupola surges upward in a graceful curve, marvelously unifying the whole vast building to become the city's single most vital and distinctive feature.* Florentines abroad do not say they are homesick, but rather "sick for the dome."

In successfully completing this project, Brunelleschi established the basis for all subsequent large-scale structures, and his accomplishment is acknowledged by modern engineers as one the greatest construction achievements of all time. In addition, it represents one of the first major breaks with the past in respect to the personal and individual responsibility of the architect *per se*. All through the Middle Ages, artists had been subject to the control of the church, the occasional royal patron, and later the guilds. Most large-scale work was the result of the common effort of many; the individual contributions merged in the overall undertaking, and the identity of the artists remained mostly unrecognized. There was no special distinction for those who practiced architecture, painting, or sculpture, as all craftsmen were lumped together. Many engaged in several pursuits, often designing clothing, armor, coats-of-arms, furniture, and other household equipment. Now Brunelleschi, having given up his goldsmith and sculpturing endeavors, had specialized in architecture and had insisted on taking personal responsibility for designing and raising the dome relatively free of direct supervision by the guilds, the church, or government.

A portion of the exterior between the top of the drum and the cupola itself remains unfinished. Brunelleschi's plan for this part

* The dome of Hagia Sophia, built in Constantinople in 535, is smaller, much lower, and surrounded by buttresses.

was lost after his death and a later attempt to complete it with a row of small arches was interrupted, after only one side was finished, by an unfavorable public response, probably because the new work tended to break the upward flow of the basic scheme. To this day, nothing more has ever been done.

As if he were not busy enough planning and building the cupola, Brunelleschi was also at work at the same time on several other projects of the greatest importance: the Foundling Hospital, the church of San Lorenzo, and the Pazzi Chapel. In attacking these problems, Brunelleschi was aided by the Roman author Vitruvius whose writings on architecture had recently (1410) been discovered. These had emphasized the importance of mathematical symmetry in achieving proper proportions, especially the use of the square and the circle, which were considered the two perfect shapes. Vitruvius also pointed out the relationship of these geometrical forms to the parts of the ideal human figure and stated that their use in architecture should have some rational correspondence to the scale of man's physique.

Beginning from these theories to work out his drawings in one over-all advance plan, independent of traditional procedures, and aided by his own rediscovery of the principles of perspective, Brunelleschi was commissioned by the Arte della Seta to design and construct as a charitable guild enterprise, the Spedale or Ospedale degli Innocenti (Hospital for Foundlings), one of the first such institutions in Europe and still in existence. Only the loggia across the front need concern us because that part of the building completed in the early 1420s, represents a complete break with the traditional architecture and may be said to be the first true Renaissance structure. It is distinguished by a long series of delicate, round arches, behind each of which is incorporated a square, domed bay, not cross-vaulted, but in the classical manner. Similarly, the Corinthian columns, capitals, corbels, and semicircular arches are derived from Roman types, while the windows with their low pediments in the story above are indebted to those in the Baptistery, which Brunelleschi and his contemporaries thought was originally a pagan temple. There were accordingly few concessions to the immediate architectural practices of the times, though the overhanging eaves, a traditional Florentine feature, still remain; and for the first time, a completely rational

View of the loggia of the Foundling Hospital (*right*) on the Piazza Santissima Annunziata before the encroachment of the automobile.

design, strung out on a generous horizontal line, open and inviting, was created, to become the model on which a whole generation of artists drew. The other buildings, for example, surrounding the piazza, which incidentally constitutes a perfect square in keeping with the Renaissance rule of balance, were designed later with the same elegance of line and color to complement the loggia of the Innocenti.

About the same time (1423), Giovanni di Bicci de'Medici selected Brunelleschi to plan and construct at his parish of San Lorenzo an entirely new type of building of great originality and beauty, the first Renaissance church. He retained the basic basilican ground plan used since classical times, but instead of the irrational proportions found in churches like Santa Croce, he arranged everything according to a definite mathematical relationship: the square of the crossing is repeated exactly in the transepts and choir and four times in the nave, while the aisle bays and the side chapels are each one-fourth and one-eighth these areas respectively. The many side chapels for the resident

The lucid and harmonious interior of Brunelleschi's church of San Lorenzo looking toward the high altar.

monks—San Lorenzo, like Santa Croce, was a monastery church —are now in better proportion to the whole and recessed in alcoves behind semicircular arches similar in rhythm to those that he places along the nave above the tall Corinthian columns of *pietra serena*, that cool, clear, blue-gray stone called "serene." Elsewhere throughout the church, the square and the circle are used repeatedly. In addition, following hints from other classical writers, Brunelleschi keeps the interior relatively simple, free of decorations and statues, so that the basic architectural forms and members, articulated against the background of white walls, are permitted to register without interference their full effect. Especially dramatic, in contrast to the crude unfinished façade outside, is the initial view on entering the nave, its clean lines fortunately still free of any later additions or funeral monuments, which presents to the eye a beautifully integrated and harmonious arrangement and a radical break with the Gothic style.

To an even stricter formula, he laid out an adjoining room at the end of the left transept, known as the Old Sacristy (finished in 1428), which was especially designed for the Medici family and

The Old Sacristy at San Lorenzo, designed by Brunelleschi and embellished by Donatello (1428).

where Giovanni di Bicci was soon to be buried with his wife. Here, Brunelleschi was able to exploit not only classical architectural form but the ideal of the centralized plan itself, also derived from Roman buildings, whereby he based everything on either a square or a circle. The room is a perfect cube, on top of which has been placed a hemispheric dome, all the walls and surfaces being divided into squares, double squares, circles, and half-circles, according to a mathematical system of proportion which, if experimental, is also highly effective.

All the great architects that followed studied this jewel-like room, and in fact, its immediate success directly led to Brunelleschi's next project, started soon after (1430), when another important family, the Pazzi, also bankers, commissioned him to design and build a similar but larger centralized structure, a chapel for them adjacent to Santa Croce. A sophisticated version of the Old Sacristy, it also contains some new features, especially in the exterior, which is made up of a most original portico of Corinthian columns supporting a barrel vaulting across the front and pierced

(*left*) The exterior of Brunelleschi's Pazzi Chapel, begun 1430, at Santa Croce. (*right*) The sophisticated simplicity of the interior of the Pazzi Chapel.

at right angles by an impressive entrance arch. Over the door is the classical triangular pediment; while inside, the deceptive simplicity and purity of the design are heightened by the stark white of the lime plastered walls and the contrasting gray of *pietra serena*.

Many of the decorative details of both the Pazzi Chapel and the Old Sacristy in San Lorenzo are by Donatello. In particular, the freely designed bronze doors, the columns and pediments framing them, and the crude but dramatic polychrome stucco roundels and reliefs in the Old Sacristy are all by Donatello. Although these details are admirable in themselves, there have been those, including Brunelleschi, who felt that some of this work was out of phase with the architecture of the room. But this is not surprising, as it was Donatello, more than anyone, who ignored architectural considerations in his enthusiasm for sculptural expression.

During those years, Ghiberti was again commissioned by the Signoria to provide yet another pair of doors for the Baptistery to be hung at the east entrance, opposite the Duomo. The chancellor, Leonardo Bruni, was selected to specify the subject matter— stories from the Old Testament—some of which, in line with the chancellor's main preoccupation, have marked political overtones. Accordingly, Ghiberti commenced the painstakingly precise work of designing, modeling, and casting what would become his masterpiece after more than two decades of labor. Again, though he would discard the Gothic framework of his earlier doors and exploit the new discoveries by Brunelleschi and Donatello in perspective, anatomy, and classic motifs, his overall concept is of a pictorial nature, more akin to the painter's art, and his work continues to be characterized by the stylized linear rhythms and elegant details of the Late Gothic. Nevertheless, the result amazed his contemporaries, and he was hailed as having created portals suitable for the gates of Paradise, by which name they have ever since been known.

Meanwhile, another artist was setting about to revolutionize painting. This was the young genius Masaccio (he died at 26), whose fresco of the *Holy Trinity* (1425), to be seen in Santa Maria Novella, may be considered the first work in that medium to incorporate the new theories of the Florentine Renaissance. It

A panel (the story of Esau and Jacob) from Ghiberti's second set of bronze doors for the Baptistery, reflecting the new mastery in relief of perspective, classical proportion, and realistic detail.

is true that he had the advantage of Brunelleschi's achievements in scientific perspective, proportion, and classical form, as well as Donatello's sculptural realism, all of which contributions are evident in the fresco, but it remains a fact that he was the first to exploit them in paint. Of even greater importance, though, are the cycle of frescoes he produced in the Brancacci Chapel of Santa Maria del Carmine in Oltrarno a few years later (1427), especially the *Expulsion from Paradise* and the *Tribute Money*, where painting for the first time can be said to have entered its modern phase and where all the lessons of the past, stemming back to the large-scale, three-dimensional volume of Giotto's work, have combined in a most dramatic expression of spatial, plastic, and realistic values. Scientific perspective is for the first time fully exploited, but not so much by architectural forms as by the arrangement of figures, and not so much by line as by atmospheric effects of light and shade. Without exception, scholars and artists have universally praised these paintings for

The central section of Masaccio's fresco *The Tribute Money* (1427), wherein Christ instructs Peter to "render unto Caesar the things which be Caesar's."

their lifelike realism, their expressive human qualities, and their technical advances, especially in atmospheric perspective, making them the single most important step between the frescoes of Giotto and Michelangelo.

In the meantime, a second long series of wars with Milan were taking place (1422–33), which also involved fighting with neighboring Lucca, one of the few Tuscan towns still independent of Florence. The war proved very costly to sustain, requiring the adoption of new taxes, in particular a direct levy on the estimated fair return on capital (gold, money, jewels, land, buildings, animals, and inventories) called the *catasto*, remarkable not only because it fell most heavily on the very merchants who agreed to it, but also because it was perhaps the first income tax ever imposed in Europe.

The war went badly from the start and accomplished less than nothing. Lucca would not be defeated, and Florence was fortunate to finally arrange a peace treaty. Partly to ward off criticism, which would tend to fall on those families, headed by the Albizzi, that had gradually concentrated political power in their hands, and partly to eliminate a potential rival, the Medici were singled out as responsible for the wasteful conflict and charged with treason. Giovanni di Bicci had recently died, so it was his son Cosimo, now head of the family, his relatives, and their close supporters who were arrested, found guilty, and banished from the city (1433). However, exile did not seriously impair the basis of the Medici's influence, which was rooted in the vast size and scope of their European banking operations, as well as in the reputation and personality of Cosimo, who, before his father's death, had been the bank's and often the city's official representative abroad in the courts of Europe. To the chagrin of his enemies, Cosimo proceeded to Venice, where he was received not as a fugitive but with the acclaim due more the head of a state.

As it turned out, the Albizzi faction in Florence, no longer all-powerful, within one short year (1434) lost control of the government to supporters of the Medici, and Cosimo was invited to return. From that time on, and for the remainder of his life, Cosimo remained the single most important Florentine citizen and the effective head of the government. He was so, however, unofficially and from behind the scenes, and, though he several times served short terms as gonfalonier and as member of the treasury board, he generally left the honors of office to others. Again, none of the political institutions were disturbed, except that the method of election to the priorate was subjected to even tighter control, so that Cosimo was invariably able to place his own men in the Palazzo Vecchio. That it was possible for him to maintain his position over so long a period was due to a number of factors: his great wealth, which he utilized to raise up those he could trust and buy off those who opposed him; a successful war against Milan in 1440 (whereby the forces of the Visconti were decisively defeated at the Battle of Anghiari in the Casentino, on which occasion Florence acquired the towns of San Sepolcro and Poppi, and out of which Cosimo was able to establish a firm alliance with the future duke of that city, Francesco Sforza); his patronage of the arts, which made Florence the indirect

beneficiary; his moderation and lack of ostentation in living—
he remained simply a banker and a commoner exciting a minimum of envy; and finally his great popularity with the lower
classes in town and country, with the lesser guilds and certain of
the big merchants. He remained always aware that broad support
was essential in case opposition became too strong and a parliament had to be called, in which event the people's will, in the
last resort, might be decisive. Republican institutions and ideals
died hard in Florence, and the populace, while admittedly more
apt to praise liberty than to actually insist upon it, preferred to
believe that their rulers enjoyed power by grace and consent
rather than by force or inherited right. Thus Cosimo, and his
son and grandson after him, consciously strove to avoid the
appearance of arbitrary power or aristocratic attitude and to
pursue a policy that would benefit the mass of the citizens as well
as themselves, much as Cicero had worked to serve the Populus
Romanus.

An example was the Council of Florence (1439), a convocation
held between the eastern and western branches of Christianity to
effect their reunion, and an event that was looked upon as one of
the greatest of the age. It had originally been planned for Ferrara,
but was moved to Florence as the result of Cosimo's efforts and
certain inducements he was able to offer. Naturally, the people of
Florence were proud to be hosts, and there were many collateral
benefits. Not only did the pope and the patriarch of Constantinople take up residence there for a long period but the Byzantine
emperor himself, his vast retinue, lay and clerical, moved into
the city. The greatest scholars of the Hellenistic world, as well as
cardinals, bishops, lay leaders, and humanist scholars from all
over Europe, appeared on the scene. Seldom, if ever, had such
an exotic and fascinating assemblage of notables been gathered
together in one place, never such colorful costumes, festivals,
processions, and parades, such learned conversations, such an
intense mingling of spirit and intellect been assembled within
living memory. Even more important, in return for the city's
financial support to resist the Turks, now seriously threatening
the Eastern Empire, the emperor provided Florentine traders with
exclusive privileges for their galleys at Byzantine ports. And
Cosimo was largely responsible. The declared purpose of it all

was never finally achieved, as the ecumenical agreements worked out were never consummated, but the city's culture, business, and reputation greatly benefited.

The origin of the Florentine Platonic Academy, devoted to an understanding of Hellenic civilization, stems from the experience of that meeting. Thereafter, especially following the fall of Constantinople to the Turks some years later in 1453, Greek scholars in droves came to Florence where, in collaboration with the humanists of the new learning and the patronage of the Medici and others, the city became the center of an unrivaled intellectual ferment. Cosimo, in particular, in addition to running his business and guiding the political destiny of the city, found time not only to keep in touch with the intellectual and artistic movements of his day but to actively support them. He befriended the wandering Greek scholars as well as the Italian ones—Marsilio Ficino, Leonardo Bruni, Carlo Marsuppini, Nicolò Niccoli—and provided generously the funds needed to search out and purchase or copy the ancient manuscripts buried in the monasteries of Europe. But it was as a patron of artists and as a collector that he has seldom been rivaled. Besides beginning his family's first accumulations of rare and beautiful objects—coins, medals, intaglios, cameos, manuscripts—Cosimo possessed an unfailing talent for selecting and inspiring the architects, sculptors, and painters who would execute his commissions, as well as a seemingly inexhaustible supply of funds to finance their works.

That is not to say, however, that everything was dependent on the Medici, nor should we exaggerate their role. On the contrary, the ground had long been in preparation. All of the elements of the Florentine Renaissance had been firmly established—the study of Greek and Roman authors, the search for philosophic and esthetic principles, the collecting and analyzing of antiquities, the introduction of new art forms. But there appears a quickening of the tempo and an increase in momentum from Cosimo's time on. Artistic production in particular, fostered not only by the Medici but also by other prosperous families, began then to reach impressive proportions, so much so that the significance and the ramifications become extremely complex and difficult to discuss in any comprehensive way. We can touch upon the high points only.

The same year that Cosimo was recalled from his short exile (1434), he ordered Brunelleschi, who was just finishing the dome of the Cathedral, to redesign and rebuild the church of the Augustinian monastery of Santo Spirito in Oltrarno, using San Lorenzo as a point of departure. The resulting plan, considered by modern critics as superior and more harmonious than the earlier basilica, encompasses a final maturity in the architect's style. There is evidence that he probably returned to Rome before commencing this building to study the ruins again and that this plan represents a new interpretation of the classical theme. For one thing, his mathematical proportions have changed for the better: the relationship of the height of the arcades and aisle bays to the height of the nave ceiling is now three to six as compared to three to five at San Lorenzo, while the nave is twice as high as it is wide and the aisle bays, exact squares, are also two times as high as wide, giving the interior a better spatial effect. For another, the transepts, which at San Lorenzo had failed to contribute to the unity of the whole, were here integrated into the arcading. Also, the side chapels have been rounded into

The nave of the church of Santo Spirito designed by Brunelleschi in his last years.

semicircular niches, repeating the rhythm of their arches, and are offset by round half-columns in between (as opposed to rectangular chapels and flat pilasters in San Lorenzo), giving the whole, expecially with the forest of full round columns at the far end, a greater unity and a stronger, more sculptural feeling that critics find important in judging architectural merit. It is a fact, however, that Brunelleschi's immediate imitators borrowed more from his work in San Lorenzo.

Meanwhile, the Duomo's cupola having been closed, the interior work of embellishment was going on beneath it in an attempt to finally finish the whole ambitious undertaking commenced over a century before. Unfortunately, the two most interesting and artistic objects ever completed for the Cathedral, the famous carved marble *cantorie* (choir lofts), which for long were installed over the doors of the two sacristies, have been removed. They may now be seen in the Museum of the Opera del Duomo.

Both *cantorie* were completed in the same year (1438), one by Donatello and the other by Luca della Robbia (1400–82), an artist who was to establish a workshop and family tradition of major importance for several generations. Though on the same scale, and designed to complement one another in their positions on either side of the high altar, affixed to the massive piers of the crossing, they differ completely in spirit and execution. Donatello's represents a band of dancing, reveling children, wildly cavorting in a sort of bacchanal. Closer scrutiny reveals a roughness, almost ugliness, in technique, but from a distance—as the *cantorie* were intended to be seen—the composition has a rhythm and vitality hard to improve upon in cold stone. Luca's is more in keeping with the architectural setting, a series of panels depicting singers and musicians in dignified and restrained attitudes—the theme is the Psalm of David (the 150th), which is inscribed around the gallery—the whole constrained within a thoroughly classical arrangement of entablature and pilasters. Both artists were working at the same time and place, and both had studied the antique, but here they have exploited their own personal interpretation of the sculptor's art: Donatello freer, more independent, emphasizing the profane, the pagan aspect of the classical age; Luca more disciplined, attempting to combine

(*above*) Donatello's cantoria (choir loft) for the Duomo: sculptural, free, rhythmical, and full of life and vigor (1438). (*below*) Luca della Robbia's cantoria: architectural, restrained, elegant, and suffused with a classical balance (1438).

A sincere expression of faith combines with the classical feeling for form in this panel from Luca della Robbia's cantoria.

The Ascension of Christ by Luca della Robbia executed in glazed terracotta (1446)—one of the first such productions in that medium as invented by the artist.

the artistry of the ancients with the sacred Christian message. Both, however, have achieved in these *cantorie* two of their greatest masterpieces in marble.

But it was in a different medium that Luca, only a few years later, was to establish a new, peculiarly Florentine art form with his sculptural reliefs in glazed and colored terracotta (baked earth).* The two earliest examples of this are here under the cupola, immediately above the sacristy doors and below where the *cantorie* once projected. These reliefs, in the shape of lunettes, and representing the Resurrection and the Ascension of Christ, established a technique that was soon employed for a thousand

* The della Robbia name comes from the red clay—*robbia*—used in the process, which involved modeling the form, coating it with chemicals, and baking it in a kiln. The exact chemical formula of Luca's glazes, his own invention and passed on by word of mouth to his descendants, has now been lost, and no one has ever been able to duplicate it. Tradition has it that it was written on a paper and sealed inside the head of one of his Madonnas.

decorative purposes in buildings all over the city. Some of the best-known glazed terracotta rosettes and medallions are those by Luca in the Pazzi Chapel and the medallions on the façade of the Foundling Hospital by his nephew Andrea.

About this time, another talented artist, Michelozzo Michelozzi (1396–1472), a follower of Brunelleschi, also caught the eye of Cosimo, who assigned him the task of rebuilding the church and monastery of San Marco, shortly before acquired by the Dominican order, an undertaking that took about five years to complete (1438–43) and was paid for by the Medici.* The new construction replaced an older group of buildings, parts of which were retained—notably the chapter house and the large refectory —but Michelozzo's work and his debt to Brunelleschi can clearly be seen throughout, especially in the cloisters, with their refreshing Renaissance forms adapted to the needs of monastic life, and the wonderful library. The latter, built on Cosimo's order to house his collections of books, one of the most valuable in the world at that time, is the finest part—light, elegant, and harmonious. It was characteristic of him to combine patronage of a religious foundation with humanist book collecting. Around the library opening off the corridors are the cells of the monks, bare and austere except for the fact that most of them contain frescoes by the hand of the last great exponent of medieval painting, one of the Dominican brotherhood, Fra Angelico (1387–1455), whose purpose here was primarily to inspire the friars and only inciden-tally to decorate. In this, the attempt to convey the spiritual side of Christianity and the love of God, he has never been sur-passed, and though his style harks back to the Gothic tradition, having acquired relatively little from his contemporaries, the unworldliness and sacred nature of his message come through clearly. For devotees of this artist, San Marco is all that need be visited, since, in addition to the frescoes, most of his altarpieces and panel paintings have also been assembled here in a gallery on the main floor.

Cosimo himself had a cell at San Marco to which he would retire on occasion to meditate and, it is said, having confessed, to

* Little of Michelozzo's work can be seen in the church itself as it was subsequently redecorated, first by Vasari, and later in the seicento by others in a restrained Baroque style.

(*left*) The first cloister at the monastery of San Marco, the work of Michelozzo (1438–43). (*right*) The library at San Marco that housed parts of the Medici book collections.

atone for some of the less admirable things he had done to maintain his power. He was apparently very conscious of the attitudes of others, for, the story goes, when it came time for him to build himself a new house, he rejected a plan prepared by Brunelleschi on the grounds that it was too grandiose for a private citizen and would have been displeasing to his adherents. Instead, he again selected Michelozzo to design a building of more modest proportions.

The resulting house—completed between 1444 and 1460 and still known as the Palazzo Medici—is partly in the Tuscan tradition but also contains some new ideas derived from ancient Rome. In the past, the tower-houses and palaces of the nobles had always been rugged and fortresslike, and though there was now less internal feuding, riots and rebellions were not uncommon. The lower story of the new dwelling therefore prudently retains a defensive character, but otherwise the whole structure takes on a new feeling and theme. It has a more generous, rather than cramped, demeanor. It is wider; the windows and doors, no

The Palazzo Medici as it appears today after having been enlarged
by the Riccardi family.

longer Gothic, are larger and of better proportion; and decorative detail, especially in the splendid massive cornice, copied from Roman buildings, is richly laid on.

Originally, the palace comprised only about half of what we see today—that portion beginning on the corner and including the first three ground floor arches on the Via Cavour and the first ten windows in each of the floors above. Much later, purchased by the Riccardi family (and hence now better known as the Palazzo Medici-Riccardi), it was extended to the north. All of the windows are divided by a colonette into double, round-headed arches, but the original ones may be distinguished from those in the later addition by the emblems of the Medici family—the seven *palle* (balls) and the three feathers within a ring—set above.

The most striking feature of the palazzo is Michelozzo's handling of the façade. The rustication of the lower third is very pronounced; the floor above, the *piano nobile*, is less rugged, being faced with evenly cut stones with channels along the joints; while on the top floor, the masonry is almost smooth. The effect is of a building of great strength and solidity, firmly anchored to the ground, but at the same time, as the eye moves upward, of a new civilized, refined character. Certain amenities appear: at the base, a stone bench where the rich man's retainers and callers could rest, and at the corner, two wide entrances, one on each street, which opened into an airy loggia where he could have been seen conducting his affairs. Later, these two portals were closed up by Michelangelo with his famous "kneeling" windows.

Crowning the building is the massive, daring cornice of classical inspiration, replacing the traditional tiled eaves. Though in proportion to the whole structure and handsome in design, it has been criticized as rather too heavy for the upper story and for the small string courses that separate the three floors.

Inside, a new approach is also clearly visible and the semifortress feeling of the exterior is completely gone. The storage areas, stables, and workshops have been removed from view and replaced by spacious rooms on the ground floor used to welcome visitors. These are grouped around a harmonious and symmetrical courtyard in the center, open to the sky, and no longer cramped or medieval. Michelozzo, too, was concerned to employ regular

The courtyard of the Palazzo Medici, which illustrates the effect
of the Renaissance on domestic architecture.

geometric forms, especially the square and the circle. The original
building itself formed a cube, while the square courtyard is
decorated with round medallions and its arches are semicircular,
as are those over the windows. Later critics were to detect a number of faults in the design of this courtyard. The colonnade,
which is taken bodily from Brunelleschi's Foundling Hospital
and bent around the four sides, is weak at the corners, where
later architects would have replaced the columns with heavier,
solid piers; the frieze is too high; the windows above are not
properly placed, being too close at the angles. Nevertheless, this
was one of the first attempts at a conscious search for beauty and
logic in the Florentine house.

The best-known room within the *palazzo*—the little chapel
on an upper floor—seems almost to have been an afterthought, as
Michelozzo had to squeeze it into a small, irregular space in a
corner of the original building. But its disadvantages as to shape
were cleverly offset by the architect, who designed the beautiful
marble floor, the carved walnut stalls, the fluted pilasters, and the
coffered ceiling, and especially by the magnificent frescoes

The chapel in the Palazzo Medici designed by Michelozzo and frescoed by Gozzoli (1459).

executed by Benozzo Gozzoli (1420–98), a student of Fra Angelico. With barely any natural light to work by, it is hard to understand how the painter managed to produce some of the most colorful pictures in Florence. The subject matter, probably prescribed by Cosimo's son, Piero, who was fond of the courtly Late Gothic style, is not profound but complicated. The artist has mixed together a religious scene—the Procession of the Magi—with some other event, real or imagined, from Italian history, the subject of which is still unclear but may have been the Council of Florence. In addition, there are hundreds of portraits of contemporaries, including that of the artist himself, all set in a fantastic landscape of cliffs, woods, and fields and with villas and castles scattered here and there reminiscent of Gentile da Fabriano's painting, *Adoration of the Magi* (1423) now in the Uffizi, the greatest Florentine example of the Late Gothic.

But the real significance of the fresco, with its crowds of church and lay leaders, their retinues and retainers, lies in how it expresses one version of the ideals of the times, which, giving its due to humanist liberation of society, seen in the frank and confident facial expressions of the participants, is still very conscious of the immediate past, described by the artist in terms of dress, equipage, sport, and buildings, and even in the romantic countryside itself. In other words, though the painting unmistakably suggests the importance of man's earthly role and his ability to guide his destiny, there is a strong admixture of traditional religious sentiment and medieval mysticism, of chivalry and the feudal order that had passed, all expressed in an art form that fuses these Late Gothic pictorial allusions with the new interest in human appearance and personality.

Following Cosimo's lead, other merchants and bankers soon were planning and building new *palazzi*. One of these was Luca Pitti, a rival of the Medici, who, determined to outdo Cosimo, commissioned an imposing house to be built in Oltrarno, presumably specifying among other things that its windows be at least as large as the main doorway in the Medici palace. Though the original building, thereafter known as the Palazzo Pitti, comprised only a fraction of the massive structure that exists today—a cube containing the central doorway and the two doorways on either side (since converted to windows) together with

The central portion of the façade of the Palazzo Pitti (mid-quattrocento).

the middle seven windows on each floor above—the intention from the beginning was to create something massive and imposing. Also its site is not within the intimate city center, as was Cosimo's, but removed from its neighbors in haughty isolation on a slight hill.

The original plan called for windows similar in design to Michelozzo's, but they were unfortunately never completed and were filled in later with brick and casements. Luca Pitti apparently wanted no sheltering cornice but only some formal balustrades, and the palace is almost devoid of ornament. However, its rugged façade of huge, rough-cut stones, many of which were quarried on the site, and its present monumental proportions, due to repeated enlargements later on by the grand dukes, lend it the aspect of a house more befitting the Olympian gods than mere mortals.

Here, as in the other *palazzo*, the architects have been able to combine something of the traditional Florentine feeling (originally

Etruscan) of massiveness and strength with the civilizing effect of classical refinements. Both buildings for the first time emphasize the horizontal rather than the vertical—wider, lower, and cube-shaped, and no longer the towering fortress—while all trace of Gothic influence has been left behind. Architecturally they are important because they were later copied extensively throughout Italy and Europe.

The Palazzo Strozzi on the Via Tornabuoni, which was begun by another banking family a little later, is merely a refinement and enlargement of the Medici Palace. For example, the rustication of the façade is more even and uniform, the string courses are more pronounced, the cornice and the courtyard more grand and imposing. Perhaps because of its too logical perfection and its great size, it lacks the same attraction, but it is still one of the most imposing houses ever built for a private citizen and another example of the pride and the resources of the Florentine banking families.

Of greater interest in the story of Renaissance civic architecture is the Palazzo Rucellai, nearby on the Via Vigna Nuova, built between 1446 and 1451. It was designed for the famous Rucellai family, who had first made their fortune in the cloth trade, by Leon Battista Alberti (1404–72), another highly talented Florentine architect on a par with Brunelleschi. Both men drew their inspiration from ancient Rome, and the work of both appealed more to the mind than the emotions, but whereas Brunelleschi had been primarily interested in practical architectural schemes and structural building techniques, Alberti sought to deduce from his studies a theory of esthetics covering art in general. He, in fact, wrote a number of books attempting to set down the rules governing painting and sculpture as well as architecture, At one point, he comments: "I shall define Beauty to be a harmony of all the parts, in whatsoever subject it appears, fitted together with such proportion and connection that nothing could be added, diminished, or altered but for the worse"—a generalization that he then attempts to translate into actual rules and guidelines. Like Leonardo da Vinci after him, he came close to the Florentine ideal of the whole, complete man, versatile to an amazing degree, taking the entire world as his province and developing his thoughts and theories not only out of his vast reading of classical texts but also out of his wide experience. He studied the Latin and Greek authors, excelled at sports and riding, wrote books on horsebreeding and criminal law, on oratory and art, wrote comedies, songs, ballads, sonnets, and fables. It was he who made the oft-quoted statement, the hallmark of Renaissance confidence, "Man can do all things if he will."

The tangible result of applying his ideas to an actual building happily may be seen in the Palazzo Rucellai, where the first attempt was made systematically to treat the entire façade of a palace in a thoroughly classical manner. All functional and military character has now disappeared, and the design is for appearance' sake alone. A mathematical relationship enters into every feature of the façade, which has a far more complex and elegant look than the Medici Palace, though it may lack the structural integrity. Its most distinguishing elements are the three entablatures supported by pilasters in between, the idea for which may have been taken from the Roman Colosseum and is the first such use since classical times. The capitals of the pilasters have been modified according to Alberti's taste, and they support richly decorative architraves and friezes incorporating the device of the Rucellai sail. There are no heavy bossed stones, but only squared blocks, smooth and regular, and for the first time the main doors have lost the traditional arch and appear as formalized rectangular shapes. The overriding cornice has been carefully thought out—large enough to crown the building as a whole, but not so massive as to be out of proportion to the entablatures below or to the upper story itself, which it renders complete. It was Alberti's intention that the façade should be symmetrical—that is, eight bays wide—but the last one on the right was unfortunately never finished and must be supplied by the imagination.

Few, at first, followed his lead, particularly in Florence, where palace architecture continued for a time to repeat the Brunelleschi and Michelozzo theme, but ultimately this gave way to Alberti's ideas.

Immediately across the street may be seen the loggia of the Palazzo Rucellai, also designed by Alberti (1468) and recently beautifully restored. In the quattrocento, every great house had a loggia (a covered, arcaded porch) either incorporated within or located close by, a place not only for the transaction of business

The façade of the Palazzo Rucellai designed by Alberti (1468).

affairs but also for the celebration of marriages, births, and other important family occasions. The physical openness of the loggia was indicative of a society that conducted much of its daily affairs and many of its celebrations literally in the streets. People required no invitation on these occasions because everyone was welcome, regardless of status. In later centuries, under the grand dukes, when the customs and habits of behavior changed and social events were restricted to the upper classes and held behind palace walls, many of the *loggie* were closed up and used for shops or other purposes.

To Alberti is due another outstanding achievement: the completion of the half-finished façade of the nearby church of Santa Maria Novella, also on a commission from the Rucellai, patrons of that church, who supplied the funds. The problem was to unite the architect's new Renaissance concepts to the older existing part—the lower half—without upsetting the balance or jarring the eye, and the result is remarkably successful. Some compromises were necessary to achieve this, as, for example, the repeating of the rectangular marble designs in the upper half to correspond with the older work below, and the use of the

The half-medieval half-Renaissance façade of the church of Santa Maria Novella.

heavy corner pilasters, added by Alberti, and those above supporting the upper entablature with their courses of alternating black
and white, which pick up a similar theme in the Gothic arches
of the tombs at the base.

But, for the rest, he firmly grafted on the new Renaissance
forms, such as the four great Corinthian columns, the doorway,
the frieze and cornice, the pediment at the top, and, to cover up
the two sloping roofs over the nave aisles, the famous reversed
volutes or scrolls, an invention widely copied later. Completed
in 1470, as the Roman numerals, MCCCCLXX, on the façade
confirm, it is a kind of textbook of decorative church architecture, combining Romanesque, Gothic, and early Renaissance
characteristics.

In addition to the architects, a whole new generation of
painters and sculptors were coming on the scene, who, throughout
the middle of the century, generated a torrent of work inspired
to one degree or another by the pioneering of Brunelleschi in
perspective, Donatello in realism, and Masaccio in applying these
discoveries to painting. One of the painters was Domenico
Veneziano (1400–61), who, not a native of Florence, settled there
and was employed frequently by the Medici. His debt to both
Masaccio and Donatello may be seen in his masterpiece in the
Uffizi, the *Sacra Conversazione* (Sacred Conversation), which he
painted about 1448. (In the *Sacra Conversazione*, a favorite theme
for quattrocento painters, the Madonna, enthroned in an architectural setting, "converses" with the saints that surround her.)
Veneziano's unique contribution is the mellowing or toning
down, by means of a new spatial lightness and airiness, of what
had become too bright, decorative Gothic color effects, an
important aspect of painting to be fully exploited by the
Florentines.

Another painter was Domenico's pupil, Piero della Francesca
(1420–92), from eastern Tuscany, who studied in Florence and
made highly original contributions to Renaissance painting by
his novel use of mathematical perspective and geometrical shapes
in the arrangements of his compositions, and especially in the formation and placement of the objects and human figures therein.
Little of his work remains in Florence, but there are two portraits

(1460s) of the duke and duchess of Urbino by his hand in the Uffizi which, in addition to the uncompromising reality of their solid, blocklike faces, also reveal in the background one of the first convincing pieces of Italian landscape painting, its exactness and unity establishing a precedent for the many Tuscan painters that followed, including the great Leonardo da Vinci, who sought to capture the beauty of the surrounding countryside.

Two other talented artists who were also devoted, perhaps excessively, to the new science of optics, perspective, and foreshortening were Paolo Uccello (1397–1475) and Andrea del Castagno (1421–57). The former combined these discoveries with the older decorative Gothic tradition and a fertile imagination to produce fantasy pictures of geometric shapes, rhythms, and colors, an example of which is his famous painting of the *Battle of San Romano* (1456) in the Uffizi, one of three of a series commissioned by the Medici that originally hung in their palace on the Via Larga. The other, Andrea del Castagno, breaking more decisively with the past, provides a dramatic and forceful representation of the religious themes he selects, though sometimes succumbing to a rather cold, austere statement, as in his frescoes in the church of the Santissima Annunziata (1455) and his large *Last Supper* in the Monastery of Sant'Apollonia (1445).

Finally there was Fra Filippo Lippi (1406–69), the inconstant and worldly friar, who, the opposite of that other painter-cleric, Fra Angelico, delights in the pleasures of the earth and in reproducing with a new exactness all the details of nature and the individuality of human faces, though always within the context of a religious subject. He was the first painter to emphasize the beauty of movement and vibrant line, foretelling the work of Botticelli, whose teacher he was; his *Madonna and Child with Angels* in the Uffizi (about 1455) is a good example.

Perhaps of all the artists, none benefited more from Cosimo's interest and patronage than Donatello, who enjoyed a long, productive life. His famous bronze *David*, now at the Bargello, the first freestanding nude figure cast since ancient times, was commissioned by Cosimo (in the 1430s), who set it up in the courtyard of his new palace to symbolize the city's triumph over stronger, Goliath-like enemies, in particular Milan. In this work critics believe Donatello attempted to combine elements from his studies of Greek sculpture (the languid stance, the features, the helmet) not only with the biblical theme of David, but also with the Christian belief of man's ultimate dependence on God's help, expressed by the immature, unaggressive nature of the face and figure, obviously lacking the Greek attributes of will and strength. The statue was thus symbolic of the Platonic Academy's ideal of uniting Greek culture with Christian piety. At the same time, it is also important as representing the final separation of sculpture from its dependence on an architectural setting and well illustrates Donatello's particular concern with realism and human personality. These latter characteristics of the sculptor, however, are even more dramatically expressed in his later works, as for instance in the haggard, ascetic figure known as the Penitent Magdalen.

Among the other sculptors of the period, the one of first importance is Bernardo Rossellino (1409–64), who is known especially for the tomb in Santa Croce that he designed and executed (1447) for Florence's great chancellor Leonardo Bruni. This was the first such memorial to incorporate all of the spirit and motifs of the classical revival—the pilasters supporting the round arch above, the Roman eagles and the classical sarcophagus, the portrait head study of the recumbent deceased, his brow in laurel wreaths and his hands clasping a book, significantly not a Bible but one of his own works—and it greatly influenced similar work thereafter. The purely religious aspects are played down. No saints or virtues appear to mark his passing from this earthly life, and the Madonna in a medallion under the arch is only a small part of the decorative scheme. (This tomb should be compared with an earlier one, from 1427, for Pope John XXIII in the Baptistery by Donatello and Michelozzo. Though the artists employed Renaissance concepts—the sarcophagus, the effigy on the bier, the shell lunette behind the Virgin and Child—it represents, with its figures of the Virtues below, a transitional phase, more religious in spirit than Rossellino's.)

Bernardo's workshop, in the tradition of Ghiberti, became the training ground for many of his younger contemporaries and the source of the revival of realistic portrait sculpture, an art form that attained great popularity in the latter half of the quattrocento, owing in part to the Renaissance penchant for

Leonardo Bruni's tomb in Santa Croce by Rossellino (1447). The epitaph reads in part, "history is in mourning, eloquence is silent, and the muses cannot restrain their tears."

glorifying individuals of merit or beauty. One of those who followed his lead was Desiderio da Settignano (1428–64), master of delicacy and sensitivity, who excelled in carving children and young women, but whose most famous single work, like Rossellino's before him, is another tomb in Santa Croce, executed about fifteen years later, this one for Carlo Marsuppini, Bruni's successor as chancellor. Less architectural and less solemn than the earlier one, with its floating ribbons, garlands, festoons of leaves, and lively *putti* (cherubs), it seems almost to celebrate life, not death.

Other sculptors—Bernardo's brother, Antonio Rossellino (1427–79), who excelled at portrait busts; Mino da Fiesole (1431–84), follower of Desiderio; and the two brothers da Maiano, Giuliano (1432–90) and Benedetto (1442–97)—carried on the so-called serene or sweet style in the tradition of Ghiberti and Luca della Robbia.

More animated and vigorous were Antonio Pollaiuolo (1431–1498) and Andrea del Verrocchio (1435–88), both of whom, influenced more by Donatello, made use of dynamic movement and vitality in carving the human face and figure and were the first to produce statues so balanced and arranged as to be viewed to equal advantage from any angle. All these artists are represented within close proximity in several rooms of the Bargello where their similarities and differences may be compared and appreciated A few works by the last two, who were also painters, are in the Uffizi.

Verrocchio's wonderful bronze casting of *Christ and Doubting Thomas* is at Orsanmichele in the only Renaissance niche there, one designed earlier by Donatello. Originally, it was intended to accommodate only one figure, but Verrocchio solved the problem ingeniously. Christ stands slightly raised within the arch as in a doorway, while the saint approaches from outside, tentatively reaching forward to touch the wound. The superb realism and expressiveness of the faces and hands and the virtuosity of the flowing robes amply testify to the artist's reputation. Here, on the east wall of the building, from across the narrow street, especially with a morning sun clearly defining the shadows, one can scan at a glance the three niches on that side and note in the figures three successive styles: Ghiberti's Gothic *St. John the Baptist* (1414), Verrocchio's fully developed Renaissance group (1480), and the later Mannerist artist Giambologna's *St. Luke* (1601).

Perhaps the single most comprehensive example of the style and work of this period is summed up in a small chapel at San Miniato, where the leading Florentine figures in all three branches of the fine arts joined in a cooperative effort. It is called the Chapel of the Cardinal of Portugal, after a young prince of royal blood, who happened to die in Florence in 1459 and was buried there. Brunelleschi's pupil, Antonio Manetti, designed the overall plan; the Rossellino brothers executed the tomb and the sculptures; Luca della Robbia created the terracotta decorations; while Antonio Pollaiuolo and his brother painted the altarpiece and, along with Baldovinetti, frescoed the walls. All were completed in 1468. Each artist attempted to coordinate his work harmoniously with that of the others to produce an ensemble of Renaissance art unique in Florence.

The fall of Constantinople to the Turks in 1453 had the effect of temporarily unifying the warring Italian states, formalized in the Peace of Lodi (1454), and ushering in a period of relative calm lasting some forty years. An important element therein, the strong Florentine alliance with the Sforza of Milan, a policy vigorously adhered to by the Medici, contributed measurably to this end. Even following Cosimo's death in 1464, when disgruntled forces reared up within and without the city to attempt the overthrow of his son and heir Piero, bold action on the part of the Medici nipped the uprising in the bud, ensuring a continuation of the alliance. But Piero, whose health was poor throughout his life, ruled as the tacitly recognized head of the state for only five years when death took him away in 1469. (Both Cosimo and Piero are buried in San Lorenzo. Cosimo's grave is marked only by the inscription *Pater Patriae* (Father of his Country), an honorary title conferred on him, as it was on Cicero, by official decree of his fellow citizens.)

The mantle of leadership fell on Piero's eldest son, Lorenzo, aged 20, around whom, despite his youth, the dominant political forces of the town rallied. Few men have made a greater impression on their contemporaries or have been the subject of so much searching inquiry by historians as Lorenzo, known within his

Tomb in Santa Croce of the Florentine chancellor and humanist
Carlo Marsuppini by Desiderio (1462).

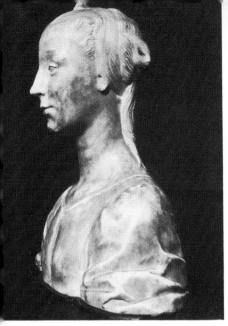

(*above left*) Portrait bust of young woman by Desiderio. (*right*) Portrait bust by Mino da Fiesole of Piero de' Medici, father of Lorenzo the Magnificent (1454). (*below left*) The features of Pietro Mellini, prosperous Florentine merchant, immortalized by Benedetto da Maiano (1474). (*right*) Young girl, thought to be Lucrezia Donati, the mistress of Lorenzo the Magnificent, by Verrocchio (whose name means "true eye").

Verrocchio's *Christ and St. Thomas* (finished 1483) occupies a niche at Orsanmichele.

own lifetime as *Il Magnifico* (the Magnificent). Many have been his detractors, but the consensus now seems to be that, despite a calculating shrewdness and at times a certain ruthlessness employed to preserve both his position and the safety of the state, he combined in his person the best qualities of both the active and the contemplative life and came finally to constitute a kind of standard by which to judge other men of his time. Certainly there is no disagreement that he decisively influenced almost all phases of life in his native town—politics, business, philosophy, poetry, music, art, sport, pageantry—few aspects of which did not receive his personal interest and attention. He was described as having a joyful, friendly nature, a strong physical endurance, and an inquiring, purposeful mind. In addition to running the family bank and a number of farms, he found time to study Greek, geometry, and architecture, write hymns, carnival songs, and excellent poetry, underwrite the copying or acquisition of hundreds of manuscripts, support and encourage scholars such as Poliziano and Pico della Mirandola, and become the acknowledged mentor of the group known as the Platonic Academy. Though not as a great a builder as his grandfather—the bank no longer returned as large a profit—he had the same sure instinct for beauty, and as a collector of antiques, gems, glass, and stoneware he excelled. Also as a generous patron of the arts, he was among the first to encourage and subsidize the regular teaching of mosaic-making, painting, and sculpture, principally in his gardens at San Marco, where he employed many artists and discovered the young Michelangelo.

At the same time, he loved the out-of-doors—hunting and sports—bred racehorses, and staged several extravagant jousts and tournaments in the Piazza Santa Croce. But to an unprecedented degree he was continually engaged in time-consuming political affairs of the most delicate and complicated nature, being in constant touch not only with the rulers and ambassadors of the various Italian states and the pope, but with many of the crowned heads of Europe. Moreover, he had to do so, not as the official head of state, but by working cautiously from behind the scenes through loyal friends and associates. As had been the case with Cosimo and Piero, Lorenzo did not regularly serve in high office, but exercised power through intermediate councils and committees the membership of which he usually controlled. Inevitably, he was criticized during his lifetime for usurping too much power, but Florentines of the next century were to look back on his era of relative peace and stability with pride and admiration. Force he had sometimes used, but always with reason and moderation, and his policies for the welfare of the state had been well balanced. In fact, this concept of balance was often applied to Lorenzo, both in handling of foreign affairs—the balance of power between the states of the peninsula—and in maintaining domestic equilibrium —the sharing of rights and privileges among the classes. Altogether, Lorenzo fulfilled to a high degree the ideals of the age of the versatile, fully confident, positive thinking, and wholly rational, complete man.

By far the most dramatic and important episode of Lorenzo's entire career centered around the events leading to and issuing from what is known as the Pazzi Conspiracy.

Even during those years after the Treaty of Lodi (1454), when Italy enjoyed a relative degree of peace and political stability stemming largely from the alliance between Florence and Milan, trouble was always breaking out in the area known as the Romagna. This territory to the east of Tuscany centering around Bologna and Ravenna was divided into numerous small local tyrannies. In theory, each recognized the pope as overlord, as did the districts of the Marches, Umbria, and Latium to the south (making up the State of the Church), but in practice they were largely independent and treated as pawns and buffers by the ever-scheming larger states. By 1474, a new, aggressive pope, Sixtus IV—the same Sixtus who was to commission the building of the famous Sistine Chapel in the Vatican that bears his name— occupied St. Peter's chair and was eager to consolidate politically once and for all these papal territories. His strenuous moves in this direction, expecially his attempts to take over several small towns on the borders of Tuscany, soon alienated Lorenzo, who put every obstacle short of war in the pope's way.

Frustrated in his attempt to deal with the Florentine leader, Sixtus gave his tacit blessing to a plan concocted by a diverse group of malcontents and deadly enemies of the Medici to assassinate Lorenzo and his brother Giuliano, as a means of changing Florentine policy. Among those involved in the scheme was the scion of one of Florence's oldest banking families, head of its Roman branch and a hater of Lorenzo, Francesco Pazzi, who was to lend his name to the plot, which, if successful, would, he hoped, elevate him to a position of civic leadership. The details were complicated, but the idea was to do away with Lorenzo and Giuliano on the first occasion when they would be in the same place and unguarded. After several miscalculations, the opportunity presented itself at a time (April 26, 1478) when the Medici would be attending high mass in the recently completed cathedral. At the appointed moment, the assassins threw themselves on their unsuspecting victims, while simultaneously their accomplices with a body of armed men stormed the Palazzo Vecchio to take over the seat of government. Giuliano was stabbed to death immediately, but the much more important Lorenzo fought off his assailants and miraculously escaped, taking refuge in the north sacristy behind Luca della Robbia's beautiful bronze doors. Saved by a mere chance, Lorenzo, reacting with lightning speed, ordered his friends and retainers to counterattack. From the moment it was known he had survived, the people rallied and the plot was doomed. Within hours, all of the conspirators were rounded up and butchered by the mob or hanged by their necks from the windows of the Palazzo Vecchio. Lorenzo emerged as a hero of heroes, but Sixtus, incensed by the massacre of his adherents, clapped an interdict on the city, excommunicated Lorenzo and the *priori*, and demanded retribution. Being denied, he ordered his troops to move north and attack.

The pope and his allies were able to muster superior military strength, and during the following year (1479) penetrated deeply into Florentine territory. Florence, depending on the usual mercenaries and unable to get adequate help from Milan, found itself not only on the defensive but facing a probable military defeat. In this emergency, Lorenzo secretly arranged to present himself personally within the enemy camp, hoping by this extraordinary tactic to make the pope see the advantages of negotiation and the folly of advertising to the world Italy's divisions and animosities. This was a bold diplomatic gamble. On the one hand, he risked his life by putting himself at the mercy of his antagonists. On the other, there was no assurance that any peace plan he was able to work out might not be rejected by his fellow citizens, for his task was to surrender on terms favorable enough to the pope, but not so adverse as to lose his following at home. Fortunately for himself and for Florence, he was successful, and after three months of delicate give and take, surrendering some territory (later recovered), paying an indemnity, and agreeing to release those of the Pazzi Conspiracy still in jail, he was able to return not only with a satisfactory peace treaty (February 1480) but also with an official papal pardon for the city.

Aside from Lorenzo's personal diplomacy, the single most important reason Sixtus and his allies were willing to come to terms was the growing threat of foreign intervention from outside Italy. Not only were the victorious and aggressive Turks a serious concern, but also covetous eyes were being cast in the direction of the peninsula by the Holy Roman emperor, by Spain, and especially by France, which had for decades been waiting for the right moment to revive its ancient claims and invade. Lorenzo had seen this more clearly than anyone and had worked diligently to avoid war between the Italian states. Also, of course, Florence was not militarily strong, and peace far better served its main commercial interests. But though a general policy might be worked out and agreed upon, innumerable complications could frustrate its implementation. For example, Florence, by long tradition and its vital business interests, needed to remain on good terms with the French king, as many of its commercial and banking houses, and especially the Medici bank, did a thriving business in France. Thus Lorenzo, while attempting on the one hand to form an Italian coalition aimed at discouraging the French, had, on the other, to do it with cunning and discretion so as not to offend his best customers. That he was able to do so throughout the remainder of his life is a measure of his ability.

The great energy and time that Lorenzo devoted to his many intellectual and political activities were given at the expense of the conduct of his business affairs, which, unlike his father and grandfather, he left mainly to others. Under Cosimo, the Medici bank had grown into one of the largest institutions of its kind in Europe, conducting a business as varied as it was successful. Medici agents, acting for the pope, collected taxes, rents, and fees for remission to Rome or searched for classical manuscripts for the Vatican collection. If a new bishop was to be appointed, the official papers might be delivered by the bank on condition it could collect from the new appointee whatever inaugural dues and assessments were owing before taking possession of his see. Acting for the Calimala, arrangements for a shipment of wool from the Cotswolds in England to Pisa would be worked out or perhaps the entire cargo would be purchased outright for resale. In the other direction, and acting for the Seta, the bank might handle the transportation and sale of Florentine silks and remit the funds. And so on into a myriad of transactions.

The breach with Rome was only temporary, but owing to general mismanagement and to substantial defaults on loans made by the London and Bruges offices, requiring that they be closed around 1480, the financial strength of the Medici bank underwent a gradual diminishment. This was aggravated by the tremendous expenses Lorenzo was put to in maintaining houses and villas, patronizing the arts, entertaining foreign personages, and conducting diplomatic embassies, for which he claimed he was never recompensed by the city but which led to accusations that he had mixed and augmented his own purse with state funds. In fact, Lorenzo's most vulnerable point of criticism lay in his monetary policies, and he was repeatedly charged with mismanaging state funds, assessing taxes unfairly, and debasing the coinage.

However, other Florentine business houses, especially those connected with the Calimala and the Lana, also experienced a similar contraction of prosperity near the end of the quattrocento. This was caused by the slow loss of the Florentine advantage in processing woolen cloth as other cities and countries, especially in the north, began to employ the same manufacturing techniques and to restrict foreign imports. It is true that compensating markets were sought and found in the Mediterranean area, and also that the weaving, processing, and dyeing of silk rapidly supplanted the primacy of the older product, but there is no question that the total volume of Florentine trade began to decline, a trend that was to accelerate in the next century.*

* The number of business houses connected with the Lana dropped from 166 to 88 during the cinquecento, and many Florentine banks were out of business when the century turned.

This, however, was scarcely apparent to Lorenzo's fellow citizens, especially the upper classes, whose enthusiasm, optimism, and confidence were reaching their climax. One can hardly wonder that art turned in the direction it did, if we consider the emphasis that increasingly manifested itself throughout quattrocento Florence on enjoying life on earth to the full. Public festivals, processions and pageants, jousts and tournaments sponsored by the Medici and others, carnivals, celebrations of victories, religious holidays and feasts, elaborate weddings and funerals were repeatedly staged. Great efforts went into building and decorating triumphal arches and allegorical floats, and much attention was given to personal dress, arms, and armor. Painting, in particular, which earlier had been concerned exclusively with subject matter of a sacred nature, now portrayed military battles, historical episodes, pagan and mythological themes—especially those concerned with Venus, Hercules, and Mars. Something of this spirit is clearly conveyed in the paintings of Gozzoli and Uccello, as it is with another Florentine painter of the next generation, Domenico Ghirlandaio (1449–94). Not now considered of the first rank, he is nevertheless important not only because his work illustrates so well the actual life of the times— rooms, dress, and other details—but also because his many portraits crystallize the mental attitudes and concerns of his contemporaries, who have so decidedly left the Middle Ages behind. Though Ghirlandaio's works are often set in a religious context, there is nothing left of religious feeling, and every portrayal simply records for posterity the Florentine quattrocento —the people, the genre, and the world of the senses—in a realistic, earthy manner and as their surface characteristics dictate. The best examples of this are his frescoes commissioned by associates of the Medici, the Sassetti family, in Santa Trinita (1485), depicting scenes from the life of St. Francis and containing numerous portraits, including Lorenzo himself, and those in Santa Maria Novella (1490), also full of portraits—the Medici, the Tornabuoni, members of the Platonic Academy, artists.

Another artist working at the same time, but of greater ability, was Sandro Botticelli (1444–1510), who, like Ghirlandaio, captured, at least in his earlier period, the verve and zest for living that characterized the era and also created some of the most pleasing, most sophisticated pictures ever painted. His work, much of it concentrated in three rooms of the Uffizi, incorporating idealism and realism, religious and pagan themes, sensual and spiritual love, the joy of living with the deepest pathos, the appearance of simple allegory with a mysticism that still defies unraveling (especially in the two large Venus paintings with their delicious flow of line and superb craftsmanship), remains the ultimate expression of the Age of Lorenzo. Here is the visible statement of all that was going on intellectually and artistically at the apogee of the Florentine Renaissance: the pageantry, the love of grace and beauty and balance, the attempt to reconcile Christian belief with humanism and the Neo-Platonic philosophy, the confidence in the secular attitude, and the belief in the dignity and power of man.

Finally, from the same period must be mentioned that universally acclaimed genius and most diverse man of the Renaissance, he who has been called also the greatest painter of all times, Leonardo da Vinci (1452–1519). Though Florence claims him and he periodically worked there during Lorenzo's lifetime and after, he spent much of his time and talents in northern Italy and France, and most of his relatively small amount of finished work is not in Florence but dispersed elsewhere. The Uffizi does possess several examples, however: two pictures by his teacher, Verrocchio, in which Leonardo had a definite hand, a controversial work of his youth—*The Annunciation*—and the unfinished *Adoration of the Magi* (1481). This latter painting, though carried only to the point where color was just being applied, represents a highly sophisticated attempt to present the familiar Christian theme in terms of all the recently perfected techniques and theories of the art. The careful preparation Leonardo made in working out the composition and figure arrangements can be seen even more clearly in the preliminary drawing for the painting, also fortunately preserved in the Uffizi, which reveals the complexity of the geometry, as well as the rationale of the figures in their apparently casual dispositions. For the first time, the scientific and artistic approaches unite in equal perfection, producing not only a convincing unity of the many diverse elements but also that special quality of mysticism appropriate both to the subject matter and to the ideals of the Platonic Academy.

Confining ourselves to the story of Florence, we cannot pursue Leonardo's manifold efforts in many directions, as sculptor, engineer, student of anatomy and biology, musician, architect, inventor, and military planner, as well as painter, but can only note in passing that he was an end product of the many new interests let loose by the Renaissance and, in the particular field of painting, the culminating focus of all the studies and talents of the quattrocento. While Botticelli in the end permitted his emotions to dominate his work, Leonardo, who more than anyone else tried to synthesize science and art, imposing his great intellect on everything he undertook, ultimately permitted the artist in him to give way to the scientist. But in the process, the techniques and concepts employed in painting—whether scientific perspective, the effects of atmosphere (*sfumato*) achieved by the use of indistinct outlines, the tactile feeling of form by means of light and dark (*chiaroscuro*), composition and draftsmanship, the study of nature and anatomy—were brought to perfection in his work, and everything that followed branched off in one or another direction from it.

It is not recorded that Leonardo and Lorenzo were very close, and the latter did nothing to discourage the artist from leaving Florence. But Lorenzo had given his teacher, Verrocchio, many commissions, including that for the magnificent bronze and marble tomb for his father, Piero, in the Old Sacristy of San Lorenzo; and he was literally the discoverer of Michelangelo, whom he took into his house and supported when the artist was still a youth. Various of the Medici were the principal patrons of Botticelli, and, in fact, the inspiration and import of the painter's greatest works—those of his middle period, including the two Venus pictures and the two *tondo* (round) paintings of the Madonna (1475–85)—can be traced to his close association with Lorenzo's circle of friends in the Platonic Academy.

The Academy, despite its name, was never a formal institution, as we understand the term, but simply a social gathering of like-minded men—poets, scholars, and intellectuals, including Cristoforo Landino, Marsilio Ficino, Poliziano, Pico della Mirandola, and Luigi Pulci—who enjoyed reading and discussing the great Greek and Latin authors with special emphasis on Plato. They usually met at one of the Medici villas, and Lorenzo was not only their host and patron but the catalyst that stimulated the group. Besides being close friends, they were bound together by the underlying, commonly shared belief that the ancient Greeks had discovered a system of immutable laws governing nature, man, and esthetics, on which they had based their thought processes, their writings, and their approach to government and art. The hope, though it proved vain, was that these principles, rediscovered, would lead to a new Golden Age. The Academy's influence upon educated Italians, however, was great, and the Platonic philosophy on which it rested was thereby introduced into European art and letters of the next century. The translations and commentaries of Ficino, Pico, Marsuppini, and Poliziano; the work of Alberti in architectural and esthetic theory; of Botticelli and Leonardo in painting; of Rossellino, Desiderio, and Verrocchio in sculpture—all served as mediums through which passed the concepts derived from Greek and Roman studies into the mainstream of European thought and practice.

The great emphasis that was laid on every aspect of the classical heritage, not only on the discovery and reinterpretation of ancient texts, but also on the physical fragments of architecture and sculpture being unearthed piece by piece, has been seen by some as a handicap to creativity, but this is only partly true. Salutati, Bruni, and others had indeed studied the Roman authors diligently and had concluded that their style and content were superior to the medieval texts, but this does not detract from the originality or quality of their own writings. And, just as the Florentines employed the structure of Greek and Latin literature to refine and sharpen the Tuscan vernacular in the writing of poetry and prose, so they took the art forms of the past and fashioned them into new, native creations. Florentine Renaissance art, in any of its branches, can never be mistaken for classical work, not only because its purposes differed but because it is also in fact a new style. Perhaps it is in painting that the characteristics of this new style—its special intellectual content, its economy of means, its balance and proportion, its awareness of line, and its sober use of color—are most clearly obvious. Certainly the painters were not inhibited or constrained by the past, as the ancient wall paintings had virtually disappeared, so that there was nothing to copy or revive. Instead, their work, though naturally drawing on prior traditions, was truly experimental and original in technology, composition, perspective, anatomy, and subject matter, and especially in their direct approach to the study of nature.

The goal of the Academy had been to mine the Greek philosophers of their approach to life and ordering of society so as to discover the principles that would lead to the ideal life, combining contemplation with action, and at the same time to try to reconcile humanism with Christianity. To a degree they succeeded, and Lorenzo himself came closest to the ideal. But ultimately, having enthroned Reason, they could not help also undermine Faith. Even the churchmen, who would have been expected to resist, became intoxicated with the revival of classicism. Some became the greatest of connoisseurs and collectors, as materialistic as the laity. Also the artists, though often attempting to clothe their paintings in religious guise, at least in the quattrocento, permitted their work to be overshadowed by worldly or pagan aspects. A tension was therefore to grow between the idea of the complete man, conscious of his power to achieve, and the Christian concept of man reconciled to humility and the will of his creator.

To the Florentine people, who always had a streak of austerity in them and who at times in the past had risen up to oppose worldliness and corruption in the church, all this became too sophisticated and unintelligible. The intellectuals, by both example and teaching, had gradually moved away from the old standards, and the people, having perhaps become satiated with display and guilty of conscience, were vulnerable to appeals for reform. These were soon supplied with a vengeance by a monk of San Marco named Girolamo Savonarola, who was elected prior of the monastery in 1490. Not a native of Florence but long a resident, he violently disapproved of a mental climate foreign to his ascetic temperament. Claiming to be divinely inspired, he sought to undo the teachings of humanism, to correct the morals of the citizenry and the church, and even to reconstitute the city government. In response to his fervent preaching, a state of mind soon developed among the people that was presently to upset the social and cultural structure of the city and the political power of the Medici.

Fortunately for Lorenzo, or more likely because of him, this waited until after his death. It would have hardly seemed possible to him or his followers that the world they had helped to build and in which they were so optimistic could fall apart in so brief a time. Their emphasis on humanistic studies and classical philosophy, on the search for beauty and logic in nature and art, and their apparently successful attempts to reconcile all this with Christianity seemed to them only the beginning in man's ability to civilize himself and to create the good life. But highly intricate and unpredictable international factors—religious, political, economic, geographic, military—were at work on a scale and of a complexity that scarcely could be anticipated, much less guided, by the leaders of one or more puny Italian city-states. The same year Lorenzo died—1492—a Genoese explorer was discovering the new world, a fact that would soon alter the direction and thrust of Europe's attention, reorient the world's trade routes, and deprive Italy of its long-honored privilege as the center of commerce. Ironically, Columbus had been decisively inspired to undertake his first voyage across the Atlantic after an exchange of letters and maps in the late 1470s with another Italian, the Florentine cartographer and astronomer, Paolo Toscanelli (1397–1482), who first advocated sailing west to reach the Indies; while the earliest explorer to follow in Columbus's wake and to realize that it was not Cathay but actually a new continent that had been discovered was also a prominent Florentine, the navigator, Amerigo Vespucci. It was, in fact, Amerigo's wider range of exploration and his more objective reports that made clearer to Europe the momentous nature of the new discovery and, unfair though it was, resulted in the new continent's being named after a Florentine. At the same time, France and Spain had grown into powerful nations with which no single Italian state could possibly compete directly. And ahead also lay the disrupting and, for Italy, catastrophic events of the Reformation and the Counter-Reformation.

As far as Florence was concerned, the period from the death of Lorenzo to the city's surrender in 1530 to the combined forces of its enemies constitutes the last chapter of its existence as an independent self-ruling state and the gradual unraveling of the Florentine Renaissance. The immediate cause for this was twofold. In the first place, the nature of the opposition to the Medici changed its character after Lorenzo's passing, from that of a narrow group of jealous, competing families to a broadly based, popular reaction which questioned the legitimacy of Medici rule, their privileges, and the mortality of their system. Even more decisive was the French invasion, which, long threatened due to that country's claim to the Kingdom of Naples, took place in 1494, opening the eyes of all Italians to the power of the French monarchy and army. A force of 45,000 men armed with superior weapons swept over the Alps and down the peninsula without any effective resistance. Disunited and weak, Milan, Florence, Rome, and finally Naples, one by one, surrendered or made the necessary concessions. Florence, traditionally accommodating to French demands, attempted cooperation. In the process, Lorenzo's sons, having bungled the negotiations and unable to cope with either the domestic or foreign situation, lost the support of the citizens and were forced to abandon the city abruptly, ending exactly sixty years of Medici rule.* Immediately, a drastic reform of the constitution was undertaken with the main purpose of broadening the scope of participation in the government so as to limit the influence of any one man or family. A Grand Council of Five Hundred (on the Venetian model) was constituted, to be made up of several successive groups of citizens with prescribed qualifications, who were to choose the Signoria and other officials and to pass the laws. This permitted, in addition to the greater guildsmen, a large number of middle-class citizens to take an active part in the government. Instrumental in effecting these changes was the monk, Savonarola. Like Lorenzo, he is a subject of great controversy, but it is now generally conceded that his first interest was in reforming the church and the morals of the citizens and that he became enmeshed in the strife and discord of politics only later, as a consequence. But regardless of motive, his eloquence and great following among the common people soon made him not only a potent influence but almost the arbiter of all

* Lorenzo, the first of the Medici to marry outside the city's bourgeoisie (into the aristocratic Orsini family of Rome), had three sons: Piero, who died a few years after his banishment; Giovanni, who was made a cardinal as a favor to Lorenzo and later became Pope Leo X; Giuliano, known as the duke of Nemours from a title given him by the French king.

decisions taken within the city for a period of several years and therefore a focal point of faction.

The story of his rise to prominence and his undoing is one that we cannot examine in detail. In short, it was his passionate sermons first delivered at San Marco and then in the Duomo to huge sympathetic crowds that firmly established his reputation and following.* Humanism and all its works were emphatically denounced, and those who placed their faith in the Greek philosophers and Roman poets rather than in the saints and apostles were admonished and warned of an impending doom. Mobs of intimidated citizens were organized into reform bodies to spy and to collect all evidence of human vanity—wigs, pictures, masks, cards, dice, cosmetics, costumes, hats, mirrors, even books and musical instruments—which were forcibly confiscated and set afire in huge pyres in the Piazza Signoria. But his crusading zeal, uncompromising policies, and fanatical single-mindedness soon alienated important groups: the larger merchants, those that remained of the Medici party, those discomfited by his reforms, and finally the church hierarchy, reaching all the way to the pope himself, at whose corruption and worldly ways Savonarola lashed out in a fury. A series of letters protesting the immorality and laxity in the church went out over his signature, one of which to the king of France urging the deposing of the pope and the calling of a general council fell into the hands of the pope's friends. But unable to bribe him—he was offered a cardinal's hat, which he refused—or to tolerate his high-handed methods or telling criticism, his enemies set about to discredit him in the eyes of the people.

An ingenious plot was devised to accomplish this end. A monk from the Franciscan order at Santa Croce was induced to challenge Savonarola to the ancient test of ordeal by fire. An elaborate spectacle was arranged in the Piazza della Signoria where the two monks were to walk through a tunnel of searing flame, the survivor to prove or disprove the authenticity of Savonarola's preaching and prophecies. A great crowd gathered on the appointed day, April 7, 1498, but, as had been planned by

* Savonarola's cell in San Marco and a few of his possessions that have been preserved there, including his books and handwritten sermons, may be seen on the upper floor of the monastery.

the authorities, an interminable series of objections and conditions were raised until, darkness falling, the test was called off and the blame was publicly placed on Savonarola. The people, cheated of the show, rioted. Almost overnight, the Dominican's following melted away, and the Signoria, now feeling it safe, had him arrested on a trumped-up charge of heresy.* For several weeks, he was repeatedly tortured until they had wrung from him a confession sufficient for their purposes. Shortly thereafter, he was tried, convicted, and put to death in front of the Palazzo Vecchio before a huge crowd.

Thus ended a remarkable personality—a popular leader and the conscience of the people, or, as others would have it, an intolerant and opinionated demagogue—who, challenging the tenets of the new civilization, had tried to bring about a moral revolution and failed. Savonarola really believed that the Florentines should return to a simpler, less worldly philosophy and give up the search for rational truths in place of revealed truths. Unfortunately, however, in attacking humanism for its emphasis on man rather than God, he had also attacked one of the healthiest developments of the quattrocento, the positive, confident attitude of mind, one of the important sources of Renaissance achievement. There is no doubt that Italian society had drifted a long way from the ideals and concepts of the prior age. The old moral codes and restraints were no longer fashionable. The emphasis was on man— a free spirit and an end unto himself, on his fine clothes, stately palaces, and pleasant country villas, on grander and more frequent public pageants, on art and music and pagan literature, on luxuries of all kinds. God had not been totally forgotten, simply demoted. Savonarola had prophesied that punishment would follow, and ensuing events seemed to vindicate him, for after his death there was no end of disasters for Italy and especially for Florence: the divisive intrigues of the banished Medici, the chaos that followed in the wake of repeated foreign invasions, and the confused Italian attempts to repulse them, the rebellion of vassal cities, financial and economic reverses, renewed visitations of the plague.

Savonarola's influence had been felt not only by the masses but also by many of the intellectuals—Pico and Poliziano both fell

* Ironically, the one man who could have saved him, Charles VIII, king of France, died that same day.

under his spell and both asked to be buried at San Marco. The same was true of many of the artists, including Michelangelo, who often heard his sermons, and especially Botticelli, who became a devoted disciple, turned away from paganism to piety in his work, and later gave up painting altogether. And there were others farther away—Erasmus and Luther—who heard his message and remembered it.

A marble disc set into the pavement of the Piazza della Signoria marks the spot where Savonarola was hanged and his body burned and records the date: May 23, 1498—the same spot where he had earlier burned the vanities. But there are other reminders of the period here. In front of the Palazzo Vecchio stands Donatello's famous *Judith Slaying Holofernes*, originally commissioned by Cosimo and for many years the centerpiece of a fountain in his home on the Via Larga, but with the expulsion of the Medici transferred here in 1495 as a warning to tyrants, as the inscription at the base tells us. At the same time, a new, grandiose room was added to the back of the palace under the direction of Simone Pollaiuolo to house the meetings of the new Council of the Five Hundred and hence called the Salone dei Cinquecento, the walls of which for a short time echoed the strident voice of Savonarola urging his reforms. The paintings and statues here are all of the following century, but some contemporary and excellent late quattrocento work may be seen in two older adjoining rooms which were redecorated at this time by Benedetto and Giuliano da Maiano: the Audience Hall, where the priors received citizens and foreign representatives, and especially the Room of the Lilies, so called from the gold fleur-de-lis symbolizing the link with France. In the latter may be seen on the east wall the remains of two Gothic windows which indicate the original style and extent of the palace before the additions. The most outstanding features of these rooms are the splendid, ornate gilded ceilings; two beautifully carved marble doorways, one severely classical and the other more elaborate; and, in the spirit of the times, Domenico Ghirlandaio's frescoes of Roman heroes (Brutus, Cicero, etc.) from the Republican era.

As the quattrocento approached its end, the situation facing Florence and Italy had altered drastically in the intervening one

(*above*) The Audience Hall (about 1480) in the Palazzo Vecchio, with frescoes illustrating the history of the Roman hero, Camillus. (*below*) Room of the Lilies (Palazzo Vecchio), showing the older Gothic windows and Ghirlandaio's frescoes (1485).

(*left*) Carved portal and inlaid doors in the Room of the Lilies by the brothers da Maiano (1480). (*right*) Michelangelo's unfinished but impressive *Brutus* (Bargello).

hundred years. No longer were the states of the peninsula to play merely local roles on an Italian stage; they were to be caught up by much larger forces operating on a wider scale. So, too, the cultural and artistic advances that Italy had nursed and brought to maturity could no longer be contained within their native boundaries, but, as with all new ideas when their time has come, readily found a welcome reception elsewhere. Thus, humanism in all its aspects no longer was to remain an exclusively Italian plant. Instead, its seeds, blowing in the winds of change, were to take root in foreign but compatible environments and to sprout up and flower in new and different forms, each variant, however, clearly stamped with its common heritage.

It had been a revolutionary century, one in which Florence played a key role, and one that served as both a watershed and a link between the superstitions of the 14th century and the scientific and exploratory discoveries of the 16th century, between the Gothic art and feudal order of the older society and the revived classicism and nation-states of the new, between the age of faith and the age of reason.

The Culmination and Dispersal of the Florentine Legacy: 1500 to 1600

With the death of Savonarola, the Florentines turned their attention outward again to the problem of Italy as a whole. The French, only temporarily successful in their first attempt, soon mounted another invasion, crossing over into Italy with a fresh army (1499), determined this time permanently to occupy the entire peninsula, step by step. They quickly subdued the plain of Lombardy, making Milan their headquarters and supply point, and moved on south through Tuscany. The Florentines as usual decided to cooperate for favors returned, but to their chagrin were soon surprised to learn that the French army had been stopped below Rome by the combined forces of Naples and its ally, Spain. With this confrontation between France and Spain began the see-saw struggle that was to last for almost three decades for the control of Italy, and Florence, motivated by traditional bonds, commercial arrangements, and what proved to be an error in judgment, throughout sided with the ultimate loser, France.

The first phase of the conflict dragged on until 1512, when, faced by an alliance of Venice, Naples, and Spain, welded together by the fiery Pope Julius II, France reluctantly was forced to abandon its conquests and retreat back over the Alps. Florence, having supported the wrong side, helpless before such a combination and with a Spanish army pouring into the Valley of the Arno, quickly sued for peace, agreeing to pay a large indemnity and, because its republican government was anathema to Julius, to abolish the Grand Council and to accept the Medici back as protectors of the city in the persons of Lorenzo's surviving sons and the pope's close collaborators, Cardinal Giovanni and his brother, Giuliano, together with their nephew (son of their dead brother, Piero), another Lorenzo.* Thus by papal and

* Both the brother Giuliano and the nephew Lorenzo were married to princesses of the French royal house, the oldest in Europe. No longer were the Medici satisfied with local bourgeois brides, or even with daughters of the Italian aristocratic families. Nor were they to remain commoners, as both men accepted dukedoms in the same year, 1516. Giuliano becoming the duke of Nemours and the young Lorenzo, duke of Urbino.

Spanish power, the Medici returned to Florence not as private citizens, but as absolute rulers.

In the following year (1513), Julius died and Cardinal Giovanni was elected to the papacy, taking the name Leo X, whereupon he assumed, from his august new station, not only the temporal power of the Papal States, but also an authority, unquestioned by the overawed citizenry, over his native town, which he treated as his own personal possession. However, Italy was not to remain for long in the equilibrium imposed by the Spanish, for within a few years there came to the French throne a new king, young and vigorous, Francis I, who was determined to reactivate the abandoned campaign to conquer the peninsula and before long had repossessed the Milanese state as a first step. Also at about the same time (1516), the Spanish and Neapolitan thrones fell vacant and inherited a new occupant, Charles of Austria, the young grandson of Ferdinand of Aragon and Isabella of Castille on his mother's side, and of Holy Roman Emperor Maximilian on his father's. Half Spanish and half German, he shortly thereafter was elected, in addition to his other titles, Holy Roman Emperor, becoming Charles V and the most powerful ruler in Europe. Not content with sovereignty over Spain, the Kingdom of Naples, and most of Germany and Austria, he was also determined to enlarge his Italian domain and sought the cooperation of the Medici pope, Leo X. An alliance was worked out between them (1521) for the purpose of again driving the French from Italian soil, with the understanding that afterward Charles would retain hegemony over certain parts of Italy, while in return he would assist the pope militarily in maintaining his hold on the reluctant cities in the Romagna, Umbria, and Tuscany, especially Florence, over which his holiness claimed sovereignty.

War was thus resumed for another decade, battles raging up and down the peninsula, no longer conducted by small groups of mercenaries wary of serious encounters but by national armies armed with cannon and bloodthirsty appetites. Italy was left in shambles. Leo did not live to see the outcome, but was succeeded by another Medici, his cousin, who became Clement VII (1523), under whom the alliance between pope and emperor was maintained.* For a time, it appeared as if the French might prevail, and

* A joint portrait of Leo and Clement, by Raphael, may be seen in the Uffizi.

this emboldened their faithful allies, the Florentines, to defy Clement, again throw out the Medici representatives (1527), re-establish the republic and the Grand Council, and dedicate themselves anew to the defense of their independence. It was an audacious but foredoomed gesture, for within another short year of fighting, the French army, decimated by plague, was totally defeated and forced out of Italy for good (1528). When the situation was confirmed the following year in a treaty between Charles and Francis, Milan and the other Italian states, with the notable exception of Florence, quickly came to terms with the all-powerful emperor, on whose head the imperial crown was now ceremoniously placed by Clement himself. In return, the pope demanded a free hand in central Italy and, if need be to bring Florence to heel, the use of imperial troops. Utterly alone, the Florentines attempted to negotiate, but Clement would accept nothing less than total acquiescence and an end to the republican government. Faced with this intransigence, and in spite of its military weakness, the city bravely prepared to defend itself. Clement was equally determined to teach the rebellious citizens a lesson. Imperial troops soon surrounded the city, and so began in the winter of 1529–30 the famous siege of Florence, the subject of many paintings, histories, and legends.

The city's walls were in good repair and massive enough to withstand the bombardment that soon rained down upon them from the primitive imperial cannons. Also new fortifications had been completed under Michelangelo's direction around the dominating strategic hill of San Miniato, which was stubbornly denied to the enemy. Assault after assault was beaten back until attempts to take the city by storm were suspended in favor of a siege so as to force a surrender by starvation. The struggle there-fore reduced itself to sporadic but bloody conflicts between roving detachments of troops from both sides attempting to convoy or intercept provisions en route to the doomed city. The citizens fought heroically and well, but month by month they were worn down, their lifelines cut, and their food stocks exhausted. Faced finally with starvation, they at last agreed to surrender (August 12, 1530), to pay a sum of money to the imperial troops, and to readmit the pope's Medici relatives on condition that the citizens be permitted to retain certain of their civil and property rights. But no sooner had the gates been opened than Clement took his revenge. The city was occupied by soldiers, and the leaders of the erstwhile republic were rounded up, tortured, exiled, and slain, their properties confiscated. All vestiges of the old constitution, including not only the Grand Council but the institution of the Signoria, were swept away into oblivion. A Medici youth, Alessandro, recently married to a daughter of Charles V, was declared lord and duke of the city, and the demoralized citizens were subjected by force to the combined will of pope and emperor.*

So, at the behest of one of its own progeny, ended the independence and republican constitution of Florence, sustained and cherished for so long, but now once and for all blotted out. Clement was thus able to reinstate his family in his native town, but altogether his reign and that of his predecessor, Leo, had been nothing but one long series of unmitigated disasters. Before Clement was finally laid to rest in 1534, he was to see the Medici policies fanning the flames of the Reformation, bankrupting the papacy morally and financially, contributing to the loss of England and northern Germany to Catholicism, to the terrible and disgraceful sack of Rome, to Spain's domination of Italy, and, not least, to the undoing of Florence and the snuffing out of its freedom.

Before the final and heroic end of the republic actually occurred, however, there remained a culminating surge in the long effluence of Florentine art, examples of which are still scattered about the city. But a great deal more of the product of Florentine genius and training is dispersed elsewhere, indicative of a trend whereby other centers of wealth and influence—Milan, Rome, Venice, Bologna, Paris, Madrid—were by the end of the quattrocento attracting the artists away. Very few of Leonardo's fabulous works are in Florence, and a great number of Michelangelo's are located in Rome and other places. But enough remains to indicate the mood and direction of the times. Painting had of course continued right along, through all the vicissitudes, ever more refined and sophisticated, under the dominating influence of

* Alessandro was the son of the duke of Urbino and half-brother of Catherine de' Medici, who was to become the wife of Henry II of France.

Leonardo—still one of the great glories of Florentine achievement, but no longer a Florentine monopoly. With the turn of the century began the great period of Venetian art (Bellini, Carpaccio, Giorgione, Titian, Tintoretto, Veronese), the major work of Leonardo's followers in Milan (Sodoma, Luini), and the greatest achievements of the Umbrian school by Pinturicchio, Perugino, and Raphael, who were so decisively to influence the art and tastes of Rome and the Vatican throughout the early cinquecento—the period of the High Renaissance.

Among the chief Florentine painters of this period, Leonardo's influence may clearly be seen in the work of Lorenzo di Credi (1456–1537) and Piero di Cosimo (1462–1515)—see Lorenzo's masterpiece *The Annunciation* and Piero's *Immaculate Conception*, both in the Uffizi—as well as in the latter's two more famous pupils Fra Bartolommeo (1475–1517) and Andrea del Sarto (1486–1531), both of whom were also affected by the pervasive authority of Michelangelo. In addition, Bartolommeo fell under the spell of Savonarola's teachings, actively sided with the monk's cause, joined the Dominican order (hence the *Fra*), burned all his paintings of the nude, and thereafter painted only for religious purposes (much of his later work is in San Marco). Andrea del Sarto, on the other hand, though almost always depicting religious themes, was more preoccupied with the human, wordly side of existence. In fact, his masterpiece, the *Madonna of the Harpies* (1517), together with Michelangelo's only easel painting, *The Holy Family* (or *Doni Tondo*, 1506), both in the Uffizi, are considered by those competent to judge as the highest expressions of the attempt to reconcile traditional religious feeling with the principles of humanism and Platonic philosophy. In addition, Andrea's picture also masterfully combines all of the technical advances achieved by his mentors—"Leonardo's nuances, Raphael's proportion, and Michelangelo's monumentality"—but, of course, never quite equaling any of them in their creativity, their range, or their special genius. Andrea's work may also be seen in the Pitti, in the atrium of Santissima Annunziata, and in the refectory of the Monastery of San Salvi, where he painted his best known fresco, a *Last Supper* (1527). Though not equal in profundity, it has often been compared with Leonardo's more famous one in Milan (1498), as well as with Ghirlandaio's *Last*

Supper in Ognissanti (1480) and Andrea del Castagno's in the convent of Sant' Apollonia (1450), to both of which it is superior.

It was during those years, between the death of Savonarola and the end of the republic, that Michelangelo Buonarroti burst upon the world to become the most renowned and sought-after artist in Europe and a legend within his own lifetime. He did not think of himself as either a painter or an architect, though he was to excel at both, but principally as a sculptor, and it was to sculpture that he devoted most of his life. In fact, it was while chipping away at a block of marble in the Medici gardens that Lorenzo the Magnificent had discovered him as a youth. Subsequently, he worked and traveled throughout Italy, much of the time actually engaged in the painful labor of extracting huge blocks of marble from the quarries at Carrara and struggling to finish the many and conflicting commissions, most of which were on an immense scale, that he received from his demanding and difficult patrons. Pope Leo X, for example, ordered him to design and build a façade for San Lorenzo. The resulting plan,

The rough brick front of the church of San Lorenzo, as it is today and substantially as Michelangelo saw it.

elaborate and studded with statues, was never carried out due to its scale and cost and the unending difficulties, but Michelangelo wasted several years on the project (1517–19) acquiring and transporting some of the marble from the quarries to Florence.* Even the confident architects of the 19th century had not the will to tackle the façade and today it remains as bare and crude as when it was built.

Perhaps no other single life more fully encompasses the period of the High Renaissance to the last gasp of its creative energies, partly because he survived a long time (his dates are 1475 to 1564) but also because he was intimately associated with so many of the important events and personalities of his era. He has been called The Titan because seldom has there been concentrated in one person such creative power. Everything in him was dynamic, explosive, seeking to release itself—his emotions, his temperament, his strength, his sensitivity, his talents. Sometimes they were misdirected, frustrated, and wasted, more often than not through the fault of his patrons, but when he was free to master them and channel them, his creations are beyond compare. Many were left incomplete because of the trials and tribulations under which he labored, but this does not interfere with their esthetic merit, and even enhances it.

In Florence, the Bargello contains a number of his lesser-known works, including a *Bacchus* carved in his youth (1496) and a *Brutus* executed when he was sixty-five. But it is in the Accademia delle Belle Arti and at San Lorenzo that his native city keeps his greatest creations. In the former is his famous *David*, carved (1501–3) out of a massive, irregular block of marble that other sculptors had given up on. So ingeniously did he design the figure that when it finally emerged from within, every inch of the full height of the huge block had been utilized, and the Florentines beheld, in contrast to the adolescent statues of David carved earlier by Donatello and Verrocchio, a superhuman giant, symbol of fortitude, strength, and independence. Here is a foretaste of Michelangelo's special quality—the embodiment of "action in repose," of forces held in tension, of the Platonic idea of the body as the earthly prison of the soul, much as the stone

---

* The plan has been preserved at the Casa Buonarroti along with other works by Michelangelo.

The gallery of the Accademia delle Belle Arti where Michelangelo's *David* (1503) and *Captives* (1518) are displayed.

block had been the prison of the statue. Gone is any trace of Goliath's corpse (the severed head in each of the earlier works), and the exact moment depicted is left unclear. That is, the narrative side of the subject is subordinated to the expression of an aspect of human character, namely the Greek quality of human will, the essential ingredient for resistance to the tyranny threatening the republic. This is further emphasized by the purposeful distortions of the oversized head and hands. This statue marked a break in the Florentine sculptural tradition of an ever-more-perfect realization of individual personality and convincing realism in favor of a more subtle revelation of a concept. When it was unveiled, it was placed in front of the Palazzo Vecchio, where it remained exposed to the elements for over 350 years. In 1873, it was finally moved to the gallery of the Accademia delle Belle Arti.

In the Accademia also are Michelangelo's lesser-known but interesting *Captives*, sometimes called *Prisoners* or *Slaves* (about 1518–19), themselves unfinished and part of another momentous, never completed scheme. These partly realized figures struggling to free themselves from the marble were doubtless intended to express man's eternal effort to free himself from the baser forces of nature and his own brutishness in trying to gain the salvation of his soul. It has been suggested that these, like others of his incomplete works, were left so intentionally by the artist, but this is highly improbable. It is true, however, that, as he matured, Michelangelo seems to have become reconciled to the unfinished state of many of his works once the essential idea had begun to emerge from the stone. Here the inherent qualities of the material itself help to express, not individualized characteristics, real or ideal, but generalized human emotions or concepts.

More famous and even more deeply profound are the figures he carved for the New Sacristy at San Lorenzo (1524–34), wherein realism and observation from nature serve only as a starting point for the expression of ideas in stone. The project was commissioned by Pope Clement VII, and, though called a sacristy, was intended as a mausoleum for the later members of the Medici family to complement the earlier Old Sacristy at the opposite transept where the founders of the dynasty were buried.* Both rooms are of the same size and proportion and both utilize a similar dark and light color scheme, but the New Sacristy, all of the architectural elements of which were also designed by Michelangelo, produces quite a different effect. Gone is the serenity, the logic, and the sense of restraint of Brunelleschi. Instead, Michelangelo has approached architecture as he did sculpture and adapted the conventional rules to his own purposes. All the classical motifs are here, but they are assembled illogically and emotionally, as if the tensions and strains the artist so often experienced personally and expressed in his human figures have been translated into the architecture. No longer is the design a purposeful end in itself, each part structurally logical, but the walls, sculptured in articulated planes, the blind doorways and windows, the cornices—lacking a frieze below and seemingly without support—the original but bizarre decorative elements, altogether seem to provide a staging for some other message, and,

* Apparently there were to have been four tombs: for Lorenzo the Magnificent; his assassinated brother, Giuliano; his son, the younger Giuliano, duke of Nemours; and his grandson, the younger Lorenzo, duke of Urbino—all buried here.

Michelangelo's New Sacristy at San Lorenzo, burial place of the Medici, with his effigy of the younger Giuliano above the figures of *Night* and *Day* (1524–34).

though spectacularly arranged, contribute to a feeling of uncertainty and doubt. Brunelleschi's straightforward statement and confidence have been replaced by a more sophisticated but less happy view of man's destiny. Perhaps this is understandable considering the conditions of turmoil in Italy and the artist's sensibilities during those years.

The tombs themselves remain incomplete and the overall plan in doubt—Michelangelo burned his drawings before he died so that no other artist could take credit for completion. He finished only six of the many sculptures planned, those for the tombs of the younger Giuliano and the younger Lorenzo, but these have been acclaimed by critics throughout the ages as among the most powerful, expressive, and human works ever produced. At the same time, their true meaning has caused unending speculation. The prevailing interpretation is that the two monumental seated figures clothed in classical military uniforms, each turning his head to the spot where the Magnificent is buried, portray Lorenzo's son and grandson. They are not, however, intended as likenesses at all ("Who will know the difference a thousand years from now?" Michelangelo is said to have remarked), but are merely excuses for art and represent the Platonic ideal of the active and contemplative life, the one rising to issue commands, the other pondering some weighty problem. Though dressed in the trappings of wealth and power, they seem conscious of their fragile mortality, ever the victims of passing time, symbolized by the reclining figures below—*Dawn*, *Day*, *Twilight*, and *Night* —eroding and frustrating both thought and action in men. These latter statues convey in their contorted postures and sliding-off positions a feeling of unrest and internal stress, characteristics of the coming Mannerist style. Dawn awakens reluctantly, not really refreshed, alongside the tired figure of Dusk, who has ended his day's work but is not satisfied with it. Opposite are the tortured figures of Night, restlessly attempting to recover strength and Day, tensely confronting life's unending problems. The anguish and struggle as well as the beauty and strength that pervade human existence are obvious, but the artist's personal intentions and their real significance remain obscure. Perhaps even Michelangelo did not know, and the mystery they invoke is the most appropriate response ever elicited by a monument dedicated to the riddle of life, death, and the beyond.

One thing is certain—here is the end of the traditional Florentine contribution to art and the beginning of Mannerism and the Baroque. Florentine moderation gives way to Roman exuberance. An even more obvious departure is evident in the Laurentian Library, also at San Lorenzo, which Michelangelo was designing concurrently with the New Sacristy to house the Medici book collection. The most interesting part, the vestibule, continues and exaggerates the trend already set. Everything is contrary to the older rules: the broken pediments above the entrance, the scroll brackets that sustain nothing, the columns set, not outside, but within the walls, the blank niches, the flowing riverlike staircase, dramatic and unprecedented. The whole thing is fascinating but bizarre and disquieting.

Meanwhile another architect, Baccio d'Agnolo, was also departing from the conventional approach by introducing a contemporary Roman influence into a Florentine palace façade with the building of the Palazzo Bartolini-Salimbeni on the Piazza

Commemorative tomb (New Sacristy) to the younger Lorenzo de' Medici, with the personifications of *Twilight* and *Dawn* below.

(*above*) The vestibule and stairs of the Laurentian Library at San Lorenzo designed by Michelangelo in the 1520s. (*below left*) Old photo before restoration work of the Palazzo Bartolini-Salimbeni (1520–29) by Baccio d'Agnolo. (*below right*) Portrait bust, possibly of Machiavelli, by Antonio Pollaiuolo.

Santa Trinita (1520–29). For the first time in the long development of the Florentine house, little remains of the older Tuscan tradition—all is now elegance and sophistication. The linear design of the structure itself gives way to a kind of sculptural or plastic treatment of the various parts—the alternating triangular and rounded pediments over the square windows (even the Palazzo Rucellai's were round-headed, uniform, and unembellished), the deep niches, the projecting cornices—all creating *chiaroscuro* effects of light and shadow against the smooth walls, features heretofore reserved for church façades. The architect was satirized and ridiculed by his fellow citizens for the building's pretentiousness and exotic importations, but it nevertheless set the path on which the other Florentine palace builders were to follow. (See, for example, the Palazzo Larderel, of 1580, also on the Via Tornabuoni, and the Palazzo Uguccioni, of 1550, in the Piazza della Signoria.)

For several centuries, far-reaching events had weakened the foundation of Christian belief throughout Europe: the failure of the Crusades and the advance of Muslim power; the accumulation of wealth and the rise of the universities outside the sphere of the church; the worldliness and corruption of the clergy; the emphasis placed by the papacy, not on spiritual matters but on its temporal domain; the discovery of the pre-Christian, pagan world free of the problems of original sin and a punitive hell.

Throughout the quattrocento, the Florentine humanists especially had continuously undermined the Christian concept that all things happened according to a divine plan, replacing this with the idea that man, a rational being, was largely responsible for working out his own destiny.

In this spirit, a number of professional humanists, many of them Florentine, had undertaken the writing of history, modeling their works after the classical authors, especially Caesar, Sallust, and Livy. A pattern of arrangement, content, and style had evolved based on the idea that the purpose of historical research was to deduce from past experience moral and ethical principles which could guide future actions. The belief was that by analyzing the actions of leaders of states and armies in the past, lessons could be drawn for the future. The underlying assumption was that man's thoughts, speeches, and acts could decisively influence the course of events and that from a combination of intelligence and *virtù* good results would pertain. To implement this approach, however, the humanist historians, following the ancient writers, concentrated almost exclusively on wars and foreign affairs, paid little attention to internal struggles and political institutions, selected only those happenings and reference sources that bolstered their premises, and confined their inquiries generally within the narrow sphere of inter-city-state affairs.

But in the first several decades of the cinquecento two of the century's greatest writers, both Florentines, Niccolò Machiavelli (1469–1527) and Francesco Guicciardini (1483–1540),* first broke away from these constrictions and, at the same time, in the course of analyzing their country's history and government, set down their appraisal of Italy's political predicament and the possibilities of a solution. Both held high office in the Florentine government and both were forced into premature retirement and into the subsequent writing that was to make them famous.

Machiavelli's contribution was to put new and decisive emphasis on politics in all its ramifications and its unique apartness from all other human activities. Thus, he disagreed with the earlier humanists whose judgments of generals and politicians were based on conventional (and Christian) moral principles pertaining to all men. Machiavelli rather considered such moral restraints inapplicable to those engaged in political life and ultimately a threat to the existence of the regime in power, since rival states and factions might not share similar scruples. While he recognized reason as indispensable to satisfactory political decisions, he placed more importance on will and force. Contrary to general belief, this did not imply that be believed only in tyranny and disfavored a republican form of government. On the contrary, he argued that a republic might be the ideal form of government for Florence since a wider sharing of power would insure a stronger state with a stronger will. Together, he

* The Machiavelli and Guicciardini families maintained palaces on the street leading south from the Ponte Vecchio. The Palazzo Guicciardini, which is still owned by that family, narrowly escaped destruction by the demolitions along the river in 1944, but the house of the Machiavellis was severely damaged.

thought, reason and will in leaders free of moral restraint could formulate and carry out political actions that could successfully guide and preserve the state.

Machiavelli, however, continued the practice of selecting those factual situations that served to fit his theories, whereas Guicciardini attempted for the first time to challenge sources and otherwise try to arrive at factual accuracy and causal connections. More important, while Machiavelli died just before the triumph of Charles V in Italy and the final collapse of all hope of freedom and independence for the Italian states, Guicciardini lived on, profoundly shocked at the helplessness of Italy's leaders to control the course of events. As a result, his later writings clearly abandoned the older assumption that reasonable men could guide the ship of state safely to port, for the more pessimistic view that political leaders, no matter how astute, were often helpless to steer a course through perilous seas without ending in disaster. The experience of the period 1527–30, including the sack of Rome, the surrender of Florence, and the total victory of foreign powers, despite all that Italian scheming and fighting could do, had confirmed in him those beliefs and altered his purpose in writing history. Thereafter, he viewed its function, generally accepted by subsequent historians, as primairly to recount man's activities, not to provide sure answers to future conduct, but to point out what man is capable of both achieving and enduring, indispensable elements of his pride and dignity.

But much of Machiavelli's writings, and Guicciardini's before his disillusionment, were concerned not with history or political philosophy *per se*, but with the practical politics and military problems of their country. In sum, they looked upon Italy as weak and disorganized while its neighbors, France and Spain, were united and powerful. Shrewdly aware that unity would not come about through cooperation, they believed that the only solution was to raise up a strong leader who would stop at nothing, use every means, fair or foul, to achieve his purpose. They were also convinced that no living Italian secular prince could command national respect and that the only alternative was for the papacy to assume the burden of this responsibility for political unification, not only because of its unique position but also because it had been largely responsible for the divisions of

Italy in the past. Being loyal Florentines (and also hopeful of employment), both Machiavelli and Guicciardini looked to the two Medici popes, Leo X and Clement VII, to fill this role.

There were, however, certain complications, for the pope, in theory at least, supposedly the very fountainhead of morality, was now freely to engage in any subterfuge, in any trick or device, in any immorality to effect political unity, while at the same time he was to attempt to reform the abuses within the religious establishment in order to regain the respect of the population. The Christian ethic that leaders, like common men, must conform to a uniform moral code is replaced in favor of the Roman principle that any act to create or to preserve the existence of the state is justified, while the main function of the Holy See is to provide a focal point of political power for wordly ends.

Neither Medici pope was to achieve this hoped-for result, not because either had any scruples or foresaw any moral difficulties, but only because their goals and their means were too limited. They were more concerned with the Romagna, Umbria, and Tuscany than with Italy as a whole, more interested in fostering art than church reform. So while each state, including that of the papacy, was selfishly pursuing its own private, limited ends, the matter was taken out of Italian hands and the unification of the peninsula was accomplished by Spanish power.

Thus, to the shambles in which the Catholic Church had fallen was added the ruin of many of the Italian temporal regimes. Small wonder that serious doubt arose in Italy in the 16th century about Renaissance man's ability to work out his destiny, and about the real merits of Italian civilization, or that a lack of confidence and a certain skepticism gripped the intellectuals and the artists.

In Tuscany, the Medici were restored to power, first in the person of Alessandro, who was named duke of Florence, and then after his assassination in 1537 in the person of his cousin, Cosimo, the closest male relative. The latter, whose immediate descendants were to rule that state for over two hundred years, fulfilled many of Machiavelli's requirements for a strong leader, though not on a national scale as he had hoped, and dependent, in the last analysis, on the power of Spain. On Cosimo's assumption of power in 1537, he set about to establish his regime in accordance with the principles set forth by Machiavelli—namely, that any act, moral or immoral, was justified to preserve and strengthen his power over the state. His enemies were exiled or killed, no republican institutions of any kind were permitted to usurp even a fraction of his total sovereignty, and the rights of citizens, high and low, were defined and limited strictly within his sway and pleasure. He ruled with an iron hand and once and for all consolidated the state of Tuscany into an obedient, integrated entity, an important addition to which was accomplished by his forceful incorporation of Siena and its territories in 1556. His title Cosimo I, grand duke of Tuscany, dates from this time.

Even Cosimo's predecessor, Alessandro, had commenced the process of isolating himself from the people. His residence in the Medici Palace was no longer open to the citizens, but instead his household was turned into a ducal court and the building was surrounded by armed retainers. He also commenced the building of an immense fortress adjoining the city wall on the north to quarter his soldiery, its purpose more to insure internal security than to bolster the defenses against attack from without. It survives intact today and is known as the Fortezza da Basso, or lower fort, to distinguish it from another one built a few years later by Cosimo's son on the other side of the Arno on the hill of San Giorgio and called the Fortezza del Belvedere (now a spectacular viewpoint and museum).

The even more ambitious Cosimo could not content himself long with the Medici Palace on the Via Larga, and shortly after his acquisition of power he determined, so as to emphasize to the citizens that he and the government were synonymous, to make over and enlarge as his official residence the old Palazzo Vecchio itself, the erstwhile seat of the priors and of the republican government. For this purpose, he had the architect Giovanni del Tasso join onto the rear of the palace a large addition on two levels opening off the Hall of the Five Hundred, henceforth known as the State Apartments. Into these he and his family moved a few years later (1540), even though their decorations were incomplete, while his personal bodyguard, the Swiss Lancers, took up their stations around the Piazza della Signoria and in the adjacent loggia henceforth known by the name Loggia dei Lanzi.

The State Apartments are interesting rooms for those who wish to catch the flavor of the new century and to understand the attitude of mind of the new ruler and the artists dependent on him. Gone are pictorial allusions to religious or republican themes. Instead, the walls and ceilings of the rooms are covered with paintings and frescoes dedicated to pagan subjects or commemorating and eulogizing members of the Medici family (Cosimo Pater Patriae, Lorenzo the Magnificent, Leo X, Clement VII, etc.) and depicting their triumphs in the context of Florentine history. These works, together with the many figures and ornamental decor in stucco, the carved and gilded ceilings and doorways, were all devised and executed by the prolific Giorgio Vasari (1511–74) with the help of numerous assistants. The paintings themselves, though uniformly mediocre or worse, are of historical and human interest. They also illustrate the direction in which the arts had been moving in Florence for about a generation, away from quattrocento realism toward what later critics were to label as Mannerism—a stylistic link between the art of the High Renaissance and the Baroque.

Mannerism has been defined by contrasting to the conscious, objective harmony and logic of the classical tradition and the careful study of nature, its propensity toward the subjective, the artificial, the exaggerated. The style was prompted by political and religious tensions and by Michelangelo's works of genius, which his contemporaries were unable to surpass. Its first practitioners, the Florentine artists maturing after the turn of the century, were disturbed by the disquieting events of the age and became introspective and emotional. In sculpture, this expressed itself in affected, contorted poses, disproportionate parts (for example, the heads), and the elongation of forms (necks and hands). These characteristics also appeared in painting, and compositions became stylized and dramatic, draperies complicated and unnatural, color harsh. Two main currents, often contradictory, developed in pictorial art, one anticlassical and emotional, giving vent to the tension of the times; the other academic and elegant, seemingly having mastered that tension, but both somewhat contrived or "mannered." A number of paintings in the Uffizi provide good examples of these two trends: the former in the *Moses* of Rosso Fiorentino showing clearly

Michelangelo's influence, and also in *The Supper at Emmaus* by Andrea del Sarto's pupil Pontormo, both executed as early as the 1520s; the latter trend in Parmigianino's *Madonna with the Long Neck* of 1535 with its elegant, elongated figures and forms (including a purposeless row of columns behind) and in Bronzino's many portraits overly concerned with pose and courtly bearing, his subjects appearing coldly unreal and remote from the flesh-and-blood people they portray.

All in all, the Mannerist painters disregarded their predecessors' attempts to produce an ever more objective perfection in their work, in favor of their own more personal, subjective interpretation. That is, the accepted "rules" regarding light, anatomy, color, and composition are exaggerated either by their free interpretation or by a too strict or academic adherence to form rather than substance. Art was thus turning toward a more sophisticated audience, and the style quickly spread to all the courts of Europe.

In any case, Vasari became Cosimo's official court painter and architect and proceeded gradually to transform the interior of almost the entire Palazzo Vecchio into the condition in which we now find it. He also took charge of completely redecorating the great Hall of the Five Hundred, which he transformed into an audience and reception hall for the duke. The vast cycle of frescoes on the walls represents Florentine military victories (against Pisa, Siena, etc.) and triumphant moments of Cosimo's reign and, on the vast ceiling, more of the same together with representations of the various cities and dependencies of the duchy.*

Finally, even the oldest part of the palace, the rooms facing the piazza, which had previously been occupied by the Signoria, were taken in hand by Vasari and redone for Duke Cosimo's wife, Eleonora of Toledo (he, like his cousin Alessandro, had also taken a royal Spanish wife) whose name they bear. They include (in order) a vestibule and private chapel (with paintings by

* Vasari's greatest achievements were not his art works but his writings. His *Ragionamenti* explains in detail the content and background of the many subjects and incidents he depicted in the frescoes of the Palazzo Vecchio, while his *Lives of the Artists*, his masterpiece, is probably the single most valuable source for our knowledge of his recent contemporaries.

Bronzino), a reception room for the ladies of the court, a dining room, a work room, and lastly Eleonora's private chamber. But the most artistic rooms in the entire palace are on the floor just below, two small retreats built for the duke and his son, Francesco, called the Studiolo (de Francesco) and the Tesoretto (de Cosimo). Both were designed by Vasari but owe much of their perfection to other Mannerist artists who created the many small pictures and sculptures: Bronzino, Giambologna, Ammannati. The former room, a study shaped like a jewel casket, records on its walls such subjects dear to the age (and the Medici) as the progress of science and industry and episodes from Greek mythology, as well as two outstanding portraits of the duke and his wife by Bronzino. The latter room, a treasury for precious objects that were locked away in the carved cabinets, has frescoes illustrating the fine arts.

At about the same time (1560–70), Vasari was busy demolishing some older buildings between the Palazzo Vecchio and the river and constructing his architectural masterpiece, the Fabbrica dei Magistrati (Building of the Magistrates), soon known as the Uffizi (offices), as it was built for the purpose of concentrating the city's administrative and judicial officials, recently cleared out of the Palazzo Vecchio, under one roof, easily accessible to the duke. In a narrow, crowded area Vasari determined not to build a solid overpowering pile, but rather ingeniously to open up the space by means of a long scenographic esplanade formed by the two matching façades of the new structure, thus forging a link between the piazza and the Arno, which can be seen through the great arch at the far end that connects the two parts of the building. Vasari drew on ideas from Michelangelo, but the final design, with its columns and statues in niches along the ground floor and its light elegant upper stories, is most original and one of the period's greatest architectural achievements.

From the beginning, the building also housed parts of the duke's archives and collections and was soon occupied by his goldsmiths, silversmiths, and craftsmen in porcelain and mosaic. The most impressive part, the *galleria* forming the topmost floor, is mainly the work of Vasari's successor, Bernardo Buontalenti, who transformed (1574) the loggia into the magnificent frescoed display we see today and built the octagonal *tribuna* and adjoining rooms where the nucleus of the Medici collections was soon

The Studiolo in the Palazzo Vecchio decorated by Mannerist artists and including a portrait of Duke Cosimo I by Bronzino (1570).

The two matching wings of the Uffizi, designed by Vasari (1560–
70), which leads from the Arno to the Palazzo Vecchio.

The Galleria of the Uffizi, designed by Buontalenti in 1574 for the display of the Medici collections.

arranged. Here, for the first time, an architect consciously set about creating a place to display art, not in the random way princes had done before, but with an organic unity and purpose. There seems to have been an implicit recognition that the Florentine Renaissance had reached its peak and that it was time to turn and contemplate its past achievements. Further, the collections could be utilized to educate the public (which was admitted) and to increase the prestige of the government.

In line with this self-conscious awareness of the importance of the arts, these same years saw the founding in 1562 under the sponsorship of the duke and the guidance of Vasari of the Accademia delle Belle Arti (Academy of Fine Arts) composed of some sixty Florentine artists with Michelangelo as its honorary head (he was in Rome at the time and died two years later). Henceforth the Accademia crystallized the direction in which art in Florence had been moving for some time—the trend and developing style of Mannerism.

Only Michelangelo, independent as always, failed to conform to the movement he had started. In particular, he refused to concern himself with the subject matter of literary symbolism—allegorical or rhetorical figures representing human sins and virtues, so dear to Vasari and his followers—and, while the younger artists continued to paint hundreds of religious subjects minus any religious feeling or fervor, the older master underwent a true reconversion to the faith and rededicated his efforts to convey the inner meaning—not the externals—of man's ideal objective, the salvation of his soul. This is vividly apparent in all the works of his later years, a good example of which is his last work in sculpture, a Deposition, known as the Florentine Pietà, now in the Duomo. Michelangelo worked on it off and on almost to his death in 1564, but, dissatisfied, left it unfinished. Later on, a follower attempted to complete the figure of Mary Magdalen on the left but only isolated it from the rest of the composition. There is no question of the sincere religious content of the group, and the agony of the moment is expressed both in the angular, twisted body of Christ and in the sad, compassionate countenance of Nicodemus (actually a self portrait of Michelangelo) supporting the body from above.

(*left*) Michelangelo's last work in sculpture, the *Florentine Pietà*.
(*right*) Giambologna's Mannerist statue, *The Rape of the Sabines* (1583).

As for the rest, sculpture followed painting, and effect became more important than content. A message was no longer implicit in the artists' work, but "art for art's sake" sufficed. Bartolomeo Ammannati's Neptune fountain in the Piazza della Signoria was put together during those years (1560–75), and though the awkward central figure was a failure by the artist's own admission, the surrounding, supporting elements—the nymphs and satyrs—are wonderful examples of the Mannerist style. So, too, are Cellini's *Perseus* (1553) and Giambologna's spiral group of three figures, *The Rape of the Sabines* (1583), now under the Loggia dei Lanzi. Both are superb creations of artistic virtuosity but, lacking any real human rapport, do not attempt any religious, moral, or political communication. The conservative understatement and compactness of the Renaissance period have been replaced by dramatization and conflict, implicit in the outstretched arms. The *Perseus*, though still retaining the superb realism of the High Renaissance, also conveys the same cold remoteness of a Bronzino portrait and includes a number of Mannerist characteristics: the bizarre helmet, the writhing hair and dripping blood of Medusa's head; while the overadorned base with its small statuettes in distorted poses and with mannered gestures is an excuse for the display of technical skill, a characteristic also found in the architecture of the time. Like sculpture, it tended to subordinate logic and simplicity to decorative effect, as for example Vasari's freely mixed use of architectural elements in his design for the Uffizi and in the concurrent remodeling of the Palazzo Pitti.

Cosimo and Eleonora, having decided that the Palazzo Vecchio was too confining for both courtly residence and seat of government, purchased the Pitti Palace and engaged Ammannati to enlarge and redecorate it for the accommodation of the royal household. He accordingly set about closing up the arches on the ground floor with Michelangelesque windows, reconstituting the interior and building two massive wings to the rear and the courtyard between (finished in the 1560s). The visual effect of these extensions from a distance is better than up close, but the exaggerated overlay of banded patterns in rough stone (much of which was quarried on the spot) masks the essentials of the architecture. The intention, however, was that the rear of the palace, and

(*left*) Giambologna's *St. Luke* at Orsanmichele displaying the Mannerist pose. (*right*) Cellini's official portrait bust of the all-powerful grand duke, Cosimo I. (*below*) Rear wings and court-yard of the Palazzo Pitti by Ammannati and the amphitheater of the Boboli Gardens.

especially the courtyard, should serve as a monumental backdrop for the amphitheater and the terraces above, also being laid out at this time by Ammannati and his successor, Buontalenti—the beginnings of the famous Boboli Gardens—and where from Cosimo's time onward were held elaborate open-air musicals and theatrical spectacles, royal weddings, tournaments, jousts, and masked balls, which drew the attention of all Europe.

The surrounding gardens with their grottos, pools, fountains, statues, and carefully placed paths and trees gradually assumed over the next century the shapes we see today, while at the same time the palace was twice widened to its present size. Inside went on a continuous program of building stairways and halls and adorning them with elaborate stuccos and frescoed ceilings some of which, by Pietro da Cortona (1596–1669) and Volterrano (1611–89), with their highly original illusions of space and light and soaring architecture, seem literally to burst the confining limits of the rooms themselves. Finally, the last major feature, the frontal wings extending down to the street with their enormous stone blocks, rivaling those piled up by the Etruscans in earlier times, were added, it is said, not only for appearance' sake but to stabilize the huge building and prevent it from slipping down the hill.

To Vasari credit is also due for the ingenious corridor linking the offices of the city administration in the Uffizi with the new residence of Duke Cosimo in the Pitti Palace. This he constructed in the year 1566 over the top of the shops on the Ponte Vecchio and then through and behind the various buildings on the Via Guicciardini, so that the duke would not have to go down into the streets but could walk back and forth at his pleasure. The shops on the bridge had for years been occupied by the city's butchers, but as the odoriferous nature of their trade was apparently not pleasing to the duke, they were relegated to other quarters and the shops henceforth, as they are today, were rented only to goldsmiths and jewelers.

Those same years (1566–69) saw the complete rebuilding of the next bridge downstream, the Ponte Santa Trinita, by Ammannati (probably on a sketch idea by Michelangelo), who produced in this famous landmark one of the most graceful bridges in the world. Ordered specifically by Cosimo—the marble scrolls on the

The Santa Trinita bridge by Ammannati (1566–69) looking toward Oltrarno.

arches honor him—to replace an earlier span swept away by flood, it was to be not just a means of crossing the river, but an embellishment to the city at the most central crossing point of the Arno and a suitable link between the two palace-lined streets of Via Tornabuoni and Via Maggio. The resulting bridge with the unique curve of its three delicate arches is a masterpiece of design and strength. The peculiarity of its curve has in fact intrigued engineers for centuries, and numerous attempts have been made to reduce it to some regular geometric formula, without success. It has therefore been concluded that Ammannati simply established the basic requirements—number of arches, height and breadth of span, need for maximum opening to accommodate the Arno in flood, etc.—and then drew the curve freehand. The result was not only beautiful but daring, having a much longer and flatter leap from pier to pier than most previous bridges (the ratio is 7 to 1 of width to height as opposed to what had been the customary 3 or 4 to 1) and its stability was accordingly questioned. But in fact it proved sturdy enough, withstanding centuries of traffic and periodic floods right up to its destruction by the Germans in 1944.

Altogether, Cosimo's reign was dynamic and purposeful, though for his enemies also cruel and unmerciful, and if the people lost what liberty they had retained under his forbears, at least they enjoyed the benefits of his constructive dictatorship. He did what he could to encourage industry in a lagging economy, built much-needed roads, drained marshes, established schools, academies, and experimental botanical gardens at Pisa and Siena as well as at Florence, and began the conversion of Leghorn into a seaport and Portoferraio into a naval base. He drew up a new criminal code for Tuscany, and the laws he promulgated were considered just. Though dependent on the Spanish crown (Spain maintained armed strongpoints in Tuscany as well as other parts of Italy), he tried diligently to retain some independence of action. Fortresses were built, and he created a permanent army. He also began the formation of a navy and established for its financial support and esprit de corps an honorary naval order with religious trappings called the Knights of Santo Stefano (1562). The navy was successfully used, in cooperation with the papal and other Italian states, to clear the Mediterranean of the Turks and the Barbary pirates, while the Order of Santo Stefano flattered the vanity of those upper classes who, no longer involved in trade or industry and eager for ducal recognition and titular dignity, were invited to join.

The gradual redirection of trading activity toward the Atlantic and the contraction of Italian participation had caused much of Florentine family wealth to flow into the enlargement and improvement of agricultural landholdings and country villas, which also served as more suitable bases for aristocratic life and pretentions. In this context and with other devices, there rapidly developed a royal court, itself the logical outcome of the dynastic ambitions of the Medici from Lorenzo on. Inevitably, Cosimo found himself progressively removed from any genuine contact with the people, and he lived and worked surrounded by his military and civil officials, a few favorite artists and architects, and his ever-present bodyguard. But after a reign of 37 years, the regime was very solidly established by the time of Cosimo's death in 1574, so that despite the weakness and political incompetence of his first successor, his eldest son, Francesco, no change occurred in the nature of the Tuscan constitution. Francesco, caring little for government, spent most of his attention on matters of art and science and, though married to a niece of Emperor Charles V, spent most of his time with Bianca Cappello, for long his mistress and later, after the death of the grand duchess, his second wife. (The palace provided for Bianca, with a secret underground passageway to the Pitti, may be seen at Via Maggio, No. 26.)

Francesco died in 1587 without male heirs, so it was his brother, Ferdinando, who succeeded him and who, more like their father Cosimo, soon had all the reins of government firmly in hand. Popular, capable, and ambitious, Ferdinando undertook numerous large-scale projects, completing the port of Leghorn and building up his navy under the auspices of the Order of Santo Stefano. He tried to govern sensibly, restrain the excesses of the clergy, and become less dependent on Spain—he married Christine of Lorraine, a French rather than Spanish royal princess. He, too, was interested in the arts. He collected many fine classical pieces, including *The Wrestlers* and *The Knife-Grinder*, now in the Tribune of the Uffizi, and he commenced in 1604 the building of the family mausoleum, the Chapel of the Princes behind San Lorenzo, an example of Florentine Baroque. To accomplish the interior decoration of this ambitious project there was founded the Manufactory of Pietra Dura, a school and factory for the designing and cutting of marble and rare stones, still in existence. All of the grand dukes, their wives and children have been buried in the mausoleum, whose vast walls are entirely covered in marble and whose interior is today regarded as cold and overdone, though noteworthy for the scope and technical skill entailed, to say nothing of the expense. Easier to admire, however, are other products of this technique of inlaying marble, which has become a Florentine specialty—art objects of intarsia on a smaller scale, especially a number of remarkable tables on display in the Pitti.

Ferdinando also encouraged experiment and innovation in music and science. The opera—the combining of a continuous musical score, not just musical interludes, with a stage play—was invented in Florence and first sung before the royal court in

(*above*) The Tribune of the Uffizi, where the choicest pieces of the Medici collections have long been displayed, including (from *left* to *right*) *The Wrestlers*, *The Medici Venus*, and *The Knife-Grinder*. (*below left*) The marble-encrusted interior of the Princes' Chapel (early 1600s). (*right*) The 17th-century façade of Ognissanti, an example of Florentine Baroque.

1597, while under Ferdinando's auspices and protection (and that of his son) Galileo carried out much of his work.

Near the end of the 16th century, to commemorate his reign and that of his father, whose character and achievements he emulated, Ferdinando commissioned Giambologna to design and cast two imposing equestrian statues, one of Cosimo, which was set up in the Piazza della Signoria, and the other of himself, assigned to the Piazza Santissima Annunziata. In earlier times, such monuments were unheard of in republican Florence, implying as they did aristocratic rank and tyrannical power. But times had changed. On the pedestal of the former were placed bronze reliefs representing the most important moments in the reign of Cosimo I: (1) his acceptance as ducal successor by the Florentines, (2) his triumphal entry into Siena, and (3) the culminating glory, the ceremony bestowing on him the title of grand duke of Tuscany. On the pedestal of Ferdinando's statue may be seen his private crest and device—a swarm of bees—symbolizing what he hoped would be his well-ordered subjects gathering wealth as bees do honey.

Unfortunately, this optimistic forecast perished with Ferdinando's death (1609), for the history of Tuscany and of the later Medici who followed his rule is one of continuous, if gradual, exhaustion and decay. Throughout the 17th and into the 18th century, Ferdinando's son, grandson, and greatgrandson (Cosimo II died in 1620, Ferdinando II in 1670, Cosimo III in 1723) struggled to carry on the Medici tradition of leadership but, owing to external forces beyond their control and even more to weaknesses of character and mistaken policies, were largely responsible for the impoverishment and decadence of the state.

The Long Quiescence: 1600 to 1860

The pattern of development was quickly set during the short reign of Cosimo II (he died at 31), who, not well in body or mind, permitted his superstitious mother and wife, both completely under the insidious influence of corrupt clergy and scheming courtiers, to dictate everything that passed for government policy, even the arrangement in his will that they should continue to dominate the state during the minority of his son, Ferdinando

II, who succeeded him. It is significant that the once powerful Medici bank was closed during this time, no longer prosperous and no longer a suitable connection for a prince.

On the surface, it seemed for a time that the new reign of Ferdinando II might be happy. Tournaments, jousts, and musical pageants repeatedly filled the piazzas of Florence and the gardens behind the Pitti, and a shrewd marriage was arranged for the young prince with Vittoria of the Della Rovere, the only surviving heir of the dukes of Urbino. Though as it turned out, due to the pope's intransigence, she was unable to retain title to the duchy itself, she at least brought all of that family's personal possessions, including a fabulous collection of paintings to augment that of the Medici—for example, Titian's *Reclining Venus* in the Uffizi and Raphael's portrait of Pope Julius II in the Pitti. Many of the rooms in the Pitti and in the various royal villas were frescoed during this period, often illustrating mythological or dynastic themes in an amazingly deceptive and clever way, creating the illusion of fantastic, elaborate architectural and sculptural forms. Also, another new academy was founded (1657) —the Accademia del Cimento (Academy of Tests or Experiments) —Europe's first scientific institution dedicated to testing by experiment physical principles and theories and their practical application.

Throughout the quattrocento and the cinquecento, progress had been made in various scientific fields, as the hampering prejudices from the Middle Ages were gradually left behind. The ancient writers had been studied, their theories elaborated upon and later challenged. Medicine, for example, and particularly anatomy, came to rest more on observable phenomena, such as through dissection, rather than on the specious theories of Hippocrates or Galen or on superstitions.* Similarly, chemistry was separated from alchemy and astronomy from astrology. But it was not until the Florentine Galileo Galilei (1564–1642) that science can be said to have entered its modern phase, when for the first time a scientist adopted within his speciality—in Galileo's case, physics and astronomy—systematic, thorough methods of

---

* The sickness known as influenza, for instance, was so called from the belief that it was caused by the influence (*influenza* in Italian) of an unsatisfactory conjunction of the planets.

One of the deceptively painted 17th-century ceilings in the
Museo degli Argenti of the Palazzo Pitti.

experiment, observation, presentation of data, and deductive
conclusions. In this way, while under the patronage and
encouragement of the Medici grand dukes, he made his greatest
contributions to scientific knowledge, namely, the proof of
Copernicus' theory of the solar system and his formulation of the
laws of motion.

Ferdinando II's reign also saw the construction of a new type
of theater, in the structural sense, which became the prototype
of many that were subsequently built throughout Europe.
Called the Pergola, it consisted of tiered rows of boxes in the
shape of a horseshoe facing the stage. It opened in midcentury
and was strongly patronized by the court and the landed aristocracy, now amply supplied with leisure time for the active pursuit
of music and the theater.

But behind the outward show, the extravagance and pomp,
the serious problems of the country were ignored. Other states
now dominated trade and industry, and the wool and silk business
in Tuscany had languished. However, the expenses of the regime

increased, so taxes were raised and raised again, further discouraging commerce and agriculture, in a vicious circle. The clergy, owning much but providing no revenue, controlled the royal family and through them all the offices. The inquisitors of the Counter-Reformation became almost a branch of government, conducting their investigations into every corner of social existence and their trials and tortures with the full support of the ducal court. Religious intolerance and moral strictures increased in severity, and spies were everywhere, until the country's only hope lay in a change of rule. Unfortunately, however, the situation grew even worse under the next duke, Cosimo III. Weighed down by a bitter marriage—his French wife could not stand Tuscany and spent most of her life in Paris—he, too, succumbed to the worst possible advice from the female members of the family and became merely a pawn of the courtiers and clerics who surrounded him. Self-defeating laws further discouraged business, and taxes became intolerable. Every transaction, no matter how trivial, every commodity passing through the markets, must bear a tax—various percentages of the proceeds of every real estate sale, of marriage dowries, of court recoveries reverted to the state. A new income tax was imposed, of course excluding the clergy, but its enforcement was difficult because it was so tenaciously resisted. Certain industries were brought under the monopolistic control of a few families who paid enormous sums to the grand duke for the privilege, and violators of these regulations were regularly condemned to the galleys. Punishments became more severe and frequent, and the death penalty was often imposed—as many as six prisoners a day were executed in the Bargello during 1683.

Beggars were everywhere, and the populace suffered recurrent plagues and famines. Some land in the *contado* ceased to be worked, brigandage increased, and bread riots occurred. The population of Pisa, Siena, and other cities gradually declined—that of Florence dropped to 50,000; grass grew in many streets, and some palaces fell empty and were closed up.

Much of the state revenue was funneled into the improvement and maintenance of the vast Medici properties, especially, in addition to the Pitti, the many villas kept by the family for purposes of formal entertainment or to which the court repaired at different seasons for sport or other country pleasures.* Cosimo III's two sons and his brother, the cardinal, also spent money hand over fist, each maintaining his own retinue and adherents, traveling from city to city when they were not moving from villa to villa. Another part of state revenues was diverted into the coffers of one or another favorite monastery or church, evidence of which may be seen in the numerous 17th century embellishments—ceilings, altars, paintings—scattered throughout the city. There are not, however, many important structural landmarks of note in Florence from this period, and the city accepted only a small fraction of the Baroque style, emanating from Rome, that was so enthusiastically adopted by the rest of Italy and all Catholic Europe during the Counter-Reformation. For example, during the 17th century, while Rome was building so many of its magnificent fountains, practically none appeared in Florence. Apparently the flowing, gushing nature of water, which so well complements the many swelling Baroque basins, pools, and fountains in Rome that contain or channel it, ran contrary to the Florentine character, which has been called miserly, hard, and too practical for aquatic luxuries, and to a city that to this day still relies on an antiquated, inadequate water system.

Two church façades from the first part of the century, one applied to the front of Santa Trinita by Buontalenti, and another —more successful—built onto the front of the church of Ognissanti by his pupil Matteo Nigetti, illustrate the restrained use of the new Baroque style in Florence. The latter façade especially, with its regular, strict balance, its rather sober articulation and its modest use of embellishment, contains little of the true spirit of Roman Baroque architecture with its liquid, unfolding quality, its expressive energy and exuberance. Nor does it have any of that theatrical illusionism that reaches out to embrace the viewer or the space around it—almost a definition of the Baroque. Even so, when the façade was unveiled, the Florentines severely criticized Nigetti for his innovations.

Practically nothing is left of the original monastic building of Ognissanti with the exception of the 13th-century campanile.

* Poggio Imperiale, Poggio a Caiano, Pratolino, Lapeggi, Castello, Petraia, Artimino.

The cloister was built in the quattrocento, and the interior of the church itself was completely remodeled in the cinquecento by Vasari and again in the seicento. It is interesting to note, however, that in the latter years the church and monastery passed by ducal command from the long custody of the Umilati to that of the Franciscans—from the productive weavers of wool to the non-productive mendicants—symptomatic of the declining cloth trade and the condition of Florence.

Nearby, on the Arno, is a secular example of 17th century Florentine architecture, the impressive Palazzo Corsini, built between 1649 and 1656. This is the logical and ultimate development of the Florentine palazzo, having progressed from the crude, vertical, fortresslike tower houses, through the logically proportioned cubical shapes of the Renaissance period, down to this commodious, more open building strung out on a horizontal line along the river. Its features are elegant and restrained, the walls flat, the fenestration regular, and its decor simplified. There are few signs of Baroque convolutions or sculptural effects,

The conservative exterior of the Palazzo Corsini (1649–56) conceals a more elaborate interior and a large private collection of art.

though the balustrades, rows of statues along the roof, and the detailing of the windows indicate the era. Here again, as in the church of San Frediano across the river, built a few years later, with its arresting and distinctive little cupola, is a reminder of how little headway the full Baroque style made in Florence without first being filtered through the traditional Tuscan reserve.

There is, however, at least one partial exception in Florence: the interior of the sumptuous church and monastery of Santissima Annunziata (Most Holy Annunciation), on the piazza of that name, but even this cannot compare with the full exploitation of the style in Rome and elsewhere.

The history of the Annunziata goes back to the 1200s, when a religious brotherhood of Florentine origin, the Servitors of Mary, established an oratory to her honor in the open fields outside the second circuit of walls. An idea of what this modest original structure looked like may be had from two views carved on a funeral monument dating from that time and still preserved in the cloisters. Also in the 1200s, according to tradition, a fresco of the Annunciation was painted for the church which, like the holy picture at Orsanmichele, acquired a reputation for performing miracles and a tremendous following among the people. The cult of the Virgin, and the countless paintings it inspired, was especially prevalent in Tuscany during the duecento as Mary represented the ideals of humility, peace, and trust during a time of excessive ambition, conflict, and suspicion between citizens and communes. The episode of the Annunciation in particular held a strong appeal, promising as it did a new life of hope for all mankind. Here, amid the thousands of votive offerings and candles, and in the presence of the miraculous fresco, the pilgrims to the Virgin's shrine could lose themselves in prayer.

The church was several times enlarged during the following centuries to accommodate the throngs that worshipped there, especially on the feast days of the Virgin, and the monastery buildings were continually added to. In the 1400s, the whole complex took on its present structural form under the direction of Michelozzo, Alberti, and others whose architectural ideas can be seen in the cloisters and in the shape of the round-domed tribune, or choir, behind the main altar, designed to implement architectural theories based on the centralized plan. Subsequently, the portico outside in front and the arcading opposite the Foundling Hospital were built to continue the theme laid down by Brunelleschi, so creating the most pleasing piazza in Florence. But the impression one takes away of the church itself is of quite a different nature. Inside, every square inch of surface has been overlaid with an unbelievably rich display of colored marbles and ornament—stuccos, paintings, sculptures, and gildings in extravagant profusion, including a remarkable ceiling by Volterrano. Most of this work, and especially the overall effect, belongs to the 17th century when the Baroque was in full swing, and is a good example of that style's special emphasis on integrating as many art forms as possible—painting and gilding, carving and mosaic, precious metal work, *pietra dura*, stucco—with the overall architectural theme in one momentous visual experience. The whole ensemble, though somewhat overawing at first sight, is worth pursuing in some detail, as here can be found examples of work of the city's greatest artists, ranging from the central current of the Florentine Renaissance through its last phases into Mannerism and the Baroque.

The entrance cloister was mostly frescoed in the early 1500s by artist members of the Company of St. Luke, a confraternity of painters (Andrea del Sarto, Pontormo, Rosso Fiorentino, Franciabigio), hinting at the beginning of Mannerism, while inside the church are works by Andrea del Castagno, Bernardo Rossellino, Andrea del Sarto, Bronzino, Baccio Bandinelli, Giambologna, and Francavilla illustrating the progress of painting and sculpture through the late quattrocento and cinquecento.* But the great mass of frescoes and decorative work giving the church its Baroque character dates from the 1600s.

The Chapel of the Madonna, which enshrines the sacred fresco of the Annunciation, combines elements from several epochs. The general design, consisting of four Corinthian columns holding up an especially beautiful, massive entablature carved with festooned leaves and the Medici arms (it was commissioned

* A number of the members of the Order of St. Luke (Pontormo, Pietro Tacca, Franciabigio, Vasari, Cellini, Andrea del Sarto, Bandinelli, Giambologna) are buried in the Annunziata or in the Company's small chapel off the cloister.

The Chapel of the Madonna in Santissima Annunziata, the
most sumptuous shrine in Florence.

by Cosimo Pater Patriae's son Piero) and surrounded by a bronze grill, is by Michelozzo (1448), carried out by Pagno Portigiani and others. The silver altar, angels, and screen over the fresco—uncovered only on special occasions—the votive candelabra and other furnishings, and the florid cupola erupting above the entablature (by Volterrano) are all of the 1600s—an example of the Baroque literally swelling out of and enveloping the Renaissance.

The Annunziata long enjoyed the patronage of the grand dukes, who commissioned many of its works and saw to the lavish adornment of walls and floors with porphyry, jasper, and other marbles. They often attended services there, watching in private from behind a grating called the Prince's Window high in the nave.

In addition to receiving financial and political support from the Tuscan government, the church establishment, and especially the monastic orders, enjoyed almost complete control over education. As a result, and because employment opportunities were scarce, many youths inevitably entered monasteries and convents until their numbers became an additional heavy burden on the rest of the population. In spite, therefore, of the continual search for new revenues, the tremendous expenses of the court and church establishment required frugality elsewhere. As an instance, the army and navy dwindled to a fraction of their former strength and were poorly equipped and dispirited. Many of the forts, falling into ruin, were unmanned and useless. The Fortezza da Basso in Florence, the third largest after those in Leghorn and Portoferraio, had a garrison of only 100 men by the end of the 17th century. The nation's weaknesses—economic, financial, military—were no secret, and the store of respect and consideration once shown by other rulers, which had been accumulated by Cosimo I, was gradually dissipated. Only with the pope's assistance and by continually placating the other powers—siding alternately with Spain, France, or the emperor, depending on who at the moment seemed stronger—was Tuscany able to remain independent of direct foreign intervention.

Such was the state of Tuscany when Cosimo III died in 1723 and his surviving son, Gian Gastone, and daughter, Anna Maria, the last generation of the Medici, prepared to play out their final roles. Neither of them had heirs, and the problem of succession had long been anticipated by their father. Much discussion and correspondence between the rulers of Europe centered on this problem, and many solutions were considered. The emperor claimed that Tuscany, or at least part of it, had long been an imperial fief and that Alessandro de' Medici had been named duke by the Emperor Charles V; but France and Spain, too, had claims. Some thought that sovereignty should return to the citizens, since Cosimo I and his line had been selected by the Florentines (though admittedly with the emperor's approval) and the present title of grand duke was first conferred by the pope. Cosimo III tried for general agreement on several solutions, but without success, and at the time of his death the question remained unanswered, though by then it was effectively out of the Medici's hands. Tuscany had become a mere bargaining counter between the larger powers.

Gian Gastone, already dissipated and broken in spirit, succeeded to the grand dukedom at the age of 52. For a time, he tried to correct some of the worst mistakes of his predecessors, relieving the tax burden, demoting some clerics, disbanding the spy network, and freeing political and religious prisoners. He also suspended the death penalty, protected certain scholars, and tried to separate the functions of church and state. But his good intentions were short lived, and, depressed by the inconsequence with which he and Tuscany were treated by the powers and by a most unfortunate marriage (his wife, like his mother, hated Florence and would never live there), he soon succumbed to a degenerate, hopeless existence, confined behind the walls of the Pitti. Years went by without his appearing in public, and then he would show himself, drunken and disheveled, only to still the rumors of his demise. Finally, he took to his bed, where he remained the last years of his life, dying in 1737.

In the meantime, it had been finally decided the year before, by Spain, France, England, and Austria at the Peace of Vienna, that Tuscany should revert to Imperial Austria in the person of Francis of Lorraine (married to Maria Theresa, the daughter of the emperor, and destined to succeed his father-in-law), in return for which he was to cede the territories of Lorraine to France while Spain received other concessions. These exchanges took place on Gian Gastone's death, Austrian troops replacing the Spanish garrisons previously stationed on Tuscan soil, and the new grand duke, henceforth styled Francesco II, formally entered Florence. He did so after passing through an arch of triumph hastily built in his honor and still standing in the Piazza della Libertà. Of no particular merit, it is one of the few examples in Florence of the neoclassical style, which, like the Baroque style before it, never really caught on. Preferring to return to his wife and the court life in Vienna, the new grand duke remained in Florence only about a month, and he ruled Tuscany through an agent who took up residence in the Pitti. The Medici, however, were not quite finished, for Gian Gastone's sister Anna Maria lived on in a separate part of the palace, disdaining any relationship with the Austrians, continuing to maintain herself in the elaborate style that had become synonymous with the name Medici, and continually adding to the family's collections— many of the Flemish and German paintings were acquired by her.

But the most important act of her life, and one that by itself almost redeemed all the failings of her immediate ancestors, was the provision in her final testament leaving in perpetuity all of her family's private property to the city of Florence for the benefit of the people of all nations, with the understanding that none of it was ever to be removed therefrom. Though she was helpless to dispose of the sovereignty or the government of the state or the succession, she left to the people everything else that the Medici had acquired over the centuries: the palaces, the villas, the family chapels and burial places, including the contents of the New Sacristy at San Lorenzo, the libraries, the tapestries, the collections of Etruscan and classical antiquities, the silver and gold work, maiolica, armor, bronzes, ivories, rare gems and stonework, the coins and medals once belonging to Lorenzo the Magnificent, the furniture and plates, and, most important, the statues and paintings. So while other dynasties and other cities (Ferrara, Mantua, Modena, etc.) saw their treasures dispersed, Florence was fortunate to retain everything both intact and accessible.

The arrangement that turned the Tuscan grand duchy over to the Austrian Empire, much as if it were no more than part of any large real estate transaction and which took no account whatever of the opinion of the people, did not endear the new regime to the Florentines. They, of course, had had little if any confidence or respect for the last of the Medici, but they had become accustomed to their peculiarities and even sympathetic to their all-too-obvious weaknesses and sufferings. In addition, whatever hopes had been entertained for an improvement in the decadent condition of the realm were soon dashed when it became evident that the new grand duke would never live in Tuscany and would take practically no interest in its innumerable problems. It was therefore not until 1765, when Francis became emperor and his brother Leopold assumed the dukedom, that a change for the better at last occurred in what had seemed a hopeless situation. Not only did Leopold take up permanent residence in Florence but he began a series of overdue and much needed reforms that were soon to earn him the deepest respect of all the citizens. Antiquated and harsh laws were repealed, the death penalty was abolished, and the Inquisition was curbed. Sorely needed hospitals were founded, and what was left of commercial trade was relieved of restrictive taxes. Most important, agriculture, for long the main surviving base of the economy, was freed from internal customs barriers, and surviving feudal inequities were removed. Also large-scale land reclamation projects were successfully undertaken.

But in 1790, Leopold was called to mount the imperial throne, and the succession to the duchy passed to his son Ferdinand III, who quickly revealed his inability to continue and build upon the progress already made. The changes his father had instigated had eased the worst burdens, but Tuscany still remained relatively backward by comparison to other countries. Industry, except for handicrafts, hardly existed, and the upper class almost without exception devoted full time to the management and improvement of their farming estates.

In the meantime, the great Florentine artistic tradition had completely withered away. A few examples of late Florentine Baroque architecture or the Florentine adaptation of the French neoclassical style may be found here and there, but they are not important; and the same can be said of painting and sculpture. Instead of encouraging anything new, the court was more than

One of the rooms in the Palazzo Pitti, almost unchanged from
the time when occupied by the grand dukes.

content to enjoy the vast collections of art already at hand. In
the Palazzo Pitti, much attention was devoted to arranging and
rearranging the many paintings that now hung from ceiling to
floor, the criterion for each picture's exact placement often
depending on the freshness of the gilding on its elaborate frame
or on the requirement that no portrait might turn its head away
from the throne.

As the 18th century closed, Italy was invaded by the armies of
Napoleon, and Tuscany, among other states, became an appen-
dage of the French Empire from 1799 to Napoleon's fall in 1814.
In that year, the Austrians returned, and the succession was
restored first in the person of Ferdinand III and then in that of his
successor, Leopold II. The second Leopold, like the first, was
reform minded, and he accepted a number of progressive changes
made during the French occupation. Moreover, he did nothing
to suppress the residue of liberal ideas they left behind which were
later to precipitate the demands for reform that preceded the
Risorgimento.

Tourism, interrupted by Napoleon, now got under way again. Throughout the 18th century, Florence had continued to be one of the principal way places on the European Grand Tour. Prices were cheap, and the surrounding countryside, tended by the loving care of both the peasants and their landlords and dotted with villas, was never more beautiful. Roads were everywhere generally improved, and it now became possible for some of the middle class to travel, though on a modest scale compared to the elaborate equipages of the wealthy, whose fancy carriages continued to ply across Europe from the north. The English in particular came well prepared, loaded down with clothing for all seasons and occasions, and with miscellaneous household implements so often lacking in even the best of Italian quarters when a winter's stay was contemplated.

Florence in those days must have been exceptionally agreeable. Tuscany was poor, but there was nothing like the misery and squalor farther south. To encourage travel, customs officials were polite and cooperative. The grand duke was easy of access to foreigners, and invitations to the many official receptions were plentiful. The Cascine, originally a pasturage reserved for the grand duke's herd and later a private royal park, had been opened to the public, and everyone who could afford a carriage was obliged to be seen there. The neoclassicism that had reached the height of its popularity during the time of Napoleon gradually faded into the cult of Romanticism, which expressed itself in Florence in the rediscovery of Gothic architecture and primitive painting. Writers and intellectuals began to give voice to liberal ideals and anti-papal feelings and to stimulate the desire of their fellow citizens for Italian unity. The foreign colony, growing rapidly and deeply involved with the new politics, now not only enjoyed the pleasant surroundings of the city but also had a cause to espouse. The duke himself was generally liked, but the system, completely lacking in any popular representation, was bound to be challenged. The first attempt in 1848 was premature, and though Leopold was forced to leave for a brief period, he returned with Austrian troops, and the revolution collapsed in a shambles.

To prevent a recurrence, he was forced into a reactionary policy, but the more stringent he became, the deeper grew the conviction that mere reform of his government was insufficient and that only through a united Italy could the new ideals be realized. It required just one decade for this to be achieved by the leaders of the Risorgimento, and when Leopold perceived that no alternative existed, he gracefully but sadly departed the Pitti, April 27, 1859, never to return, while the people looked on with mixed emotions. Thus ended after over three hundred years the Tuscan grand duchy, while simultaneously the city of Florence, so long the focal point of a small but distinct territory, found itself cast in a new, unfamiliar role within a much larger state.

For reasons of political compromise, Florence became the temporary capital of Italy. Drastic change was of course inevitable, as a result both of the unification and of the dawning industrial age. Vast properties belonging to the former grand duke, the church, the monasteries, and the aristocracy were taken over and converted to other uses. A large section of the old town center and most of the third circuit of walls were razed to the ground, and new building began on an unprecedented scale. Quite naturally, these wholesale demolitions provoked a reaction, and since then two mutually opposed attitudes of mind concerning the city's development have existed. The one, progressive and forward looking, sought to demolish and rebuild, to clean up and modernize, to leave the past behind and try to catch up with other, more advanced countries. The other attitude, more romantic and nostalgic, sought to slow down change, to preserve and restore, and to hold on to Florence's unique inheritance.

These two approaches can be seen in the city planning and architectural solutions that were carried out in trying to cope with the expansion that soon occurred and that still continues. Architects of a progressive bent, ignoring completely the Tuscan traditions, raised up countless buildings of a "modern" nature— as that term is differently defined with each passing decade— some of it highly original but most of a depressing, nondescript uniformity. Others, more traditional, have sought, with varying success, to retain to one degree or another local characteristics. Romanticism in the 1800s encouraged a rash of pseudo-Gothic buildings and restorations, as well as a number of sham Gothic church façades.* Later, the same motivations led to the indiscriminate borrowing from one or another style of the past, sometimes compounding them in a hybrid mixture to which has been given the name Eclecticism. Such products have been generally bad. There are, however, some excellent examples of new construction and restoration in one or another traditional style executed with taste and authenticity.

The struggle between the two groups is still going on, and though the advocates of modernization seem always to be winning, a great deal from the past has been preserved or beautifully restored. Of course, all cities have environmental and growth problems, but those that inflict Florence are unique. Somehow, the requirements of modern life must be satisfied, while at the same time preserving those sections of the city and its surroundings that are irreplaceable and that all the Western world counts as part of its common heritage. It would seem that when these two objectives clash, the wiser course would be to decide in favor of that which has stood the test of time, that which is beautiful or characteristic or historic as against that which is merely utilitarian and perhaps transitory. It will require a master hand, sensitive yet practical, to guide the future of Florence and guarantee its historic treasures for succeeding generations.

* The best example of the latter, the façade of the Duomo, was constructed between 1860 and 1887. The original design called for a tricuspidal, pointed roof line similar to that of Santa Croce, completed just prior, but was changed when the work was half-way along, as a result of public criticism. Instead, the upper half of the façade was completed in a so-called basilican manner, with a series of cornices and friezes designed on a horizontal line to complement similar features on the adjoining campanile, even though this somewhat interrupts the pointed style of the doorways below.

INDEX

INDEX

(Page numbers of illustrations are in bold type)